THE ENGLAND WOMEN'S FC 1972-2022 THE LIONESSES – A STATISTICAL RECORD

Dirk Karsdorp

British Library Cataloguing in Publication Data
A catalogue record for this book is available from the British Library

ISBN: 978-1-86223-497-0

Copyright © 2023, SOCCER BOOKS LIMITED (01472 696226)
72 St. Peter's Avenue, Cleethorpes, N.E. Lincolnshire, DN35 8HU, England
Web site   www.soccer-books.co.uk
e-mail   info@soccer-books.co.uk

All rights are reserved. No part of this publication may be reproduced, stored in a retrieval system or transmitted, in any form or by any means, electronic, mechanical, photocopying, recording, or otherwise, without the prior written permission of Soccer Books Limited.

Printed in the UK by 4edge Ltd.

FOREWORD

Although there is evidence that some women played football as early as the 1880's and 1890's, it was not until the time of the First World War that interest really began to take off. The profile of women in general at that time took a leap forward when many were called upon to plug the huge gap in the nation's workforce (particularly in the munitions factories) which arose when so many men were recruited into the armed forces.

This and the women's suffrage campaigns clearly boosted female involvement in sport of all kinds but their participation in the country's favourite game was warmly welcomed by the UK public who turned out in large numbers for many games. The Dick, Kerr's Ladies FC were at the pinnacle of this popularity and, on Boxing Day 1920, no fewer than 53,000 supporters turned up to see them play a match at Everton's ground, Goodison Park.

Somewhat rattled by the success of the women's game, the Football Association, in a move which today would be clearly identified as misogynistic, imposed a total ban on women's football at any of the grounds which were affiliated to the Football Association. Ostensibly this was 'because football damaged women's bodies' but, today, it is generally regarded as having been a move to prevent it from undermining (commercially) the men's game.

That this ban remained in force until it was finally revoked in 1969 can only be seen today as discriminatory, especially so in light of the fact that it even took pressure from UEFA to force that revocation!

Soon after England men's 1966 World Cup Victory the Women's Football Association was formed and, in November 1972, their hard-fought campaign led to the first-ever International match played by an England Women's representative team. It was, to say the least, fitting that this was (as with the Men's team) against Scotland, even though it came a century after the Men's first match!

Since that time the Women's Game in general has blossomed and, in particular, has gone from strength to strength since the introduction of professionalism with the formation of the Women's Super League in 2010. However, despite the development of some very talented players in recent years, it wasn't until the arrival of Sarina Wiegman as coach of the England team in September 2021 that the Lionesses were able to move to the next level. 2022 proved to be a remarkable year for the team as they went 20 matches undefeated and became European Champions with a 2-1 victory over Germany in the Euro 2022 Final.

Readers will see that, particularly for some of the early matches (and even for some relatively recent ones) it has not proved possible to locate detailed statistics. We therefore appeal to anyone who may be able to provide some of the missing information to get in touch with us via our following e-mail address:

info@soccer-books.co.uk

England Women Official International Football Matches

1. 18.11.1972   <u>Ravenscraig Stadium, Greenock</u>: Scotland - England 2-3 (2-1)
<u>Scotland</u>: Janie Houghton, June Hunter, Jean Hunter, Sandra Walker, Marion Mount, Linda Kidd, Mary Carr, Margaret McAuley, Mary Anderson, Edna Neillis, Rose Reilly.
Coach: Robert Stewart
<u>England</u>: Sue Buckett, Sandra Graham, Morag Kirkland, Paddy McGroarty, Sheila Parker, Janet Bagguley, Jean Wilson, Jeannie Allott, Pat Davies, Sylvia Gore, Lynda Hale.
Coach: Eric Worthington
<u>Goals</u>: Mary Carr (20), Rose Reilly (27) / Sylvia Gore (43), Lynda Hale (..), Jeannie Allott (89)
<u>Referee</u>: J.Clelland (Scotland)   <u>Attendance</u>: 400.

2. 22.04.1973   <u>Stade Brion, Brion (France)</u>: France - England 0-3 (0-1)
<u>France</u>: Marie-Louise Butzig, Ghislaine Royer Souef, Régine Pourveux, Nicole Mangas, Betty Goret, Colette Guyard, Claudine Die, Dominique Tedeschi, Marie-Christine Tschopp, Atmelie Binard, Michèle Wolf (36 Dominique Dewulf). Coach: Pierre Geoffroy
<u>England</u>: Susan Bucket, Jeannie Allott, Janet Bagguley, Paddy McGroarty, Sheila Parker, Pat Davies, Eileen Foreman, Ray Wilson, Sylvia Gore, Lynda Hale, Morag Kirkland.
Coach: John Adams
<u>Goals</u>: Eileen Foreman (64), Pat Davies (30, 52)
<u>Referee</u>: Marcel Bacou (France)   <u>Attendance</u>: 3,000.

3. 23.06.1973   <u>Manor Park, Nuneaton</u>: England - Scotland 8-0 (2-0)
<u>England</u>: Sue Buckett (64 Sue Whyatt), Margaret Miks, Morag Kirkland, Paddy McGroarty, Sheila Parker, Wendy Owen, Lynda Hale, Janet Bagguley (71 Julia Manning), Pat Firth (71 Eileen Foreman), Jeannie Allott, Pat Davies. Coach: John Adams
<u>Scotland</u>: Gerry Chalmers, Margaret Wilson, Susan Ferries, Linda Kidd, Sheila Begbie, Mary Anderson (40 Ann Morrison), Rose Reilly, June Hunter, Edna Neillis, Margaret McAuley, Mary Car.
<u>Goals</u>: Patricia (Pat) Firth (25, 47, 51), Patricia (Pat) Davies (31, 63), Margaret (Paddy) McGroarty (50 pen, 70), Eileen Foreman (86).
<u>Attendance</u>: 1,310.

4. 07.09.1973   <u>Twerton Park, Bath</u>: England - Northern Ireland 5-1
<u>Goals</u>: Jeannie Allott, Lynda Hale (2x), Margaret Dunlop (og), Sylvia Gore / Sharon Gillespie

5. 09.11.1973   <u>Elm Park, Reading</u>: England - Netherlands 1-0 (1-0)
<u>England</u>: *Line-up not known*
<u>Netherlands</u>: Hanny van de Bungelaar (60 Hennie van Rooyen-Vernooij), Hennie Schlimbach-Smit, Ellen Popeyus, Marian Wellenberg, Truus Deen (36 Tonnie de Kort), Jos Andeweg-de Vroedt, Corrie de Jong-Welgraven, Jo Fuchs, José van Hoof, Tilly van Asdonck-van Rooijen, Wilma van Elderen (36 Joke van de Veen). Coach: Bert Wouterse)
<u>Goal</u>: Paddy McGroarty (34)
<u>Referee</u>: K.C.Walker (England)   <u>Attendance</u>: 3,000.

6. 17.03.1974   Wexham Park, Slough: England - Wales 5-0
England: Sue Buckett, Sue Whyatt, Margaret Miks, Wendy Owen, Sheila Parker, Morag Kirkland, Paddy McGroarty, Sue Lopez, Janet Bagguley, Lynda Hale, Pat Davies, Pat Firth, Eileen Foreman, Jeannie Allott, Leslie Stirling, Julia Manning, Sylvia Gore.
Coach: Tommy Tranter
Wales: Sheryl Evans, Gaynor Jones, Valerie Bevan, Michele Adams, Tina Cositori, Mai Griffith, Diane Totty, Julie Yale, Karen Wells, Brenda Jones, Ann Rice, Gaynor Jones, Pat Griffith, Gloria O'Connor, Pauline Parker, Linda James.   Coach: Dave Powell
Goals: Paddy McGroarty (2x), Pat Davies, Pat Firth, Julia Manning
Referee: D.Haywood (England)   Attendance: 500.

Both teams shown include the substitutes who may or may not have played.

7. 31.05.1974   Stadspark, Groningen: Netherlands - England 0-3 (0-3)
Netherlands: Hanny van de Bungelaar (.. Hennie Vernooy), …, Jos Andeweg (.. Hanneke van der Veen), Henny Smit, Tonnie de Kort, Beppie Timmer, Tilly van Rooyen, Corry Welgraven, Tine Baay (.. Anja van der Horst).   Coach: Bert Wouterse
England: Sue Buckett, Margaret Miks, …, Sue Lopez, Pat Davies, Jeannie Allott.
Coach: Tommy Tranter
Goals: Sue Lopez (11), Pat Davies (21, 30)   *(KNVB attributes the first goal to Janet Bagguley)*
Referee: Frans Derks (Netherlands)   Attendance: 1,500.

8. 07.11.1974   Plough Lane, Wimbledon: England - France 2-0 (1-0)
England: Sue Buckett, Margaret Miks, Morag Kirkland, Wendy Owen, Sheila Parker, Janet Bagguley, Sandra Choat, Pat Firth, Pat Davies, Sue Lopez, Jeannie Allott.
Coach: Tommy Tranter
France: Marie-Louise Butzig, Régine Pourveux, Nicole Carrié Cauvet, Annie Bataille, Marie-Bernadette Thomas, Renée Delahaye, Dominique Scharo, Claudine Dié, Michèle Wolf, Michèle Bariset, Dominique Dewulf.   Coach: Pierre Geoffroy
Goals: Pat Davies (13), Sue Lopez (42)
Attendance: 2,000.

9. 19.04.1975   Stadion Schützenmatte, Basel: Switzerland - England 1-3 (0-2)
Switzerland: Mirella Cina, Morena Pestoni, Antoinette Bayer (41 D.Gasparoli), Jeanette Thomet, Nadja Ripamonti, E.Meier, M.Boll, Kathy Moser, Denise Blanchet (58 S.Bachman), M.Näf, Helena Barmettler.   Coach: Libero Taddei
England: Sue Buckett, Morag Kirkland, Sheila Parker, Wendy Owen, Margaret Miks (63 Carol McCune), Jeannie Allott, Janet Bagguley, Sue Lopez, Sandra Choat, Pat Davies (56 Lorraine Dobb), Liz Deighan.   Coach: Tommy Tranter
Goals: Helena Barmettler (68) / Sandra Choat (20 pen, 29, 69)
Referee: Ernst Dörflinger (Switzerland)   Attendance: 3,000.

10. 15.06.1975   Gamla Ullevi, Gothenburg: Sweden - England 2-0 (2-0)
Sweden: Gun Hellestig (Engfors), Mary Olsson, Anette Börjesson, Ingalill Arvling, Lena Bergman Isberg, Görel Sintorn, Agneta Björck, Lona Svensson, Ann Magnusson (46 Pia Sundhage), Ann Jansson, Ann-Kristina Lindqvist. Coach: Hasse Karlsson
England: Sue Buckett, Carol McCune, Alison Leatherbarrow, Janet Bagguley, Wendy Owen, Sheila Parker, Lynda Hale, Lorraine Dobb, Elaine Badrock (30 Liz Deighan), Pauline Chilton, Jeannie Allott (48 Sandra Choat). Coach: Tommy Tranter
Goals: Ann Jansson (36, 39)
Referee: Åke Jansson (Sweden)   Attendance: 2,963.

11. 07.09.1975   Plough Lane, Wimbledon: England - Sweden 1-3 (1-1)
England: Sue Buckett, Alison Leatherbarrow (Carol McCune), Morag Kirkland, Wendy Owen, Sheila Parker, Rayner Haddon, Sandra Choat, Lorraine Dobb (Angela Smith), Elaine Badrock, Liz Deighan, Jeannie Allott. Coach: Tommy Tranter
Sweden: Sabine Piltorp, Lena Bergman Isberg, Anette Börjesson, Christina Norin (46 Ingalill Arvling), Mary Olsson, Görel Sintorn, Aulikki Suomela, Lona Svensson (42 Ulla Håkansson), Ann Jansson, Pia Sundhage, Anne Andersén (65 Lilibeth Svärd). Coach: Hasse Karlsson
Goals: Liz Deighan (..) / Pia Sundhage (34), Ulla Håkansson (47, 61)
Referee: Bartley John Homewoord (England)

12. 02.05.1976   Borough Park, Blackpool: England - Netherlands 2-1 (2-1)
England: Coach: Tommy Tranter
Netherlands: Hanny van de Bungelaar, Tilly Asdonck-van Rooijen (50 Loltje van de Mossel), Jos Andeweg-de Vroedt, Jose van Hoof (50 Sylvia Genderen), Donny de Jong-Welgraven, Aukje Kuipers (55 Christa Nannings), Ellen Popeyus, Bep Timmer, Wil de Visser, Ria van Hassel, Hennie Schlimbach-Smit. Coach: Ger Blok.
Goals: Elaine Badrock (16), Sandra Choat (30 pen) / Wil de Visser (20)
Attendance: 4,000.

13. 23.05.1976   Home Championship
                Southbury Road, Enfield: England - Scotland 5-1

14. 02.06.1976   Stadio Flaminiio, Rome: Italy - England 2-0 (1-0)
Italy: Wilma Seghetti, Rocca (41 Silvia Silvaggi), Maura Furlotti, Manola Conter, Coda, Bandini, Elena Schiavo, Sacchi (58 Greco), Betty Vignotto, Gualdi, Liliana Mammina (69 Maurizia Ciceri). Coach: Amedeo Amadei
England: Sue Buckett, Carol McCune, Morag Kirkland, Alison Leatherbarrow (63 Angie Poppy), Wendy Owen, Linda Coffin, Lorraine Dobb, Rayner Haddon, Elaine Badrock, Pat Firth, Sue Lopez. Coach: Tommy Tranter
Goals: Betty Vignotto (31, 59)
Referee: Barra (Italy)

15. 04.07.1976   Novara (Italy): Italy - England 2-1 (1-1)
Italy: Wilma Seghetti, Rocca, Maura Furlotti, Greco, Coda, Bandini, Elena Schiavo, Sacchi (60 Fery Ferraguzzi), Betty Vignotto, Gualdi, Maurizia Ciceri (70 Cherillo).
Coach: Amedeo Amadei
England: Sue Buckett, Carol McCune, Morag Kirkland, Alison Leatherbarrow, Wendy Owen, Elaine Badrock, Angie Poppy (65 Pat Chapman), Rayner Haddon, Linda Coffin, Pat Firth (46 Day), Sue Lopez.   Coach: Tommy Tranter
Goals: Maurizia Ciceri (23), Feriana (Fery) Ferraguzzi (66) / Linda Coffin (21)
Referee: Beretta (Italy)   Attendance: 1,500.

16. 26.02.1977   Longjumeau (France): France - England 0-0
France: Danielle Vatin, Patricia Mousel, Marie-Noëlle Fourdrignier Warot, Annie Bataille, Marie-Bernadette Thomas, Elisabeth Dejean, Michèle Wolf, Renée Delahaye (60 Marie-Laure Montauriol), Véronique Roy (30 Martine Thivolle), Christine Scharo (45 Armelle Binard), Marlène Farrugia.   Coach: Francis-Pierre Coche
England: Coach: Tommy Tranter
Referee: Jean Muchembled (France)   Attendance: 1,200.

17. 28.04.1977   Boothferry Park, Hull: England - Switzerland 9-1 (7-1)
England: Sue Buckett, Carol McCune, Morag Kirkland, Alison Leatherbarrow, Linda Coffin, Liz Deighan, Lynda Hale, Linda Curl (46 Sheila Parker), Eileen Foreman, Sue Lopez, Pat Chapman.   Coach: Tommy Tranter
Switzerland: M.Cina (44 E.Huber), N.Ripamonti, A.Bayer, J.Thomet, E.Näpflin (60 M.Pestoni), M.Kaufmann, M.Boll, I.Grim, F.Kretz (41 S.Kuttruff), C.Hüsler (41 J.Fontanive), H.Bartmettler.
Goals: Eileen Foreman (6, 37), Pat Chapman (22, 38, 43), Liz Deighan (27), Sheila Parker (42, 54), Linda Coffin (46) / M.Boll (39)
Referee: Robert (Bob) Matthewson (England)   Attendance: 2,800.

18. 29.05.1977   Downfield Park, Dundee: Scotland - England 2-1 (1-0)
Scotland: Elizabeth Smith, Marion Barclay, Margaret McAuley, A.Squires, Sheila Begby, Elizabeth Vinesky (85 Betty Ure), Jane Leggett, Mary O'Neill, Elizabeth Creamer (Marie Blagojevic), A.Reilly, Lorraine Spruvey.
England: Janet Milner, Alison Leatherbarrow, Josie Lee, Linda Coffin, Lorraine Dobb, Linda Curl, Elizabeth Bringham (57 Sue Lopez), Ellen Foreman, Christine Hutchinson, Pat Chapman, *Unknown*.   Coach: Tommy Tranter
Goals: Elizabeth Creamer (35), Marie Blagojevic (83) / Sue Lopez (65 pen)
Referee: J.Morrison (Scotland)   Attendance: 1,000.

19. 15.11.1977   Plough Lane, Wimbledon: England - Italy 1-0 (1-0)
England: Sue Buckett, Carol McCune, Alison Leatherbarrow, Lorraine Dobb, Linda Coffin, Linda Curl, Day, Sue Lopez, Eileen Foreman, Sheila Parker, Pat Chapman.
Coach: Tommy Tranter
Italy: Wilma Seghetti, Sossella, Maura Furlotti, Bandini, Pedrali, Fery Ferraguzzi, Greco, Babetto, Meles (53 Gualdi), Betty Vignotto, Liliana Mammina (53 Cherillo).
Coach: Amedeo Amadei
Goal: Sheila Parker (8)
Referee: Reynolds (England)

20. 30.09.1978   Sportpark Irislaan, Vlissingen: Netherlands - England 3-1 (1-0)
Netherlands: Sjoukje Leistra, Jos Andeweg-de Vroedt (15 Wil de Visser), Margaret van Dinten, Jose van Hoof, Elly Manuputty (56 Tonnie Meijerink-van de Boom), Christa Nannings, Ellen Popeyus, Edith Ramakers, Els Schoon, Wil Siereveld, Bep Timmer.
Coach: Ruud de Groot
England: Sue Buckett, …, Pat Chapman, Elaine Badrock, … (70 Debbie Bampton), …
Coach: Tommy Tranter
Goals: Jose van Hoof (30,65), Elly Manuputty (50) / Pat Chapman (60)
Referee: G.H.H.van der Linden (Netherlands)   Attendance: 1,000.

21. 28.10.1978   The Dell, Southampton: England - Belgium 3-0
England: Coach: Tommy Tranter
Belgium: Daniella Ottoy, Agnès Debock, Lutgart Dierckx, Gerda Colpaert, Maria Seymus, Conny Dubois, Anne-Marie Carrette, Monique Huybrechts, Sandra Temmerman, Marina Verdonck, Jeanine Van Buel.
Goals: Elaine Badrock (2x), Linda Curl
Attendance: 5,471.

22. 19.05.1979   Hvidovre Stadium, Copenhagen: Denmark - England 3-1 (2-0)
Denmark: Lise Olesen, Maren Barsballe, Anne Grete Holst (Kirsten Fabrin), Susanne Niemann (Hanne Larsen), Lene Pedersen, Vibeke Mortensen, Fridel Riggelsen, Jeanette Jensen, Britta Ehmsen, Lone Smidt Nielsen, Inge Hindkjær.   Coach: Bjørn Basbøll
England: Terry Wiseman, Sue Buckett, Carol McCure, Maggie Pearce, Lorraine Dobb, Linda Coffin, Linda Curl, Elaine Badrock, Julie Brown, Eileen Foremann, Sue Lopez, Pat Chapman, Liz Deighan, Alison Leatherbarrow, Debbie Bampton.   Coach: Martin Reagan
(The England team shown includes all the substitutes who may or may not have played)
Goals: Maren Barsballe (35), Anne Grete Holst (45), Hanne Larsen (49) / Sara Pollard (72)
Referee: Jørgen Mortensen (Denmark)   Attendance: 480.

23. 19.07.1979   Unofficial European Competition for Women's Football Group B
                 Sorrento (Italy): England - Finland 3-1

24. 23.07.1979   Unofficial European Competition for Women's Football Group B
                 Sorrento (Italy): England - Switzerland 2-0 (0-0)
England: Coach: Martin Reagan
Switzerland: R.Niederberger, H.Moser, S.Kutruff, S.Jufer (36 C.Hepp), H.Barmettler, S.Dolder, C.Hüsler, R.Krummenacher (48 S.Romano), E.Odermatt, N.Sauter, M.Pestoni.
Goals: *Not known*

25. 25.07.1979   Unofficial European Competition for Women's Football Semi-finals
                  Stadio San Paulo, Naples (Italy): Italy - England 3-1 (1-0)
Italy: Wilma Seghetti, Perin, Sossella, Greco, Maura Furlotti, Manfredini, Colin, Gualdi, Betty Vignotto, Fery Ferraguzzi, Blondi. Coach: Galli
England: Sue Buckett, Carol McCune, Maggie Pearce, Linda Coffin, Eileen Lillyman, Sheila Parker, Linda Curl, Liz Deighan, Debbie Mack, Sue Lopez, Pat Chapman.
Coach: Martin Reagan
Goals: Betty Vignotto (11, 65), Musumeci (70) / Linda Curl (54)

26. 27.07.1979   Unofficial European Competition for Women's Football Third place
                  Scafati (Italy): Sweden - England 0-0
Sweden: Inger Arnesson, Birgit Nilsson, Mona Åhman, Doris Hjelm (Birgitta Söderström), Anna-Karin Andersson, Anette Börjesson, Anna Svenjeby, Ann Jansson (Görel Sintorn), Karin Ödlund, Susanne Erlandsson, Pia Sundhage.
England: Terry Wiseman, Alison Leatherbarrow, Carol Thomas, Sheila Parker, Sue Lopez, Linda Coffin, Linda Curl, Pat Chapman, Eileen Lillyman, Liz Deighan, Debbie Mack (Janet Turner). Coach: Martin Reagan

Sweden won 4-3 on penalties

Penalties Sweden: Anette Börjesson, Ing-Marie Ottosson, Ann-Kristin Lindkvist, Mona Åhman.
Penalties England: Terry Wiseman, Linda Curl, Sue Lopez.

27. 13.09.1979   Boothferry Park, Hull: England - Denmark 2-2 (2-2)
England: Coach: Martin Reagan
Denmark: Inge Mikkelsen, Anne Grete Holst, Susanne Niemann, Britta Ehmsen, Jeanette Jensen, Hanne Larsen (Kirsten Fabrin), Vibeke Mortensen, Inger Pedersen, Fridel Riggelsen, Lone Smidt Nielsen, Inge Hindkjær. Coach: Bjørn Basbøll
Goals: Fridel Riggelsen (42 og), Eileen Foreman (43) /
Lone Smidt Nielsen (15), Susanne Niemann (39)
Attendance: 1,100.

28. 01.05.1980   Albertpark, Ostende: Belgium - England 2-1

29. 17.09.1980   Filbert Street, Leicester: England - Sweden 1-1 (0-0)
England: Terry Irvine, Morag Pearce, Carol Thomas, Maureen Reynolds, Leslie Stirling, Eileen Foreman, Mary Meacham (Linda Coffin), Linda Curl, Tracy Doe, Debbie Bampton, Pat Chapman. Coach: Martin Reagan
Sweden: Elisabeth Leidinge (58 Inger Arnesson), Anna Svenjeby, Helena Lundberg, Ann Jansson, Anna-Karin Andersson, Birgitta Söderström, Susanne Lundmark, Marie Arnberg (82 Ulla Håkansson), Görel Sintorn, Pia Sundhage, Karin Ödlund. Coach: Ulf Lyfors
Goals: Eileen Foreman (58) / Birgitta Söderström (85)
Referee: John Hunting (England)

10

30. 09.09.1981   Portopia
Nishigaoka Soccer Stadium, Tokyo: England - Denmark 0-1 (0-0)
England: Terry Wiseman, Carol Thomas, Angie Gallimore, Sheila Parker, Linda Coffin, Linda Curl (Gilllian Coultard), Debbie Bampton, Liz Deighan, Tracy Doe, Eileen Foreman (Christine Hutchinson), Janet Turner. Coach: Martin Reagan
Denmark: Marianne Riis (60 Gitte Hansen), Gitte Christensen, Annette Hadamer, Anne Grete Holst (55 Jette Hansen), Charlotte Nielsen-Mann, Susanne Niemann, Marian Petz, Britta Ehmsen (40 Annette Mogensen), Inger Pedersen, Fridel Riggelsen, Lone Smidt Nielsen.
Coach: Bjørn Basbøll
Goal: Inger Pedersen (49)
Attendance: 3,000.

31. 25.10.1981   Abbey Stadium, Cambridge: England - Norway 0-3
England: Coach: Martin Reagan
Norway: Rita Fjærli Teigen, Eva Amble, Grete Pedersen, Heidi Støre, Tone Irene Opseth, Ingunn Ramsfjell (Eli Landsem), Karen Espelund (Ranveig Karlsen), Marit Bjørkli, Kari Nielsen, Gunn Lisbeth Nyborg, Liv Strædet.
Goals: Gunn Lisbeth Nyborg, Grete Pedersen, Kari Nielsen
Attendance: 1,300.

32. 26.05.1982   Viskavallen, Kinna: Sweden - England 1-1 (1-1)
Sweden: Elisabeth Leidinge, Ann Jansson, Anette Börjesson, Angelica Burevik Törnqvist, Karin Åhman, Eva Andersson (62 Helene Björk Johansson), Anna Svenjeby, Camilla Andersson-Neptune (54 Anette Nicklasson, 82 Carina Samuelsson), Birgitta Söderström, Pia Sundhage, Karin Ödlund. Coach: Ulf Lyfors
England: Terry Wiseman (Terry Irvine), Morag Pearce (Lorraine Hunt), Carol Thomas, Sheila Parker, Linda Coffin, Gillian Coultard, Linda Curl, Liz Deighan, Tracy Doe, Lorraine Dobb (Christine Hutchinson), Janet Turner. Coach: Martin Reagan
Goals: Pia Sundhage (6) / Lorraine Dobb (1)
Referee: Jan Almqvist (Sweden)   Attendance: 772.

33. 11.06.1982   Pescaia: Italy - England 2-0 (1-0)
Italy: Granieri, Perin, Sossella (58 Montesi), Mariotti, Saldi, Maura Furlotti, Carolina Morace, Grilli, Betty Vignotto, Boselli (41 Secchi), Ida Golin (70 Colzani). Coach: Sergio Guenza
England: Terry Wiseman, Vicky Johnson (58 Helmsley), Carol Thomas (71 Christine Hutchinson), Sheila Parker, Lorraine Hunt, Gillian Coultard, Linda Curl, Liz Deighan, Tracy Doe, Lorraine Dobb, Janet Turner. Coach: Martin Reagan
Goals: Carolina Morace (20), Betty Vignotto (47)
Referee: Benini (Italy)

34. 19.09.1982   EURO 1984 Qualifiers
Gresty Road, Crewe: England - Northern Ireland 7-1
Goals: Kerry Davis (2x), Tracy Doe, Linda Curl (2x, 1x pen), Janet Turner, Gillian Coultard / Gillian Totten
Referee: Neil Midgley (England)

35. 03.10.1982   EURO 1984 Qualifiers
                 Boghead Park, Dumbarton: Scotland - England 0-4 (0-2)
Goals: Kerry Davies (21, 26, 56, 67)
Referee: Alexander (Scotland)

36. 07.11.1982   EURO 1984 Qualifiers
                 Dalymount Park, Dublin: Republic of Ireland - England 0-1
Republic of Ireland: Jacqueline Hogan, Catherine Byrne (66 Pauline Goggins), Nora Barrett, Catherine Fitzpatrick, Geraldine Slane, Teresa McCann, Mairead Byrne, Catherine Byrne, Angela McCabe, Annette Kealy, Denice Lyons (61 Ann Beirne).
England: Terry Wiseman, Carol Thomas, Maggie Pearce, Sheila Parker, Angela Gallimore, Gillian Coultard, Linda Curl (59 Maxime Fewkes), Liz Deighan, Tracy Doe (57 Janet Turner), Kerry Davis, Pat Chapman.   Coach: Martin Reagan
Goal: Kerry Davis
Referee: Patrick Daly (Republic of Ireland)

37. 14.05.1983   EURO 1984 Qualifiers
                 Seaview Ground, Belfast: Northern Ireland - England 0-4
Goals: Kerry Davis (2x), Linda Curl, Pat Chapman
Referee: Hugh Wilson (Northern Ireland)

38. 22.05.1983   EURO 1984 Qualifiers
                 Elland Road, Leeds: England - Scotland 2-0 (2-0)
Goals: Pat Chapman (6, 13)
Referee: David Richardson (England)

39. 11.09.1983   EURO 1984 Qualifiers
                 Elm Park, Reading: England - Republic of Ireland 6-0
Goals: Kerry Davis (2x), Angie Gallimore, Liz Deighan, Linda Curl, Catherine Fitzpatrick (og)
Referee: Alan Robinson (England)

40. 30.10.1983   The Valley, London: England - Sweden 2-2 (1-0)
England: Terry Wiseman (75 Terry Irvine), Carol Thomas, Lorraine Hanson, Angelo Gallimore, Morag Pearce, Gillian Coultard, Debbie Bampton (83 Jackie Sherrard), Liz Deighan (65' Hope Powell), Linda Curl, Kerry Davis (69 Brenda Sempare), Pat Chapman. Coach: Martin Reagan
Sweden: Inger Arnesson, Catarina Gjellan (46 Anette Nicklasson), Anette Börjesson, Helena Kihlberg-Bystedt (55 Angelica Burevik Törnqvist), Mia Kåberg Pettersson, Karin Åhman-Svensson, Anna Svenjeby, Camilla Andersen Neptune, Eleonor Hultin (55 Doris Uusitalo), Pia Sundhage, Helene Björk Johansson.   Coach: Ulf Lyfors
Goals: Kerry Davis (18), Linda Curl (50) / Anna Svenjeby (70), Helene Björk Johansson (88)
Referee: A.W.Ward (England)   Attendance: 991.

41. 08.04.1984   EURO 1984 Semi-finals
   Gresty Road Stadium, Crewe: England - Denmark 2-1 (1-0)
England: ..., Linda Curl, Liz Deighan, ...   Coach: Martin Reagan
Denmark: Gitte Hansen, Annie Gam-Pedersen, Susan MacKensie, Glennie Nielsen, Charlotte Nielsen-Mann, Jette Andersen, Kirsten Fabrin, Mette Munk Nielsen (57 Helle Pedersen), Hanne Pedersen, Lone Smidt Nielsen, Inge Hindkjær. Coach: Flemming Schultz
Goals: Linda Curl (31), Liz Deighan (51) / Inge Hindkjær (49 pen)
Referee: Kevin O'Sullivan (Republic of Ireland)   Attendance: 1,000.

42. 28.04.1984   EURO 1984 Semi-finals
   Bredbånd Nord Arena, Hjørring: Denmark - England 0-1 (0-1)
Denmark: Gitte Hansen, Birgitte Frederiksen (55 Annette Mogensen), Annie Gam-Pedersen, Glennie Nielsen, Charlotte Nielsen-Mann, Jette Andersen, Kirsten Fabrin, Hanne Larsen (46 Pia Andersen), Hanne Pedersen, Lone Smidt Nielsen, Inge Hindkjær.
Coach: Flemming Schultz
England: Terry Wiseman, Debbie Bampton, Gillian Coultard, Kerry Davis, Pat Chapman, Linda Curl, Liz Deighan, Angela Gallimore, Lorraine Hanson, Morag Pearce-Kirkland, Carol Thomas-McCune.   Coach: Martin Reagan
Goal: Debbie Bampton (44)
Referee: Kaj Natri (Finland)   Attendance: 1,439.

43. 12.05.1984   EURO 1984 Final
   Gamla Ullevi, Gothenburg: Sweden - England 1-0 (0-0)
Sweden: Elisabeth Leidinge, Karin Åhman-Svensson, Eva Andersson, Anette Börjesson, Angelica Burevik-Törnqvist, Anette Hansson, Ann Jansson, Mia Kåberg-Pettersson, Pia Sundhage, Anna Svenjeby, Lena Videkull.   Coach: Ulf Lyfors
England: Terry Wiseman, Maggie Pearce-Kirkland, Debbie Bampton, Gillian Coultard (64 Tony Brightwell), Kerry Davis, Pat Chapman (47 Janet Turner), Linda Curl, Liz Deighan, Angela Gallimore, Lorraine Hanson, Carol Thomas-McCune. Coach: Martin Reagan
Goal: Pia Sundhage (57)

44. 27.05.1984   EURO 1984 Final
   Kenilworth Stadium, Luton: England - Sweden 1-0 (1-0)
England: Terry Wiseman, Maggie Pearce-Kirkland, Linda Curl, Gillian Coultard, Pat Chapman, Lorriane Hanson, Angela Gallimore, Kerry Davis, Debbie Bampton, Carol Thomas, Liz Deighan.   Coach: Martin Reagan
Sweden: Elisabeth Leidinge, Karin Åhman-Svensson, Eva Andersson, Helene Björk-Johansson, Anette Börjesson, Angelica Burevik-Törnqvist, Ann Jansson, Mia Kåberg-Pettersson, Pia Sundhage, Anna Svenjeby, Lena Videkull (36 Doris Uusitalo).
Coach: Ulf Lyfors
Goal: Linda Curl (31)
Referee: Ignace Goris (Belgium)   Attendance: 2,567.

Sweden won 4-3 on penalties

Penalties: Linda Curl missed, Anette Börjesson 0-1, Angela Gallimore 1-1, Eva Andersson 1-2, Debbie Bampton 2-2, Helen Björk-Johansson missed, Lorraine Hanson missed, Ann Jansson 2-3, Kerry Davis 3-3, Pia Sundhage 3-4.

45. 20.08.1984   Mundialito
            Stadio Comunale Armando Picchi, Jesolo (Italy): Belgium - England 1-1
Goals: Carla Martens / Linda Curl

46. 22.08.1984   Mundialito
            Stadio Comunale Armando Picchi, Jesolo (Italy): England - West Germany 0-2 (0-0)
England: Coach: Martin Reagan
West Germany: Marion Isbert, Ingrid Zimmermann, Christel Klinzmann, Monika Steinmetz, Elke Richter, Sissy Raith (46 Eva Schute), Rike Koekkoek (Marie-Luise Gehlen), Beate Henkel, Silvia Neid, Petra Bartelmann, Anne Kreuzberg.   Coach: Gero Bisanz
Goals: Silvia Neid (46, 47)

47. 24.08.1984   Mundialito
            Stadio Comunale Armando Picchi, Jesolo (Italy): Italy - England 1-1 (1-1)
Italy: Roberta Russo, Marisa Perin, Dorio, Maria Mariotti, Paola Bonato, Fariana Ferraguzzi, Bontacchio, Carolina Morace (72 Ida Golin), Elisabeth Vignotto, Reilly (78 Langella), Mega.
England: Terry Wiseman, Carol Thomas, Jacqueline Slack, Lorraine Hanson, Angela Gallimore, Hope Powell, Debbie Bampton, Brenda Sempare (65 Liz Deighan), Marieanne Spacey, Linda Curl, Janet Turner.   Coach: Martin Reagan
Goals: Carolina Morace (25) / Linda Curl (10)
Referee: Zazza Di Torino (Italy)   Attendance: 3,000.

48. 25.08.1984   Mundialito Third Place
            Stadio Comunale Giovanni Chiggiato, Caorle (Italy): England - Belgium 2-1
Goals: Marieanne Spacey, Linda Curl / *Unknown* (pen)

49. 17.03.1985   EURO 1987 Qualifiers
            Deepdale, Preston: England - Scotland 4-0 (2-0)
Goals: Gillian Coultard (5), Janet Turner (39), Kerry Davis (53), Hope Powell (60)

50. 25.05.1985   EURO 1987 Qualifiers
            Allen Park, Antrim: Northern Ireland - England 1-8
Goals: Gillian Wilson / Kerry Davis (5x), Linda Curl (2x), Hope Powell

51. 19.08.1985   Mundialito
            Stadio Giovanni Chiggiato, Caorle (Italy): Denmark - England 1-0 (1-0)
Denmark: Gitte Hansen, Annie Gam-Pedersen, Jette Hansen, Annette Mogensen, Mette Munk Nielsen, Glennie Nielsen, Lotte Bagge (75 Linda Brogård), Kirsten Fabrin, Helle Pedersen (Mette Odgaard), Lone Smidt Nielsen, Karen Leth Hansen.   Coach: Birger Peitersen
England: Coach: Martin Reagan
Goal: Helle Pedersen (9)
Attendance: 2,000.

52. 20.08.1985   Mundialito
                  Stadio Giovanni Chiggiato, Caorle (Italy): Italy - England 1-1 (1-0)
Italy: Roberta Russo, Coda, Sandra Pierazuoli, Mega (46 Reilly), Paola Bonato, Fariana Ferraguzzi, Bontacchio, Carolina Morace, Elisabeth Vignotto, Adele Marsiletti, Ida Golin (58 Antonella Carta).
England: Terry Wiseman, Carol Thomas (65' Suzanne Law), Jacqueline Slack, Debbie Bampton, Angela Gallimore, Gillian Coultard (70' Liz Deighan), Hope Powell, Brenda Sempare, Marieanne Spacey (55' Janet Turner), Kerry Davis, Linda Curl.
Coach: Martin Reagan
Goals: Ida Golin (7) / Kerry Davis (76)
Referee: Angelelli Di Terni (Italy)   Attendance: 5,000.

53. 23.08.1985   Mundialito
                  Stadio Giovanni Chiggiato, Caorle (Italy): England - USA 3-1
England: Coach: Martin Reagan
USA: Kim Wyant (Ruth Harker), Ann Orrison, Denise Bender, Stacey Enos, Lori Henry, Laurie Bylin, Emily Pickering (Sharon McMurtry), Tuca Healy, Denise Boyer, Cindy Gordon, Michelle Akers. Coach: Mike Ryan
Goals: Marieanne Spacey, Linda Curl, Angie Gallimore / Michele Akers

54. 25.08.1985   Mundialito Final
                  Stadio Giovanni Chiggiato, Caorle (Italy): Italy - England 2-3 (1-0)
Italy: Roberta Russo, Coda, Sandra Pierazuoli, Adele Marsiletti, Paola Bonato, Fariana Ferraguzzi, Bontacchio, Carolina Morace (46 Reilly), Elisabeth Vignotto, Antonella Carta (65 Maura Furlotti), Ida Golin.
England: Terry Wiseman, Carol Thomas, Jacqueline Slack, Debbie Bampton, Lorraine Hanson, Gillian Coultard, Hope Powell, Brenda Sempare, Linda Curl, Kerry Davis, Janet Turner (46 Marieanne Spacey).   Coach: Martin Reagan
Goals: Ida Golin (40, 78) / Marieanne Spacey (49, 77), Brenda Sempare (56)
Referee: Angelelli Di Terni (Italy)   Attendance: 10,000.

55. 22.09.1985   EURO 1987 Qualifiers
                  Flower Lodge, Cork: Republic of Ireland - England 0-6 (0-3)
Republic of Ireland: Sue Kelly, Bernadette Cassidy, Linda Gorman, Catherine Fitzpatrick, Geraldine Slane, Eileen Brennan, Grainne Cross, Caroline Nagle (46 Debbie McGarry), Breeda Cummins, Teresa Hurley, Susan Mary Hayden (57 Linda Fitzwilliam).
England: Terry Wiseman, Carol Thomas, Jacqueline Slack, Debbie Bampton, Angela Gallimore (52 Suzanne Law), Gillian Coultard, Hope Powell (49 Jacqueline Sherrard), Brenda Sempare, Marieanne Spacey, Kerry Davis, Linda Curl.   Coach: Martin Reagan
Goals: Linda Curl (19, 59, 69), Hope Powell (24), Gillian Coultard (26), Brenda Sempare (72)

56. 16.03.1986   EURO 1987 Qualifiers
                  Ewood Park, Blackburn: England - Northern Ireland 10-0

57. 27.04.1986   EURO 1987 Qualifiers
                  Elm Park, Reading: England - Republic of Ireland 4-0 (1-0)
England: Terry Wiseman, Suzanne Law, Jacqueline Slack, Debbie Bampton, Angela
Gallimore, Gillian Coultard, Jacqueline Sherrard (55 Jane Stanley), Brenda Sempare,
Marieanne Spacey, Kerry Davis, Linda Curl (55 Hope Powell).   Coach: Martin Reagan
Republic of Ireland: Sue Kelly, Catherine Byrne, Pauline Goggins, Cristina Buckley, Paula
Merriman (67 Marion Leahy), Carol Purdy (50 Ann Thorpe), Loretta Cullen, Brigid Reynolds,
Bridie Flood, Denice Lyons, Patricua Hughes.
Goals: Kerry Davis (42, 77), Linda Curl (47), Sue Law (50)

58. 12.10.1986   EURO 1987 Qualifiers
                  Stark's Park, Kirkcaldy: Scotland - England 1-3 (1-2)
Goals: Marshall (13) / Kerry Davis (5), Hope Powell (7), Marieanne Spacey (75)

59. 11.06.1987   EURO 1987 NORWAY Semi-finals
                  Melløs Stadion, Moss (Norway): Sweden - England 3-2 (1-1,2-2)
Sweden: Elisabeth Leidinge, Karin Åhman-Svensson, Anette Nicklasson, Anette Börjesson
(YC), Anna Svenjeby (80 Marie Karlsson), Helena Carlsson, Gunilla Sonja Eva Axén, Eva
Andersson, Lena Videkull, Eleonor Hultin (47 Helen Björk-Johansson), Pia Sundhage.
Coach: Ulf Lyfors
England: Terry Wiseman, Brenda Sempare, Gillian Coultard, Kerry Davis, Sue Law, Linda
Curl (5 Jane Stanley, 41 Hope Powell), Debbie Bampton, Marieanne Spacey, Jackie Sherrard,
Angela Gallimore, Jackie Slack.   Coach: Martin Reagan
Goals: Anette Börjesson (2), Gunilla Sonja Eva Axén (90, 100) / Kerry Davis (1),
Linda Curl (89)
Referee: Michal Listkiewicz (Poland)   Attendance: 300.

Sweden won after extra time.

60. 13.06.1987   EURO 1987 NORWAY Third place
                  Marienlyst Stadion, Drammen (Norway): Italy - England 2-1 (2-1)
Italy: Roberta Russo, Maura Furlotti, Marina Cordenons, Paola Bonato, Marisa Perin, Maria
Mariotti, Fariana Ferraguzzi (46 Frigerio), Antonella Carta, Elisabeth Vignotto, Carolina
Morace, Ida Golin (72 Sandra Pierrazuoli).   Coach: Ettore Reccagni
England: Terry Wiseman, Brenda Sempare, Marieanne Spacey, Angela Gallimore, Kerry
Davis, Gillian Coultard, Debbie Bampton, Sue Law, Jackie Sherrard, Hope Powell (69 Linda
Curl), Lorraine Hunt.   Coach: Martin Reagan
Goals: Carolina Morace (36), Elisabeth Vignotto (45) / Kerry Davis (11 pen)
Referee: Peter Mikkelsen (Denmark)   Attendance: 504.

61. 25.10.1987   EURO 1989 Qualifiers
                  Urheilukenttä, Kirkkonummi: Finland - England 1-2 (0-0)
Finland: Marianne Sulen, Sirpa Järnfors, Ann Kaasinen, Tiina Lehtola, Maija Liukkonen-
Raitanen, Soile Ojala, Tuula Okkola-Sundman, Hanna-Mari Sarlin, Teerijoki, Anu Toikka,
Anne Virokannas.
England: Terry Wiseman, Brenda Sempare, Debbie Bampton, Gillian Coultard, Marieanne
Spacey, Linda Curl, Lorraine Hunt, Sue Law, Jackie Sherrard, Jackie Slack, Jane Stanley.
Coach: Martin Reagan
Goals: Hanna-Mari Sarlin (79) / Linda Curl (55), Jane Stanley (66)
Referee: Wieland Ziller (Germany)

62. 08.11.1987   EURO 1989 Qualifiers
              Ewood Park, Blackburn: England - Denmark 2-1 (2-1)
England: Terry Wiseman, Brenda Sempare, Debbie Bampton, Gillian Coultard, Kerry Davis, Marieanne Spacey, Lorraine Hunt, Sue Law, Jackie Sherrard, Jackie Slack, Jane Stanley. Coach: Martin Reagan
Denmark: Helle Bjerregaard, Annie Gam-Pedersen, Jette Hansen, Jannie Hansen, Bonny Madsen, Annette Mogensen, Mette Bach Kjær, Kirsten Fabrin (41 Marianne Jacobsen), Ulla Jacobsen, Pernille Obel, Helle Jensen (41 Jette Jensen).
Coach: Birger Peitersen
Goals: Marieanne Spacey (34), Kerry Davis (40 pen) / Jannie Hansen (44)
Referee: John Walter Lloyd (Wales)   Attendance: 700.

63. 08.05.1988   EURO 1989 Qualifiers
              MCH Arena, Herning: Denmark - England 2-0 (1-0)
Denmark: Helle Bjerregaard, Jannie Hansen, Bonny Madsen, Annette Mogensen, Karina Sefron, Lotte Bagge, Marianne Jacobsen, Pernille Obel (75 Jette Jensen), Helle Jensen (41 Mette Bach Kjær), Lone Smidt Nielsen, Lene Hansen. Coach: Keld Gantzhorn
England: Terry Wiseman, Brenda Sempare, Debbie Bampton, Gillian Coultard, Kerry Davis, Joanne Broadbust, Marieanne Spacey, Linda Curl, Angela Gallimore, Lorraine Hunt, Jackie Slack. Coach: Martin Reagan
Goals: Marianne Jacobsen (5), Pernille Obel (58)
Referee: Rune Larsson (Sweden)   Attendance: 1,200.

64. 22.07.1988   Mundialito
              Riva del Garda (Italy): France - England 1-1 (0-1)
France: Sylvie Josset, Sylvie Baracat (41 Hélène Hillion Guillemin), Nathalie Tarade, Marie-Christine Umdenstock, Sophie Ryckeboer Charrier, Marie-Angèle Blin (50 Véronique Bernard), Elisabeth Loisel, Marielle Breton (64' Isabelle Le Boulch), Martine Puentes, Isabelle Musset, Régine Mismacq. Coach: Aimé Mignot
England: Coach: Martin Reagan
Goals: Isabelle Musset (70) / *Unknown*

65. 27.07.1988   Mundialito Semi-finals
              Riva del Garda (Italy): England - USA **2-0**
England: Coach: Martin Reagan
USA: Allman, Werden, Henry, Hamilton, Bates (Kristine Lilly), Belkin, Higgins, Joy Biefeld, Jennings, Gebauer (Mia Hamm), April Heinrichs.
Goals: *Unknown*

66. 30.07.1988   Mundialito Final
              Arco (Italy): England - Italy 2-1 (0-0, 1-1)
England: Terry Wiseman (89 Davidson), Sue Law, Lorraine Hunt, Debbie Bampton, Jackie Sherrard, Gillian Coultard, Brenda Sempare (81 Skillcorn), Marieanne Spacey, Linda Curl, Karen Walker, Jane Stanley. Coach: Martin Reagan
Italy: Roberta Russo, Comparcola, Adele Marsiletti, Principe, Paola Bonato, Federica D'Astolfo, Bavagnoli, Bichi (54 Ferrigno), Carolina Morace, Mega, Capo. Coach: Recagni
Goals: Linda Curl (70, 98) / Carolina Morace (80)
Referee: Cafiero Di Roma (Italy)   Attendance: 1,500.

England won after extra time.

67. 21.08.1988   EURO 1989 Qualifiers
                  Klepp Stadion, Klepp: Norway - England 2-0
Norway: Hege Ludvigsen, Bjørg Storhaug, Liv Strædet, Ellen-Cathrine Scheel Aalbu, Tone Haugen (34 Turid Storhaug), Birthe Hegstad, Torill Hoch-Nielsen (68 Sissel Grude), Linda Medalen, Gunn Lisbeth Nyborg, Heidi Støre, Cathrine Zaborowski Brathen.
Coach: Erling Hokstad
England: Terry Wiseman, Debbie Bampton, Gillian Coultard, Kerry Davis, Joanne Broadbust, Marieanne Spacey, Linda Curl, Lorraine Hunt, Sue Law, Jackie Sherrard, Jane Stanley.
Coach: Martin Reagan
Goals: Ellen-Cathrine Scheel Aalbu, Linda Medalen
Referee: Bo Helén (Sweden)   Attendance: 1,517.

68. 04.09.1988   EURO 1989 Qualifiers
                  The Den, London: England - Finland 1-1
England: Terry Wiseman, Debbie Bampton, Gillian Coultard, Kerry Davis, Joanne Broadbust, Marieanne Spacey, Linda Curl, Lorraine Hunt, Sue Law, Jackie Sherrard, Jane Stanley.
Coach: Martin Reagan
Finland: Marianne Sulen, Minna Honkanen, Sirpa Järnfors, Ann Kaasinen, Tiina Lehtola *(YC)*, Anna-Maria Lehtonen, Soile Ojala *(YC)*, Tuula Okkola-Sundman, Hanna-Mari Sarlin, Merja Savolainen, Anu Toikka.
Goals: Marieanne Spacey / Ann Kaasinen
Referee: W.Keith Burge (Wales)

69. 19.09.1988   EURO 1989 Qualifiers
                  Ewood Park, Blackburn: England - Norway 1-3
England: Terry Wiseman, Debbie Bampton, Gillian Coultard, Kerry Davis, Marieanne Spacey, Karen Walker, Linda Curl, Lorraine Hunt, Sue Law, Jackie Sherrard, Jane Stanley.
Coach: Martin Reagan
Norway: Hege Ludvigsen, Bjørg Storhaug, Liv Strædet, Ellen-Cathrine Scheel Aalbu, Tone Haugen, Birthe Hegstad, Linda Medalen, Gunn Lisbeth Nyborg, Heidi Støre, Cathrine Zaborowski Brathen, Sissel Grude. Coach: Erling Hokstad.
Goals: Karen Walker / Cathrine Zaborowski Brathen, Tone Haugen, Birthe Hegstad
Referee: Frederick McKnight (England)   Attendance: 300.

70. 30.04.1989   Stark's Park, Kirkcaldy: Scotland - England 0-3

71. 13.05.1989   Four Nations Tournament
                  Stade de la Colombière, Épinal (France): England - Netherlands 0-0
England: ..., Kerry Davis, ...   Coach: Martin Reagan
Netherlands: Marleen Wissink, Marjoke de Bakker, Regina Miltenburg, Rianne van Dam, Josephina Timisela, Anja van Rooyen-Bonte, Daniëlle de Winter, Sarina Glotzbach-Wiegman, Marja Heerink, Rita Stegerink-Egberts, Nathalie Geeris (46 Ditte van de Bor).
Coach: Piet Buter

72. 14.05.1989   Four Nations Tournament
           Stade de la Colombière, Épinal (France): England - Belgium 2-0
England: Coach: Martin Reagan
Belgium: Daniella Ottoy (81 Ann Noë), Karin Buysschaert (82 Kristel Laurent), Anita Martens, Dorine Delombaerde, Krista Thys, Kenny Minnaert, Annick Coolens, Sonia Deschepper, Maryse Gevers, Marina Verdonck, Carlo Martens.
Goals: *Unknown*

73. 23.05.1989   Wembley, London: England - Sweden 0-2 (0-1)
England: Terry Wiseman (69 Tracy Davidsson), Jo Broadhurst, Janet Murrey (49 Maria Harper), Debbie Bampton, Jackie Sherrard, Brenda Sempare, Hope Powell, Gillian Coultard, Marieanne Spacey (54 Linda Curl), Kerry Davis, Jane Stanley (73 Karen Walker).
Coach: Martin Reagan
Sweden: Elisabeth Leidinge, Camilla Fors, Anette Hansson (56 Pia Syrén), Eva Zeikfalvy, Åsa Persson (55 Malin Swedberg), Ingrid Johansson, Marie Karlsson (63 Camilla Andersson-Neptune), Pia Sundhage, Helene Björk-Johansson, Lena Videkull, Ulrika Kalte (54 Eleonor Hultin). Coach: Gunilla Paijkull
Goals: Pia Sundhage (6), Lena Videkull (64)
Referee: Brian Hill (England)   Attendance: 3,150.

74. 01.10.1989   EURO 1991 Qualifiers
           Griffin Park, Brentford: England - Finland 0-0
England: Terry Wiseman, Brenda Sempare, Debbie Bampton, Gillian Coultard, Kerry Davis, Hope Powell, Marieanne Spacey, Sue Law, Janice Murray, Jackie Sherrard, Jackie Slack.
Coach: Martin Reagan
Finland: Marja Aaltonen, Sirpa Järnfors, Susanne Kuosmanen, Tiina Lehtola, Maija Liukkonen-Raitanen, Lilian Nieminen-Widjeskog, Soile Ojala, Jutta Rautiainen, Hanna-Mari Sarlin, Anette Sjölind, Anu Toikka.
Referee: Leslie Irvine (Northern Ireland)   Attendance: 2,083.

75. 11.11.1989   Loakes Park, Wycombe: England - Italy 1-1 (0-0)
England: Terry Wiseman, Tracey Davidson, Sue Law, Jackie Sherrard, Gillian Coultard, Debbie Bampton, Clare Lambert, Linda Curl, Hope Powell, Kerry Davis. Marieanne Spacey.
Coach: Martin Reagan
Italy: Giorgia Brenzan (41 Pavan), Marina Cordenons, Adele Marsiletti, Grilli (41 Mega), Maura Furlotti, Maria Mariotti, Antonella Carta, Federica D'Astolfo, Carolina Morace, Feriana (Fery) Ferraguzzi (68 Emma Iozzelli), Bianca Baldelli.   Coach: Sergio Guenza
Goals: Linda Curl (45 pen) / Federica D'Astolfo (5 pen)
Referee: Stephen Dunn (England)

76. 17.03.1990   EURO 1991 Qualifiers
                  Crackstadion, Ypres: Belgium - England 0-3 (0-2)
Belgium: Anne Noe-Haesendonck, Anita Martens, Ingrid Van Herle, Carla Martens, Annick Coolens, Ann De Vroede, Dorine Delombaerde, Peggy Demeester, Sonia Deschepper (54 Nadia Dermul), Emmanuelle Devaux, Annick van Laethem (41 Katty Yde).
England: Terry Wiseman, Brenda Sempare, Gillian Coultard *(YC)*, Kerry Davis, Hope Powell, Marieanne Spacey, Clare Lambert, Sue Law, Janice Murray, Jackie Sherrard, Jackie Slack. Coach: Martin Reagan
Goals: Hope Powell (32, 39), Brenda Sempare (66)
Referee: Hans-Peter Dellwing (Germany)

77. 07.04.1990   EURO 1991 Qualifiers
                  Bramall Lane, Sheffield: England - Belgium 1-0 (0-0)
England: Tracey Davidson, Brenda Sempare, Debbie Bampton, Gillian Coultard, Kerry Davis (72 Karen Walker), Hope Powell, Marieanne Spacey, Sue Law, Janice Murray, Jackie Sherrard, Jackie Slack (55 Clare Lambert).   Coach: Martin Reagan
Belgium: Anne Noe-Haesendonck, Anita Martens, Ingrid Van Herle (72 Nathalie Schrymecker), Carla Martens, Annick Coolens, Véronique Davister, Ann De Vroede (66 Nadia Dermul), Dorine Delombaerde, Sonia Deschepper, Emmanuelle Devaux *(YC)*, Annick van Laethem.
Goal: Gillian Coultard (63)
Referee: Eyjolfur Olafsson (Iceland)

78. 06.05.1990   Love Street, Paisley: Scotland - England 0-4 (0-2)
Scotland: E.Creamer, J.Legget, K.Vaughan (A.Smith), C.Black, S.McNaught, L.McWhinney, K.Mitchell, S.Balley, A.Donaldson (J.Rice), M.Minary (G.Gray), J.North (A.Barr).
England: Terry Wiseman (Tracey Davidson), Sue Law, Clare Lambert, Debbie Bampton, Jackie Sherrard, Gillian Coultard, Linda Curl (Gail Borman), Brenda Sempare, Marieanne Spacey (Karen Walker), T.Davis, Janice Murray.   Coach: Martin Reagan
Goals: Linda Curl (3), Gillian Coultard (27), Karen Walker (..), Gail Borman (..)

79. 12.05.1990   Wembley Stadium, London: England - Scotland 4-0
England: Tracey Davidson, Sue Law, Lou Waller, Clare Lambert, Jackie Sherrard, Gillian Coultard, Gail Borman, Brenda Sempare, Marieanne Spacey, T.Davis, Janice Murray. Coach: Martin Reagan (Used subs: Karen Walker, Stanton).
Scotland:
Goals: Jackie Sherrard, Marieanne Spacey (2x), *Unknown* (og)

80. 27.05.1990   EURO 1991 Qualifiers
                  Klepp Stadion, Kleppe: Norway - England 2-0 (0-0)
Norway: Hilde Strømsvold, Agnete Synnøve Carlsen, Liv Strædet, Trine Dyveke Tviberg, Tone Haugen, Trude Haugland (87 Turid Storhaug), Birthe Hegstad, Linda Medalen, Gunn Lisbeth Nyborg, Heidi Støre, Cathrine Zaborowski Brathen.   Coach: Even Pellerud
England: Terry Wiseman, Brenda Sempare, Debbie Bampton, Gillian Coultard, Kerry Davis, Hope Powell, Marieanne Spacey, Clare Lambert, Sue Law, Jackie Sherrard, Jane Stanley. Coach: Martin Reagan
Goals: Linda Medalen (51), Tone Haugen (76)
Referee: Kaj Østergaard (Denmark)   Attendance: 604.

81. 05.08.1990 North America Cup
National Sports Center, Blaine (USA): England - Germany 1-3 (0-0)
England: Coach: Martin Reagan
Germany: Manuela Goller, Dagmar Uebelhör, Jutta Nardenbach (41 Frauke Kuhlmann), Britta Unsleber, Sissy Raith, Petra Damm (41 Andrea Heinrich), Doris Fitschen (41 Bettina Wiegmann), Silvia Neid (41 Roswitha Bindl), Ursula Lohn, Heidi Mohr, Martina Voss (41 Gudrun Gottschlich). Coach: Gero Bisanz
Goals: *Unknown* / Ursula Lohn (46), Heidi Mohr (47, 48)
Referee: Raúl J. Domínguez (USA)

82. 09.08.1990 North America Cup
National Sports Center, Blaine (USA): England - USA 0-3
England: Coach: Martin Reagan
USA: Mary Harvey, Carla Werden, Linda Hamilton (Lori Henry), Debbie Belkin, Kristine Lilly (Tracey Bates), Shannon Higgins, Julie Foudy, Joy Biefeld, Carin Jennings (Wendy Gebauer), Michelle Akers-Stahl (Mia Hamm), April Heinrichs (Cole).
Goals: Michelle Akers-Stahl (2x), April Heinrichs

83. 11.08.1990 North America Cup
National Sports Center, Blaine (USA): England - Sovjet Union 1-1
England: Coach: Martin Reagan
Sovjet Union: Svetlana Petko, V.Ulyanova, Natalia Bunduchi, N.Gurov, G.Prikhodko (46 L.Krivonogova), Tatiana Bikeykina, L.Smirnova, Irina Aleksandrova, Elena Kononov, Irina Grigoreva, Tatyana Verezubova.
Goals: *Unknown* / Elena Kononov (80)
Referee: Majid Jay (USA)   Attendance: 1,200.

84. 18.08.1990 Wembley, London: England - Italy 1-4 (1-2)
England: Tracey Davidson, Sue Law, Jackie Slack, Barninton, Jackie Sherrard, Gillian Coultard, Hope Powell, Brenda Sempare, Stanton, Kerry Davis, Janice Murray.
Coach: Martin Reagan
Italy: Giorgia Brenzan (63 Antonino), Paola Bonato, Bertolini (16 Correra, 46 Federica D'Astolfo), Emma Iozzelli, Salmaso (63 Magistrali), Mega, Bavagnoli, Migliaccio, Carolina Morace, Feriana (Fery) Ferraguzzi, Fiorini (41 Bianca Baldelli). Coach: Sergio Guenza
Goals: Kerry Davis (42) / Carolina Morace (19, 29, 46, 60)

85. 02.09.1990 EURO 1991 Qualifiers
Old Trafford, Manchester: England - Norway 0-0
England: Terry Wiseman, Brenda Sempare, Lou Waller, Debbie Bampton, Gillian Coultard, Kerry Davis, Hope Powell, Marieanne Spacey, Clare Lambert, Jackie Sherrard, Jane Stanley.
Coach: Martin Reagan
Norway: Reidun Seth-Nysveen, Agnete Synnøve Carlsen, Liv Strædet, Tina Svensson, Trine Dyveke Tviberg, Tone Haugen (41 Ann Kristin Aarones), Birthe Hegstad, Gunn Lisbeth Nyborg, Hege Riise (41 Margunn Humlestøl Haugenes), Heidi Støre, Cathrine Zaborowski Brathen. Coach: Even Pellerud
Referee: Johannes Reygwart (Netherlands)   Attendance: 435.

86. 27.09.1990   EURO 1991 Qualifiers
              Ratina Stadion, Tampere: Finland - England 0-0
Finland: Marja Aaltonen, Ira Eskelinen, Ing Marie Holmberg, Susanne Kuosmanen, Leena Kurkisuo, Tiina Lehtola, Maija Liukkonen-Raitanen, Soile Ojala, Anne Parnila, Anette Sjölind, Anu Toikka.
England: Terry Wiseman, Brenda Sempare, Lou Waller, Debbie Bampton, Gillian Coultard, Kerry Davis, Hope Powell, Marieanne Spacey, Clare Lambert, Jackie Sherrard, Jane Stanley.
Coach: Martin Reagan
Referee: Dr. Klaus Scheurell (Germany)

87. 25.11.1990   EURO 1991 Quarter Finals
              Causeway Stadium, High Wycombe: England - Germany 1-4 (1-3)
England: Terry Wiseman, Brenda Sempare, Lou Waller, Gilian Coultard, Kerry Davis, Marieanne Spacey, Karen Walker, Clare Lambert, Janice Murray, Jackie Sherrard, Jackie Slack. Coach: Martin Reagan
Germany: Marion Isbert-Feiden, Doris Fitschen, Jutta Nardenbach, Sissy Raith, Britta Unsleber, Roswitha Bindl, Petra Damm (50 Bettina Wiegmann), Silvia Neid, Martina Voss-Tecklenburg (67 Gudrun Gottschlich), Ursula Lohn, Heidi Mohr. Coach: Gero Bisanz
Goals: Karen Walker (28) / Heidi Mohr (18, 37, 54), Ursula Lohn (34)
Referee: Jaap Uilenberg (Netherlands)   Attendance: 2,000.

88. 16.12.1990   EURO 1991 Quarter Finals
              Ruhrstadion, Bochum: Germany - England 2-0 (1-0)
Germany: Marion Isbert-Feiden, Doris Fitschen, Jutta Nardenbach, Sissy Raith, Dagmar Uebelhör (53 Susanne Brück-Messner), Britta Unsleber, Roswitha Bindl, Silvia Neid, Martina Voss-Tecklenburg, Ursula Lohn (63 Bettina Wiegmann), Heidi Mohr. Coach: Gero Bisanz
England: Terry Wiseman, Brenda Sempare, Clare Elizabeth Taylor, Lou Waller, Gillian Coultard, Kerry Davis, Marieanne Spacey, Karen Walker, Clare Lambert, Janice Murray, Jackie Sherrard. Coach: Martin Reagan
Goals: Britta Unsleber (24, 80)
Referee: Michel Girard (France)   Attendance: 3,051.

89. 20.04.1991   Adams Park, Wycombe: England - Scotland 5-0
Goals: Marieanne Spacey (3x), Karen Walker (2x)

90. 26.05.1991   Hirson (France): USA - England 3-1
USA: Kimberlee Maslin-Kammerdeiner, Carla Werden, Joy Biefeld, Debbie Belkin, Shannon Higgins, Mia Hamm (McCarthy), Kristine Lilly, Julie Foudy, April Heinrichs, Michelle Akers-Stahl, Carin Jennings.
England: Coach: John Bilton
Goals: April Heinrichs, Michelle Akers-Stahl, Carin Jennings / Gail Borman

91. 28.06.1991   Nordby Stadion, Nordby: Denmark - England 0-0
Denmark: Helle Bjerregaard, Ulla Christensen, Annie Gam-Pedersen, Bonny Madsen, Lotte Bagge (61 Anita Jørgensen), Marianne Jensen, Lisbet Kolding, Pernille Obel, Karina Sefron, Irene Stelling (61 Mette Nielsen), Annette Thychosen (78 Alice Larsen).
Coach: Keld Gantzhorn
England: Coach: John Bilton
Referee: Carl Laursen (Denmark)   Attendance: 132.

92. 30.06.1991   Nordby Stadion, Nordby: Denmark - England 3-3 (2-3)
Denmark: Helle Bjerregaard, Annie Gam-Pedersen, Bonny Madsen, Mette Nielsen, Jannie Hansen, Marianne Jacobsen, Marianne Jensen, Lisbet Kolding, Karina Sefron, Irene Stelling (Ulla Christensen), Annette Thychosen (Lotte Bagge). Coach: Keld Gantzhorn
England: Coach: John Bilton
Goals: Annie Gam-Pedersen (35, 42, 70) / Marieanne Spacey (8), Sarah Begg (18), Karen Walker (27)
Referee: Finn Lambek (Denmark)   Attendance: 300.

93. 07.09.1991   The Dell, Southampton: England - Soviet Union 2-0
Goals: Jackie Sherrard, Gillian Coultard
Attendance: 500.

94. 08.09.1991   Goldstone Ground, Brighton: England - Soviet Union 1-3
Goals: Marieanne Spacey / E.Sotnikova, Natalja Bunduki, V.Barkova

95. 18.04.1992   Euro 93 Qualifiers
                 Bescot Stadium, Walsall: England - Scotland 1-0 (0-0)
England: Tracey Davidson, Clare Elizabeth Taylor, Lou Waller, Debbie Bampton, Gillian Coultard, Marieanne Spacey, Karen Walker, Gail Borman, Sue Law, Janice Murray, Jackie Sherrard. Coach: John Bilton
Scotland: Lyall, Pauline McDonald, Linda Brown, Coleen Dailly, Faulkner, Law, Martin, Isobel McAllister, McBride, Debbie McWhinnie, Kathleen Mitchell *(YC)*.
Goal: Karen Walker (55)
Referee: John Ferry (England)

96. 17.05.1992   EURO 1993 Qualifiers
                 Huish Park, Yeovil: England - Iceland 4-0 (2-0)
England: Lesley Higgs-Shipp, Clare Elizabeth Taylor, Lou Waller, Debbie Bampton, Gillian Coultard, Marieanne Spacey, Karen Walker, Gail Borman, Sue Law, Janice Murray, Jackie Sherrard. Coach: John Bilton
Iceland: Steindóra Sigrídur Steinsdóttir, Gudrún Sæmundsdóttir, Halldóra Vanda Sigurgeirssdóttir (46 Gudrun Jona Kristjansdóttir), Audur Skúladóttir, Sigrún Sigrídur Óttarsdóttir, Ragna Loa Stefansdóttir, Ásta Breidflörd Gunnlaugsdóttir, Halldóra Sigridur Gylfadóttir, Sigurlín Jónsdóttir, Gudrídur Arney Magnúsdóttir (46 Bryndís Valsdóttir), Jónína Halla Víglundsdóttir. Coach: Sigurdur Hannesson
Goals: Debbie Bampton (38,60), Karen Walker (39), Janice Murray (58 pen)
Referee: Denis McArdle (Republic of Ireland)

97. 19.07.1992   EURO 1993 Qualifiers
                 Kópavogsvöllur Stadium, Kópavogur: Iceland - England 1-2 (0-1)
Iceland: Steindóra Sigrídur Steinsdóttir, Gudrun Jona Kristjansdóttir, Gudrún Sæmundsdóttir, Halldóra Vanda Sigurgeirssdóttir, Audur Skúladóttir, Ragna Loa Stefansdóttir, Ásta Breidflörd Gunnlaugsdóttir, Halldóra Sigridur Gylfadóttir (53 Helena Olafsdóttir), Karitas Jónsdóttir, Gudrídur Arney Magnúsdóttir (68 Gudlaug Jónsdóttir), Jónína Halla Víglundsdóttir.
Coach: Sigurdur Hannesson
England: Lesley Higgs-Shipp, Clare Elizabeth Taylor, Lou Waller, Debbie Bampton, Sammy Britton, Gillian Coultard, Karen Walker, Gail Borman, Sue Law, Janice Murray, Jackie Sherrard. Coach: John Bilton
Goals: Ragna Loa Stefansdóttir (60) / Karen Walker (13), Gail Borman (78)
Referee: Roy Helge Olsen (Norway)

98. 23.08.1992   EURO 1993 Qualifiers
McDiarmid Park, Perth: Scotland - England 0-2 (0-1)
Scotland: Lyall, Pauline McDonald, Linda Brown, Pauline Hamill, Pamela Brown, Coleen Dailly, Fowler, Law, Debbie McWhinnie, Kathleen Mitchell, Vaughan.
England: Tracey Davidson, Clare Elizabeth Taylor, Lou Waller, Debbie Bampton, Sammy Britton, Gillian Coultard, Karen Walker, Gail Borman, Sue Law, Janice Murray, Jackie Sherrard. Coach: John Bilton
Goals: Gail Borman (32, 76)
Referee: Johannes (Hans) Reygwart (Netherlands)

99. 17.10.1992   EURO 1993 Quarter-finals
Comunale Solofra, Solofra: Italy - England 3-2 (2-0)
Italy: Giorgia Brenzan, Dolores Prestifillipo, Emma Iozzelli, Marina Cordenons, Elisabeth (Betty) Bavagnoli, Adele Marsiletti, Silvia Fiorini, Federica D'Astolfo *(YC)*, Antonella Carta, Raffaela Salmaso, Carolina Morace *(YC)*. Coach: Sergio Guenza
England: Tracy Davidson, Clare Elizabeth Taylor, Lou Waller, Sammy Britton, Gillian Coultard, Kerry Davis, Marieanne Spacey, Karen Walker, Gail Borman, Janice Murray, Jackie Sherrard. Coach: John Bilton
Goals: Carolina Morace (37, 40), Silvia Fiorini (54) /
Karen Walker (73), Marieanne Spacey (79)
Referee: Gilles Veissière (France)

100. 07.11.1992   EURO 1993 Quarter-finals
AESSEAL New York Stadium, Rotherham: England - Italy 0-3 (0-0)
England: Tracy Davidson, Clare Elizabeth Taylor, Lou Waller, Debbie Bampton, Gillian Coultard, Kerry Davis, Marieanne Spacey, Karen Walker *(RC36)*, Gail Borman, Sue Law, Janice Murray. Coach: John Bilton
Italy: Stefania Antonini, Dolores Prestifillipo, Emma Iozzelli, Marina Cordenons, Betty Bavagnoli, Adele Marsiletti, Silvia Fiorini, Federica D'Astolfo *(YC)*, Antonella Carta, Raffaela Salmaso, Carolina Morace. Coach: Sergio Guenza
Goals: Adele Marsiletti (53), Carolina Morace (55, 78)
Referee: José João Mendes Pratas (Portugal)

101. 25.09.1993   EURO 1995 Qualifiers
Bezigrad Stadium, Ljubljana: Slovenia - England 0-10 (0-5)
Slovenia: Ivica Cizel, Irena Zaloznik, Anica Korpic, Andreja Dolenc, Zdenka Domincovic, Vera Horvat, Majda Karo, Andreja Lapanja, Vijolica Manxzuka, Urska Rek, Alison Skocaj.
England: Lesley Higgs-Shipp, Sammy Britton, Clare Elizabeth Taylor, Debbie Bampton, Karen Burke, Gillian Coultard, Marieanne Spacey, Karen Walker, Gail Borman, Michelle Curley, Janice Murray (75 Kerry Davis). Coach: Ted Copeland
Goals: Clare Elizabeth Taylor (20), Marieanne Spacey (22, 36, 72, 87), Gail Borman (30), Karen Walker (39, 48, 82), Kerry Davis (88)
Referee: Dimitar Ivanov Momirov (Bulgaria)

102. 06.11.1993   EURO 1995 Qualifiers
           Stadion VV Coxyde, Koksijde: Belgium - England 0-3 (0-1)
Belgium: Anne Noe-Haesendonck, Ingrid Van Herle, Kristel Vautmans, Barbara Cravillon, Dorine Delombaerde, Peggy Demeester (46 Katty Yde), Sonia Deschepper *(RC80)*, Andrea Janssens, Carine Maus (61 Annick van Laethem), Myriam Vanslembrouck, Carine Vanstraelen. Coach: Marc Van Geersom
England: Lesley Higgs-Shipp, Kirsty Pealling (87 Lou Waller), Clare Elizabeth Taylor, Debbie Bampton, Gillian Coultard, Hope Powell (70 Karen Burke), Marieanne Spacey *(YC)*, Karen Walker, Gail Borman, Michelle Curley, Janice Murray. Coach: Ted Copeland
Goals: Karen Walker (26, 87), Clare Elizabeth Taylor (83)
Referee: Tore Hollung (Norway)

103. 19.12.1993   EURO 1995 Qualifiers
           Reyno de Navarra, Pamplona: Spain - England 0-0
Spain: Maria ROSER SERRA Carandeli, MARIA Arántzazu Del Puerto ASTIZ, MARÍA ANTONIA "Toña" Is PIÑERA, María del MAR PRIETO Ibáñez, Beatriz Garcia Bernardos, Begoña Casalengua Llorente "GORO", ITZIAR BAKERO Escudero, Galedte Vargas, Esther Torner Hernandez, Begoña Iriarte, Miren Begoña JAUREGUI Ardura.
England: Lesley Higgs-Shipp, Sammy Britton, Clare Elizabeth Taylor, Debbie Bampton, Gillian Coultard, Kerry Davis, Marieanne Spacey, Karen Walker, Gail Borman, Janice Murray, Lou Waller. Coach: Ted Copeland
Referee: Fortunato Alves de Azevedo (Portugal)

104. 20.02.1994   EURO 1995 Qualifiers
           Valley Parade, Bradford: England - Spain 0-0
England: Lesley Higgs-Shipp, Kirsty Pealling, Clare Elizabeth Taylor, Debbie Bampton, Gillian Coultard, Kerry Davis, Hope Powell, Marieanne Spacey, Gail Borman, Janice Murray, Lou Waller. Coach: Ted Copeland
Spain: Maria ROSER SERRA Carandeli, MARIA Arántzazu Del Puerto ASTIZ, MARÍA ANTONIA "Toña" Is PIÑERA, ROSA CASTILLO Varó, María del MAR PRIETO Ibáñez, Beatriz Garcia Bernardos, Ainhoa Escudero Bakero, ITZIAR BAKERO Escudero, Begoña Iriarte, Miren Begoña JAUREGUI Ardura, Mercedes González Laviada.
Referee: Bragi Bergmann (Iceland)

105. 13.03.1994   EURO 1995 Qualifiers
           City Ground, Nottingham: England - Belgium 6-0 (3-0)
England: Lesley Higgs-Shipp, Sammy Britton, Kirsty Pealling, Clare Elizabeth Taylor, Debbie Bampton, Gillian Coultard, Kerry Davis, Marieanne Spacey, Karen Walker, Gail Borman, Lou Waller. Coach: Ted Copeland
Belgium: Anne Noe-Haesendonck, Ingrid Van Herle (46 Katty Yde), Kristel Vautmans, Michele Canniere, Dorine Delombaerde, Peggy Demeester, Andrea Janssens, Daniela Specogna, Peggy van Puymbroeck (79 Elly Schmidtmayer), Myriam Vanslembrouck, Carine Vanstraelen. Coach: Marc Van Geersom
Goals: Marieanne Spacey (13, 22), Karen Walker (19, 63), Kerry Davis (58), Gillian Coultard (86)
Referee: Terje Hauge (Norway)

106. 17.04.1994   EURO 1995 Qualifiers
Griffin Park, Brentford: England - Slovenia 10-0 (2-0)
England: Lesley Higgs-Shipp, Sammy Britton, Kirsty Pealling, Clare Elizabeth Taylor, Debbie Bampton, Gillian Coultard, Kerry Davis (46 Hope Powell), Marieanne Spacey, Karen Walker, Gail Borman, Lou Waller.   Coach: Ted Copeland
Slovenia: Janja Plevnik, Irena Zaloznik, Anica Korpic, Melita Balek, Andreja Dolenc, Zdenka Domincovic, Andreja Lapanja, Vijolica Manxzuka, Urska Rek, Simona Semen, Alison Skocaj.
Goals: Clare Elizabeth Taylor (1, 58), Karen Walker (14, 62), Sammy Britton (60), Gillian Coultard (65, 81), Hope Powell (71), Gail Borman (74), Marieanne Spacey (87)
Referee: Vitor Manuel Melo Pereira (Portugal)

107. 08.10.1994   EURO 1995 Quarter-finals
Laugardalsvöllur Stadium, Reykjavik: Iceland - England 1-2 (1-1)
Iceland: Sigrídur Fanney Pálsdóttir, Audur Skúladóttir, Halldóra Vanda Sigurgeirsdóttir, Gudrún Sæmundsdóttir, Andrea Olga Færseth, Ásthildur Helgadóttir, Gudlaug Jónsdóttir, Margrét Rannveig Ólafsdóttir, Sigrún Sigrídur Óttarsdóttir (69 Gudrún Jóna Kristjánsdóttir), Ragna Lóa Stefánsdóttir, Ásta Breidfjörd Gunnlaugsdóttir.   Coach: Logi Ólafsson
England: Lesley Higgs-Shipp, Kirsty Pealling (YC), Donna Smith, Clare Elizabeth Taylor, Debbie Bampton, Gillian Coultard, Kerry Davis, Marieanne Spacey, Sian Elizabeth Williams, Karen Walker, Janice Murray.   Coach: Ted Copeland
Goals: Margrét Rannveig Ólafsdóttir (31) / Gillian Coultard (5), Kerry Davis (61)
Referee: Timo Keltanen (Finland)   Attendance: 600.

108. 30.10.1994   EURO 1995 Quarter-finals
Goldstone Ground, Brighton: England - Iceland 2-1 (1-1)
England: Lesley Higgs-Shipp, Kirsty Pealling, Donna Smith, Clare Elizabeth Taylor, Debbie Bampton, Gillian Coultard, Kerry Davis (46 Lou Waller (YC)), Marieanne Spacey, Sian Elizabeth Williams, Karen Walker, Janice Murray.   Coach: Ted Copeland
Iceland: Sigrídur Fanney Pálsdóttir, Gudrún Jóna Kristjánsdóttir, Gudrún Sæmundsdóttir (YC), Halldóra Vanda Sigurgeirsdóttir, Audur Skúladóttir (37 Helga Ósk Hannesdóttir), Andrea Olga Færseth (78 Kristín Anna Arnthórsdóttir), Ásthildur Helgadóttir, Gudlaug Jónsdóttir, Margrét Rannveig Ólafsdóttir, Ragna Lóa Stefánsdóttir, Ásta Breidfjörd Gunnlaugsdóttir.
Coach: Logi Ólafsson
Goals: Gillian Coultard (13), Marieanne Spacey (65) / Ásta Breidfjörd Gunnlaugsdóttir (36)
Referee: Richard O'Hanlon (Republic of Ireland)   Attendance: 2.000

109. 11.12.1994   EURO 1995 Semi-finals
Vicarage Road, Watford: England - Germany 1-4 (1-1)
England: Lesley Higgs-Shipp, Sammy Britton, Kirsty Pealling, Clare Elizabeth Taylor, Debbie Bampton, Karen Burke, Gillian Coultard, Kerry Davis, Karen Walker, Karen Farley, Janice Murray.   Coach: Ted Copeland
Germany: Manuela Goller, Birgitt Austermühl, Anouschka Bernhard, Doris Fitschen, Sandra Minnert (46 Pia Wunderlich), Maren Meinert, Silvia Neid, Martina Voss-Tecklenburg, Bettina Wiegmann, Patricia Brocker-Grigoli (68 Birgit Prinz), Heidi Mohr.   Coach: Gero Bisanz
Goals: Karen Farley (7) / Heidi Mohr (32, 80), Patricia Brocker-Grigoli (68), Bettina Wiegmann (87 pen)
Referee: Sándor Piller (Hungary)   Attendance: 800.

110. 26.01.1995   Florence: Italy - England 1-1 (0-0)
Italy: Giorgia Brenzen, Damiana Deiana, Ferrari, Emma Iozzelli, Marina Cordenons, Pittalis (46 Tavalazzi, 61 Casu), Fiorini, Carta, Carolina Morace, Bianca Baldelli (85 Manuela Tesse), Maria Rita Guarino (66 Sberti).
England: Lesley Higgs-Skipp (46 Pauline Cope Boanas), Kirsty Pealling (46 Karen Burke), Woodhead (46' Hope Powell), Smith, Clare Elizabeth Taylor, Gillian Coultard, Marieanne Spacey, Debbie Bampton, Karen Farley, Kerry Davis, Sian Elizabeth Williams.
Coach: Ted Copeland
Goals: Carolina Morace (56) / Karen Farley (89)
Referee: Bravi (Italy)

111. 23.02.1995   EURO 1995 Semi-finals
          Ruhrstadion, Bochum: Germany - England 2-1 (1-1)
Germany: Manuela Goller, Dagmar Pohlmann (80 Ursula Lohn), Jutta Nardenbach, Birgitt Austermühl, Anouschka Bernhard, Bettina Wiegmann, Martina Voss-Tecklenburg, Heidi Mohr, Patricia Brocker Grigoli (46 Birgit Prinz), Silvia Neid, Maren Meinert.
Coach: Gero Bisanz
England: Pauline Cope Boanas, Lou Waller, Clare Elizabeth Taylor, Tina Ann Mapes, Sian Elizabeth Williams, Marieanne Spacey, Kerry Davis, Gillian Coultard, Karen Burke, Karen Farley, Karen Walker.   Coach: Ted Copeland
Goals: Lou Waller (34 og), Birgit Prinz (79) / Karen Farley (1)
Referee: Kostadin Gerginov (Bulgaria)   Attendance: 7,000.

112. 13.05.1995   Örjans Vall, Halmstad: Sweden - England 4-0 (0-0)
Sweden: Annelie Nilsson, Malin Lundgren (Helen Häglund), Pia Sundhage, Anna Pohjanen (Anneli Wahlgren), Lena Videkull, Ulrika Kalte (Malin Flink), Anneli Andelén (Anneli Olsson), Malin Lovén, Kristin Bengtsson (Åsa Lönnkvist), Susanne Fahlström (Anika Boicevic), Åsa Jakobsson.   Coach: Bengt Simonsson
England: Pauline Cope Boanas (Kerry Davis), Tina Ann Mapes, Gillian Coultard (Karen Walker), Becky Easton, Karen Farley, Hope Powell (Lesley Higgs), Brenda Sempare (Donna Smith), Marieanne Spacey (Sian Elizabeth Williams), Clare Elizabeth Taylor, Kirsty Pealling, Jo Broadhurst.   Coach: Ted Copeland
Goals: Claire Taylor (55 og), Anneli Andelén (72), Ulrika Kalte (80), Pia Sundhage (84)
Referee: Bente Folsing (Denmark)   Attendance: 427.

113. 06.06.1995   FIFA World Cup 1995 Sweden
          Olympiastadion, Helsingborg: England - Canada 3-2 (0-0)
England: Pauline Cope Boanas, Tina Ann Mapes (70 Hope Powell), Sammy Britton, Clare Elizabeth Taylor, Brenda Sempare, Karen Burke, Gillian Coultard, Marieanne Spacey, Debbie Bampton, Karen Farley, Karen Walker (75 Kerry Davis).   Coach: Ted Copeland
Canada: Carla Chin, Charmaine Hooper, Janine Helland Wood, Michelle Ring, Cathy Ross (78 Suzanne Muir), Andrea Neil, Geri Donnelly, Veronica O'Brien, Angela Kelly, Silvana Burtini, Helen Stoumbos.   Coach: Sylvie Béliveau
Goals: Gillian Coultard (51 pen, 85), Marieanne Spacey (76 pen) /
Helen Stoumbos (87), Geri Donnelly (90+1)
Referee: Eva Ödlund (Sweden)   Attendance: 655.

114. 08.06.1995   FIFA World Cup 1995 Sweden
           Tingvalla IP, Karlstad: Norway - England 2-0 (2-0)
Norway: Bente Nordby, Linda Medalen (73 Randi Leinan), Anne Nymark Andersen
Rylandsholm, Nina Nymark Andersen Jakobsen, Tina Svensson, Gro Espeseth, Merete
Myklebust, Hege Riise (85 Hege Gunnerød), Ann Kristin Aarønes, Tone Haugen, Kristin
Sandberg (66 Marianne Pettersen). Coach: Even Jostein Pellerud
England: Pauline Cope Boanas, Tina Ann Mapes, Sammy Britton (65 Kerry Davis), Clare
Elizabeth Taylor, Brenda Sempare, Karen Burke, Gillian Coultard (82 Becky Easton),
Marieanne Spacey (36 Hope Powell), Debbie Bampton, Karen Farley, Karen Walker.
Coach: Ted Copeland
Goals: Tone Haugen (7), Hege Riise (37)
Referee: Eduardo Gamboa Martinez (Chile)   Attendance: 5,520.

115. 10.06.1995   FIFA World Cup 1995 Sweden
           Tingvalla IP, Karlstad: Nigeria - England 2-3 (1-3)
Nigeria: Ann Chiejine, Yinka Kudaisi, Florence Omagbemi, Mavis Ogun, Prisca Emeafu,
Ngozi Ezeocha (44 Maureen Mmadu), Phoebe Ebimiekumo, Patience Avre (47 Nkiru
Okosieme), Ann Mukoro, Rita Nwadike, Adaku Okoroafor.   Coach: Paul Ebiye Hamilton
England: Lesley Higgs Shipp, Tina Ann Mapes, Clare Elizabeth Taylor (81 Sammy Britton),
Brenda Sempare (58 Becky Easton), Karen Burke, Gillian Coultard, Marieanne Spacey (70
Hope Powell), Debbie Bampton, Kerry Davis, Karen Farley, Karen Walker.
Coach: Ted Copeland
Goals: Adaku Okoroafor (13), Rita Nwadike (74) / Karen Farley (10, 38), Karen Walker (27)
Referee: Ingrid Jonsson (Sweden)   Attendance: 1,843.

116. 13.06.1995   FIFA World Cup 1995 Sweden
           Arosvallen, Västerås: Germany - England 3-0 (1-0)
Germany: Manuela Goller, Sandra Minnert, Anouschka Bernhard, Ursula Lohn, Silva Neid,
Maren Meinert (85' Pia Wunderlich), Martina Voss-Tecklenburg, Bettina Wiegmann, Dagmar
Pohlmann, Birgit Prinz (67 Patricia Brocker Grigoli), Heidi Mohr.   Coach: Gero Bisanz
England: Pauline Cope Boanas, Tina Ann Mapes (79 Lou Waller), Clare Elizabeth Taylor (87
Sammy Britton), Brenda Sempare, Karen Burke, Gillian Coultard (46 Becky Easton),
Marieanne Spacey, Debbie Bampton, Kerry Davis, Karen Farley, Karen Walker.
Coach: Ted Copeland
Goals: Martina Voss-Tecklenburg (41), Maren Meinert (55), Heidi Mohr (82)
Referee: Bente Ovedie Skogvang (Norway)   Attendance: 2.317.

117. 01.11.1995   EURO 1997 Qualifiers
           Roker Park Ground, Sunderland: England - Italy 1-1 (1-1)
England: Pauline Cope-Boanas, Gillian Coultard, Becky Easton, Tina Ann Mapes, Debbie
Bampton, Karen Burke, Kerry Davis, Hope Powell, Kelly Jayne Smith, Marieanne Spacey,
Karen Farley.   Coach: Ted Copeland
Italy: Giorgia Brenzan, Manuela Tesse, Elisabeth Bavagnoli, Emma Iozzelli, Marina
Cordenons, Florinda Ciardi, Federica D'Astolfo, Tatiana Zorri (25 Deiana, 57 Balducci),
Bianca Baldelli, Carolina Morace, Maria Rita Guarino.   Coach: Sergio Guenza
Goals: Gillian Coultard (33) / Carolina Morace (44)
Referee: Christine Frai (Germany)

118. 19.11.1995   EURO 1997 Qualifiers
The Valley, London: England - Croatia 5-0 (4-0)
England: Pauline Cope-Boanas, Gillian Coultard, Becky Easton, Carol Harwood, Debbie Bampton, Karen Burke, Kerry Davis, Hope Powell, Karen Farley, Kelly Jayne Smith, Karen Walker. Coach: Ted Copeland
Croatia: Anica Ganz, Marija Milas, Renate Pirsa (46 Marina Koljenik *(YC80)*), Brankica Strbac-Drljaca, Nada Besker, Marija Damjanovic (37 Tanja Kovac), Marija Matuzic *(YC12)*, Andreja Rogar, Mihaela Gurdon, Ivana Iljic (55 Mirjana Sola), Blazenka Logarusic. Coach: Maijan Gvozden
Goals: Karen Farley (22, 45), Karen Walker (27, 37), Kelly Jayne Smith (90 pen)
Referee: Vibeke Karlsen-Gabrielsen (Norway)

119. 11.02.1996 EURO 1997 Qualifiers
Campo das Portas do Sol, Benavente: Portugal - England 0-5 (0-2)
Portugal: CARLA CRISTINA Trindade Aco Correia, Anabela Fernanda Pinto Silva "BÉ", ROSALINA Maria Oliveira e Silva, CARLA Maria Filipe RODRIGUES (83 SANDRA Cristina de Castro e SILVA), OLÍVIA Maria Silva Marinho, MARIA JOÃO Fernandes Clemente Lopes XAVIER *(YC)* (70 Elvira CARLA Almeida SOARES), PATRÍCIA Alexandra Pimentel Sequeira, PAULA Adelina de Sousa REIS, CARLA Sofia Basilio COUTO *(YC)* (85 PAULA CRISTINA Dias Santos), ALFREDINA Maria Seabra da Silva *(YC)*, Anabela Guerra Conceicao "CAZUZA". Coach: Antonio Simoes
England: Pauline Cope-Boanas, Gillian Coultard, Becky Easton, Mo Marley, Debbie Bampton, Karen Burke, Kerry Davis (61 Marie-Anne Catterall), Hope Powell, Sian Elizabeth Williams, Karen Farley, Kelly Jayne Smith. Coach: Ted Copeland
Goals: Hope Powell (25), Karen Farley (33), Gillian Coultard (48), Marie-Anne Catterall (76), Karen Burke (89)
Referee: Regina Belksma-Konink (Netherlands)

120. 16.03.1996   EURO 1997 Qualifiers
Stadio San Vito, Cosenza: Italy - England 2-1 (0-1)
Italy: Giorgia Brenzan, Manuela Tesse, Elisabeth Bavagnoli, Emma Iozzelli, Marina Cordenons, Antonella Carta, Fabiana Correra, Federica D'Astolfo, Tatiana Zorri (46 Salmaso), Carolina Morace, Maria Rita Guarino. Coach: Sergio Guenza
England: Pauline Cope-Boanas, Gillian Coultard, Becky Easton (72 Tina Ann Mapes), Mo Marley (46 Carol Harwood), Debbie Bampton, Kerry Davis (78 Baley), Hope Powell, Tara Proctor, Sian Elizabeth Williams, Kelly Jayne Smith, Karen Walker. Coach: Ted Copeland
Goals: Antonella Carta (50), Carolina Morace (59) / Kelly Jayne Smith (43)
Referee: Florence Dorigny (France)

121. 18.04.1996   EURO 1997 Qualifiers
Gradski vrt, Osijek: Croatia - England 0-2 (0-2)
Croatia: Anica Ganz, Marija Milas (76 Klara Stuburic), Renate Pirsa, Katica Rumbocic, Nada Besker *(YC80)*, Marija Damjanovic (87 Tanja Kovac), Marija Matuzic, Branka Kozic, Andreja Rogar *(YC48)*, Snjezana Focic, Blazenka Logarusic. Coach: Maijan Gvozden
England: Pauline Cope-Boanas, Gillian Coultard, Mo Marley, Mary Rose Phillip, Debbie Bampton, Karen Burke, Kerry Davis (35 Vicky Exley), Hope Powell, Sian Elizabeth Williams *(YC57)*, Kelly Jayne Smith, Marie-Anne Catterall. Coach: Ted Copeland
Goals: Kelly Jayne Smith (34), Vicky Exley (38)
Referee: Galina Lazarova Doneva-Hristova (Bulgaria)

122. 19.05.1996   EURO 1997 Qualifiers
   Griffin Park, Brentford: England - Portugal 3-0 (2-0)
England: Pauline Cope-Boanas, Gillian Coultard, Kelley Few *(YC)* (55 Kimberly Jerray-Silver), Tina Ann Mapes (70 Donna Smith), Mo Marley, Mary Rose Phillip, Karen Burke, Kerry Davis, Sian Elizabeth Williams, Kelly Jayne Smith, Maria Harper-Stanton (66 Vicky Exley).   Coach: Ted Copeland
Portugal: CARLA CRISTINA Trindade Aco Correia (13 Paula CRISTINA Gomes PERA), ANA RITA Andrade Gomes (60 SANDRA SILVA de Castro e Silva), Anabela Fernanda Pinto Silva "BÉ", ROSALINA Maria Oliveira Silva, OLÍVIA Maria Silva Marinho (46 ADÍLIA Jesus Correia MARTINS), MARIA JOÃO Fernandes Clemente Lopes XAVIER *(YC)*, Ana PAULA Martins FREITAS, PATRICIA Alexandra Pimentel SEQUEIRA, CARLA Sofia Basilio COUTO, ALFREDINA Maria Seabra Silva, Anabela Guerra Conceicao "CAZUZA".
Coach: Antonio Simoes
Goals: Kerry Davis (9, 54), Kelly Jayne Smith (38)
Referee: Bente Ovedie Skogvang (Norway)

123. 08.09.1996   EURO 1997 Play-offs
   IMD Fontamar Montilla, Córdoba: Spain - England 2-1 (1-0)
Spain: Maria ROSER SERRA Carandeli, MARIA Arántzazu Del Puerto ASTIZ *(YC)*, JUDITH COROMINAS Serrats, MARÍA ANTONIA "Toña" Is PIÑERA, MARINA NOHALEZ Caballero, MAIDER CASTILLO Muga, ROSA CASTILLO Varó, YOLANDA Lara MATEOS Franco, María del MAR PRIETO Ibáñez, Arantza GONDRA Basterretxea, MARÍA LUISA PUNAL Valverde.
England: Pauline Cope-Boanas, Gillian Coultard, Becky Easton, Tina Ann Mapes, Mo Marley (46 Kelly Few), Debbie Bampton, Karen Burke, Kerry Davis (46 Maria Harper-Stanton), Hope Powell, Tara Proctor, Sue Smith.   Coach: Ted Copeland
Goals: Marie de MAR PRIETO Ibanes (8, 56) / Hope Powell (64)
Referee: Tiziana Calamosca (Italy)

124. 29.09.1996   EURO 1997 Play-offs
   Prenton Park, Tranmere: England - Spain 1-1 (0-1)
England: Pauline Cope-Boanas, Gillian Coultard, Kelly Few, Mo Marley, Debbie Bampton, Karen Burke, Kerry Davis (46 Maria Harper-Stanton), Hope Powell (46 Vicky Exley), Tara Proctor, Sian Elizabeth Williams, Kelly Jayne Smith (46 Tina Ann Mapes).
Coach: Ted Copeland
Spain: Maria ROSER SERRA Carandeli, MARIA Arántzazu Del Puerto ASTIZ, JUDITH COROMINAS Serrats *(YC)*, MARÍA ANTONIA "Toña" Is PIÑERA *(YC)*, MARINA NOHALEZ Caballero *(YC)*, MAIDER CASTILLO Muga, ROSA CASTILLO Varó, YOLANDA Lara MATEOS Franco, María del MAR PRIETO Ibáñez *(YC)*, Arantza GONDRA Basterretxea, MARÍA LUISA PUNAL Valverde.
Goals: Maria Harper-Stanton (77) / YOLANDA Lara MATEOS Franco (41)
Referee: Bente Folsing (Denmark)

125. 27.02.1997   Deepdale, Preston: England - Germany 4-6 (0-4)
England: Pauline Cope Boanas (Rachel Brown-Finnis), Hope Powell (Becky Easton), Mo Marley, Gillian Coultard, Karen Burke, Debbie Bampton (Lou Waller), Kelly Smith (Sue Smith), Kelly Few (Vicky Exley), Sian Williams, Alex Cottier, Jo Broadhurst.
Coach: Ted Copeland
Germany: Nadine Angerer (46 Silke Rottenberg), Anouschka Bernhard, Ariane Hingst, Doris Fitschen, Pia Wunderlich (46 Sonja Beate Fuss), Bettina Wiegmann, Martina Voss-Tecklenburg (46 Renate Lingor), Kerstin Stegemann (46 Katja Bornschein), Steffi Jones, Claudia Müller, Maren Meinert.   Coach: Tina Theune
Goals: Hope Powell (49 pen), Gillian Coultard (70, 78), Sue Smith (87) /
Pia Wunderlich (10, 12), Claudia Müller (25, 46, 90+1), Kelly Few (43 og)
Referee: Stephen Lodge (England)   Attendance: 1,500.

126. 09.03.1997   Bramall Lane, Sheffield: England - Scotland 6-0
England: Pauline Cope Boanas (Rachel Brown-Finnis), Tina Ann Mapes, Hope Powell (Mary-Anne Catterall), Mo Marley (Fay White), Gillian Coultard, Karen Burke, Debbie Bampton (Becky Easton), Kelly Smith, Sian Williams (Sue Smith), Alex Cottier, Jo Broadhurst.
Coach: Ted Copeland
Scotland:
Goals: Jo Broadhurst (3x), Gillian Coultard (2x), Mo Marley

127. 23.04.1997   Ruffini Stadium Turin, Torino: Italy - England 2-0 (0-0)
Italy: Brenzan, Tavalazzi, Bavagnoli (61 Deiana), Iozzelli, Nannini (63 Marchio), D'Astolfo, Zorri (46' Ulivi), Correra (59 Ulivieri), Guarino (46 Panico), Baldelli (72 Murelli), Carta.
Coach: Sergio Guenza
England: Pauline Cope Boanas (73 Rachel Brown-Finnis), Mo Marley, Gillian Coultard, Karen Burke, Debbie Bampton (57 Tina Ann Mapes), Kerry Davis, Kelly Smith (73 Sue Smith), Sian Williams (82 N.Daly), Jo Broadhurst, Mary Phillip, Pru Buckley (57 Vicky Exley).
Coach: Ted Copeland
Goals: Ulivi (75), Carta (82)
Referee: Gozzi (Italy)

128. 09.05.1997   Spartan Stadium, San Jose: USA - England 5-0 (2-0)
USA: Briana Scurry (Ducar), L.Fair, Brandi Chastain, Pearce (R.Fair), MacMillan, Tisha Venturini (Baumgardt), Julie Foudy, Kristine Lilly, Tiffeny Milbrett, Debbie Keller (Parlow), Mia Hamm (Pearman).
England: Pauline Cope Boanas (Tina Lindsay), Tina Ann Mapes, Becky Easton (Sian Williams), Hope Powell (Kelly Smith), Mo Marley, Gillian Coultard, Karen Burke, Debbie Bampton, Vicky Exley (Pru Buckley), Alex Cottier (Mary Phillip), Jo Broadhurst.
Coach: Ted Copeland
Goals: MacMillan (37), Mia Hamm (45, 51, 60), Julie Foudy (81)
Attendance: 17,358.

129. 11.05.1997   Merlo Field, Portland: USA - England 6-0 (4-0)
USA: Briana Scurry (Mead), L. Fair, Brandi Chastain, Pearce, Julie Foudy (Perman), Tisha Venturini (R. Fair), Baumgardt, Kristine Lilly, Tiffeny Milbrett, Parlow (Debbie Keller), Mia Hamm (French).
England: Pauline Cope Boanas (Sarah Reed), Tina Ann Mapes, Becky Easton (Sian Williams), Hope Powell (Kelly Smith), Mo Marley, Gillian Coultard, Karen Burke, Debbie Bampton, Vicky Exley (Pru Buckley), Alex Cottier (Mary Phillip), Jo Broadhurst.   Coach: Ted Copeland
Goals: Mia Hamm (7), Parlow (12, 39), Tiffeny Milbrett (28), Kristine Lilly (72), Debbie Keller (84)
Attendance: 5,049.

130. 08.06.1997   Åråsen Stadion, Lillestrøm: Norway - England 4-0 (4-0)
Norway: Bente Dalum Nordby, Henriette Dalseng Viker (56 Gøril Kringen), Agnete Synnøve Carlsen, Gro Espeseth, Anne Nymark Rylandsholm (77 Brit Sandaune), Marianne Iren Pettersen, Hege Riise, Heidi Støre (72 Monica Knudsen), Unni Lehn (57 Margun Haugenes), Ann Kristin Aarønes (46' Merete Myklebust), Linda Flan Medalen.
England: Pauline Cope Boanas (88 Rachel Brown-Finnis), Becky Easton, Hope Powell (88 Tina Lindsay), Mo Marley (88 Carol Harwood), Gillian Coultard, Karen Burke, Kerry Davis, Kelly Smith, Sian Williams, Lou Waller (67 Sue Smith), Jo Broadhurst (88 Vicky Exley).
Coach: Ted Copeland
Goals: Gro Espeseth (3 pen, 21), Linda Flan Medalen (23), Heidi Støre (30)
Referee: Ingrid Jonsson (Norway)   Attendance: 1,005.

131. 23.08.1997   Almondvale Stadium, Livingston: Scotland - England 0-4
Scotland:
England: Pauline Cope Boanas, Mary Phillip (Becky Easton), Sammy Britton (Danielle Murphy), Hope Powell, Mo Marley (Fay White), Gillian Coultard, Karen Burke, Pru Buckley (K.Massey), Rachel Yankey, Kerry Davis (Vicky Exley), Sue Smith (Justine Joanna Lorton). Coach: Ted Copeland
Goals: Kerry Davis (2x), Sammy Britton, Rachel Yankey

132. 25.09.1997   FIFA World Cup 1999 Qualifiers
           Paul Greifzu Stadium, Dessau: Germany - England 3-0 (1-0)
Germany: Silke Rottenberg, Doris Fitschen, Ariane Hingst (46 Sandra Smisek), Stephanie Ann Jones, Sandra Minnert, Kerstin Stegemann, Melanie Hoffmann, Bettina Wiegmann, Pia Wunderlich, Monika Meyer (75 Sonja Fuss), Birgit Prinz.   Coach: Tina Theune-Meyer
England: Rachel Brown-Finnis, Sammy Britton, Gillian Coultard, Becky Easton *(YC)*, Mo Marley, Karen Burke, Kerry Davis, Hope Powell, Sue Smith, Rachel Yankey, Jo Broadhurst *(YC)* (82 Danielle Murphy).   Coach: Ted Copeland
Goals: Monika Meyer (13), Sandra Smisek (68), Birgit Prinz (75)
Referee: Bente Ovedie Skogvang (Norway)   Attendance: 8,451.

133. 30.10.1997   FIFA World Cup 1999 Qualifiers
   Upton Park (Boleyn Ground), London: England - Netherlands 1-0 (0-0)
England: Pauline Cope-Boanas, Sammy Britton, Gillian Coultard, Becky Easton, Tina Ann Mapes, Karen Burke, Kerry Davis, Hope Powell, Sue Smith, Rachel Yankey (46 Natasha Daly, 77 Marie-Anne Catterall), Jo Broadhurst.   Coach: Ted Copeland
Netherlands: Marleen Wissink, Willemijn Lodder, Sandra van Tol, Annemieke Kiesel-Griffioen, Gilanne Louwaars (75 Elisabeth Migchelsen), Sandra Muller, Sarina Wiegman-Glotzbach, Jessica Torny, Minke van der Waals (59 Annemiek van Waarden), Vera Pauw, Sandra Roos (80 Lisette Koning).   Coach: Ruud Dokter
Goal: Sue Smith (60)
Referee: Asim Khudiev (Azerbaijan)   Attendance: 2,002.

134. 15.02.1998   Stade Jacques Fould, Alençon: France - England 3-2 (1-0)
France: Corine Lagache, Emmanuelle Sykora (65 Nelly Guilbert), Cécille Locatelli, Fabienne Prieux, Corinne Diacre, Sandrine Soubeyrand (46 Peggy Provost), Stéphanie Morel (61 Véronique Sourdin), Elodie Woock, Anne Zenoni (71 Nicole Turcot), Marinette Pichon, Hoda Lattaf.   Coach: Elisabeth Loisel
England: Pauline Cope Boanas (Rachel Brown-Finnis), Sammy Britton, Hope Powell, Mo Marley (Danielle Murphy), Gillian Coultard (Justine Joanna Lorton), Karen Burke, Sue Smith (Rachel Yankey), Kerry Davis (Mary-Anne Catterall), Becky Easton (Kate Massey), Faye White (Claire Utley), Mel Garside.   Coach: Ted Copeland
Goals: Marinette Pichon (42, 59), Hoda Lattaf (80) / Kerry Davis (57), Karen Burke (68)
Referee: Jacky Legrain (France)   Attendance: 683.

135. 08.03.1998   FIFA World Cup 1999 Qualifiers
   The Den Stadium, Millwall: England - Germany 0-1 (0-1)
England: Rachel Brown-Finnis, Sammy Britton, Gillian Coultard, Mo Marley (46 Mel Garside-Wight), Danielle Murphy, Faye White, Karen Burke, Kerry Davis (25 Becky Easton), Hope Powell (82 Claire Utley), Sue Smith, Kelly Jayne Smith.   Coach: Ted Copeland
Germany: Claudia von Lanken, Doris Fitschen, Ariane Hingst (86 Inka Grings), Stephanie Ann Jones, Sandra Minnert, Kerstin Stegemann, Stefanie Gottschlich (46 Renate Lingor), Melanie Hoffmann, Martina Voss-Tecklenburg, Birgit Prinz, Sandra Smisek (60 Monika Meyer).   Coach: Tina Theune-Meyer
Goal: Sandra Smisek (33)
Referee: Eva Ödlund (Sweden)   Attendance: 4,917.

136. 21.04.1998   The Hawthorns, West Bromwich: England - Italy 1-2 (1-0)
England: Pauline Cope Boanas (46 Rachel Brown-Finnis), Danielle Murphy, Tara Proctor (88 Mo Marley), Hope Powell, Faye White, Gillian Coultard, Claire Utley, Sammy Britton (77 Becky Easton), Jo Broadhurst (46 Alex Cottier), Mel Garside (45 Mary-Anne Catterall), Sue Smith.   Coach: Ted Copeland
Italy: Pulerà (46 Comin), Deiana, Duò (40 Miniati), Stefanelli (31 Marchio), Tavalazzi, Tesse, Guarino (46 Ulivi), Zorri (88 Iannuzzell), Panico (46 Sberti), Carta (62 Maglio), Ciardi (62 D'Astolfo).   Coach: Sergio Vatta
Goals: Faye White (5) / Sberti (70), Maglio (76)
Referee: Reed (England)

137. 14.05.1998   FIFA World Cup 1999 Qualifiers
Oldham Stadium, Oldham: England - Norway 1-2 (1-1)
England: Pauline Cope-Boanas, Sammy Britton, Gillian Coultard, Mo Marley, Faye White, Karen Burke, Hope Powell (46 Danielle Murphy), Sue Smith, Rachel Yankey, Kelly Jayne Smith, Karen Walker.   Coach: Ted Copeland
Norway: Bente Nordby, Gøril Kringen, Brit Sandaune, Henriette Dalseng Viker, Ann Kristin Aarones (90 Ingrid Camilla Fosse Sæthre), Monica Knudsen *(YC)*, Unni Lehn (46 Elisabeth Fagereng), Hege Riise, Margunn Humlestøl Haugenes, Linda Medalen, Marianne Iren Pettersen.   Coach: Per Mathias Høgmo
Goals: Faye White (45) / Monica Knudsen (39), Margunn Humlestøl Haugenes (90)
Referee: Valery Onufer (Ukraine)   Attendance: 2,380.

138. 23.05.1998   FIFA World Cup 1999 Qualifiers
Sportpark Olympia, Waalwijk: Netherlands - England 2-1 (1-1)
Netherlands: Marleen Wissink, Willemijn Lodder, Sandra van Tol, Annemieke Kiesel-Griffioen, Gilanne Louwaars, Sandra Muller (46 Minke van der Waal), Miranda Noom, Sarina Wiegman-Glotzbach, Shirley Smith, Jessica Torny (46 Elisabeth Migchelsen), Vera Pauw.   Coach: Ruud Dokter
England: Pauline Cope-Boanas, Sammy Britton, Gillian Coultard, Mo Marley (46 Becky Easton), Danielle Murphy, Faye White, Karen Burke, Sue Smith, Rachel Yankey, Kelly Jayne Smith, Karen Walker.   Coach: Ted Copeland
Goals: Miranda Noom (1, 46) / Karen Walker (19)
Referee: Khagani Mamedov (Azarbaijan)

139. 26.07.1998   Victoria Park, Dagenham: England - Sweden 0-1 (0-0)
England: Pauline Cope Boanas, Becky Easton, Mo Marley, Danielle Murphy, Sue Smith, Gillian Coultard, Karen Burke, Rachel Yankey, Sammy Britton, Kelly Smith, Karen Walker.   Coach: Ted Copeland
Sweden: Ulrika Olsson, Karolina Walfridsson Westberg, Jane Törnqvist, Åsa Lönnkvist, Kristin Bengtsson (Christin Lilja), Anna Pohjanen (Camilla Ackerfors), Cecilia Sandell (Salina Olsson), Sara Call, Malin Lovén, Hanna Ljungberg (Linda Fagerström), Victoria Sandell (Malin Moström).   Coach: Marika Domanski-Lyfors
Goal: Malin Moström (83)
Referee: Dermot Gallagher (England)   Attendance: 650.

140. 15.08.1998   FIFA World Cup 1999 Qualifiers
Åråsen Stadion, Lillestrøm: Norway - England 2-0 (0-0)
Norway: Bente Nordby, Gro Espeseth, Silje Jørgensen Anzjøn (42 Hege Gunnerød), Gøril Kringen, Brit Sandaune, Henriette Dalseng Viker, Hege Riise, Ragnhild Øren Gulbrandsen (60 Tone Gunn Frustøl Eriksen), Margunn Humlestøl Haugenes (85 Unni Lehn), Linda Medalen, Marianne Iren Pettersen.   Coach: Per Mathias Høgmo
England: Pauline Cope-Boanas, Sammy Britton, Gillian Coultard, Becky Easton, Mo Marley, Karen Burke, Sue Smith, Rachel Yankey, Jo Broadhurst (46 Tara Proctor), Kelly Jayne Smith, Karen Walker (46 Kate Massey).   Coach: Ted Copeland
Goals: Marianne Iren Pettersen (70), Brit Sandaune (89)
Referee: Jaroslav Jara (Czech Republic)   Attendance: 1,054.

141. 12.09.1998   FIFA World Cup 1999 Qualifiers
Stadionul Poiana, Câmpina: Romania - England 1-4 (0-2)
Romania: Bianca Tanasa (Lenuta Pop), Magda Abrasu, Magda Botoroaga, Petrica Neculai, Dana Pufulete, Dana Pintea, Adriana Grigore, Elena Ducan, Mirela Laslo, Gabriela Enache, Marcela Surdu. Coaches: Ion Numweiller (III) & Maria Delicoiu
England: Pauline Cope-Boanas (46 Sarah Reed), Becky Easton, Mo Marley, Danielle Murphy, Faye White, Karen Burke, Gillian Coultard, Sue Smith, Sian Elizabeth Williams, Karen Walker (46 Natasha Daly), Rachel Yankey. Coach: Hope Powell
Goals: Gabriela Enache / Rachel Yankey, Sue Smith, Karen Walker (2x)

142. 11.10.1998   FIFA World Cup 1999 Qualifiers
Adams Park, Wycombe: England - Romania 2-1 (1-1)
England: Pauline Cope-Boanas, Becky Easton, Mo Marley (46 Faye White), Danielle Murphy, Sammy Britton, Karen Burke (46 Tara Proctor), Gillian Coultard, Sue Smith, Sian Elizabeth Williams, Karen Walker, Rachel Yankey. Coach: Hope Powell
Romania: Lenuta Pop, Dana Pufulete, Elena Ducan, Petrica Neculai, Luminita Mache (Cristina Dragan), Dana Pintea, Adriana Grigore, Mirela Laslo, Mariana Ciorba, Gabriela Enache, Marcela Surdu. Coach: Maria Delicoiu
Goals: Karen Walker, Jo Broadhurst / Adriana Grigore (37)

143. 26.05.1999   Lugo di Romagna: Italy - England 4-1 (3-0)
Italy: Brenzan, Tesse (65 Pallotti), Duò, Miniati, Tavalazzi (59 Stefanelli), Marchio, Zorri (46 Deiana), D'Astolfo, Carta (55 Fiorini), Panico, Tagliacarne (46 Sberti). Caoch: Facchin
England: Rachel Brown-Finnis (46 Danielle Murphy), Faye White, Becky Easton, Marieanne Spacey (46 Justine Joanna Lorton), Mo Marley (75 Julie Fletcher), Gillian Coultard, Karen Burke, Sammy Britton (66 Reed), Karen Walker, Sue Smith, Rachel Yankey (49 Angela Banks). Coach: Hope Powell
Goals: Carta (20, 29), Panico (35, 49) / Karen Walker (86)
Referee: Calamosca (Italy)

144. 22.08.1999   Odense Stadion, Odense: Denmark - England 0-1 (0-0)
Denmark: Dorthe Larsen, Hanne Sand Christensen, Karina Christensen, Lene Terp, Katrine Søndergaard Pedersen, Janni Lund Johansen (77 Anja Møller), Christina B.Petersen (79 Linda Nissen), Mikka Hansen, Gitte Krogh, Merete Pedersen (46 Nadia Kjældgaard, Lene R.Jensen. Coach: Poul Højmose
England: Coach: Hope Powell
Goal: Karen Walker (85)
Referee: Lotte Rye Wæde (Denmark)   Attendance: 850.

145. 15.09.1999   Huish Park, Yeovil: England - France 0-1 (0-1)
England: Coach: Hope Powell
France: Corinne Lagache, Elodie Woock (63 Fabienne Prieux), Peggy Provost, Aline Riéra Ubiergo, Corinne Diacre, Stéphanie Mugneret-Béghé (85 Ellen Pogeant), Sandrine Soubeyrand, Gaëlle Blouin (80 Laurence Richoux), Angélique Roujas (80 Mélanie Briche), Anne Zenoni (73 Hoda Lattaf), Françoise Jézéquel. Coach: Elisabeth Loisel
Goal: Stéphanie Mugneret-Béghé (19)
Referee: Eva Ödlund (Sweden)   Attendance: 1,021.

146. 16.10.1999   EURO 2001 Qualifiers
Sportanlagen Trinermatten, Zofingen: Switzerland - England 0-3 (0-2)
Switzerland: Kathrin Lehmann, Janine Levitt-Helmlinger, Katja Aeschlimann, Mirjam Berz, Fabienne Dätwyler *(RC76)*, Evelyne Zimmermann *(YC30)* (46 Karin Hofstetter), Sandra Sommer (86 Irene Kunz), Sandra de Pol, Christa Meyer, Monica Di Fonzo, Cornelia Gisler (62 Beatrice (Bea) Mettler).   Coach: Simon Steiner
England: Pauline Cope-Boanas, Becky Easton, Julie Fletcher *(YC)*, Mo Marley, Danielle Murphy (74 Fara Williams), Sammy Britton, Karen Burke, Gillian Coultard, Sue Smith, Marieanne Spacey (62 Angela Banks), Karen Walker.   Coach: Hope Powell
Goals: Karen Walker (25), Karen Burke (43), Sue Smith (90)
Referee: Marianne Mattsson (Sweden)   Attendance: 800.

Sent-off: Fabienne Dätwyler (76)

147. 20.02.2000   EURO 2001 Qualifiers
Oakwell Stadium, Barnsley: England - Portugal 2-0 (2-0)
England: Pauline Cope-Boanas, Becky Easton *(YC)*, Julie Fletcher, Mo Marley, Danielle Murphy, Faye White (69 Sammy Britton), Karen Burke, Gillian Coultard, Sue Smith, Kelly Jayne Smith, Karen Walker.   Coach: Hope Powell
Portugal: CARLA CRISTINA Trindade Aco Correia, ANA RITA Andrade Gomes, Anabela Fernanda Pinto Silva "BÉ", CELISA Fenda Mendes JASSI *(YC)*, ADÍLIA Jesus Correia MARTINS (76 SUSANA Maria Silva Martins), PAULA CRISTINA Dias Santos, MARIA JOÃO Fernandes Clemente Lopes XAVIER, PATRÍCIA Alexandra Pimentel Sequeira (88 PAULA Margarida Mendes OLIVEIRA), PAULA Adelina Sousa REIS, SANDRA SILVA de Castro e Silva, SÓNIA Cristina Peixoto Teixeira Silva (68 Elisabete Jesus Rocha Matos "BETA").   Coach: GRAÇA SIMÕES
Goals: Kelly Jayne Smith (11), Karen Walker (30)
Referee: Maria Trampusch (Austria)

148. 07.03.2000   EURO 2001 Qualifiers
Carrow Road, Norwich: England - Norway 0-3 (0-3)
England: Pauline Cope-Boanas, Becky Easton (75 Vicky Exley), Julie Fletcher, Mo Marley, Danielle Murphy, Sammy Britton (79 Rachel Yankey), Karen Burke, Gillian Coultard, Sue Smith, Kelly Jayne Smith, Karen Walker (90 Marieanne Specey).   Coach: Hope Powell
Norway: Bente Nordby, Gøril Kringen, Bente Kvitland, Brit Sandaune, Anne Tønnessen, Silje Joergensen Anzjøn (73 Dagny Mellgren Haugland), Anita Rapp-Ødegaard, Hege Riise (79 Margunn Humlestøl Haugenes), Ingrid Camilla Fosse Sæthre, Ragnhild Øren Gulbrandsen, Marianne Iren Pettersen (55 Unni Lehn).   Coach: Per Mathias Høgmo
Goals: Marianne Iren Pettersen (37), Bente Kvitland (39), Anita Rapp-Ødegaard (45)
Referee: Claudine Brohet (Belgium)   Attendance: 5,142.

149. 22.04.2000   EURO 2001 Qualifiers
Estádio do Sport Grupo Sacavenense, Sacavém: Portugal - England 2-2 (1-1)
Portugal: CARLA CRISTINA Trindade Aco Correia, Anabela Fernanda Pinto Silva "BÉ", ANA RITA Andrade Gomes, CELISA Fenda Mendes JASSI, SANDRA Cristina Castro SILVA (89 CARLA Susana Anunciacao MONTEIRO), MARIA JOÃO Fernandes Clemente Lopes XAVIER, PAULA Adelina Sousa REIS, PATRÍCIA Alexandra Pimentel Sequeira, ADÍLIA Jesus Correia MARTINS, CARLA Sofia Basilio COUTO (83 Elisabete Jesus Rocha Matos "BETA"), ANABELA Loureiro Santos.   Coach: GRAÇA SIMÕES
England: Pauline Cope-Boanas, Becky Easton, Julie Fletcher, Mo Marley, Danielle Murphy, Faye White, Karen Burke, Gillian Coultard, Sue Smith, Marieanne Spacey (64 Sammy Britton), Karen Walker (84 Rachel Yankey).   Coach: Hope Powell
Goals: CARLA Sofia Basilio COUTO (7), PATRÍCIA Alexandra Pimentel Sequeira (57) / Karen Burke (40), Sue Smith (79)
Referee: Geja Mulder (Netherlands)

150. 13.05.2000   EURO 2001 Qualifiers
Memorial Ground, Bristol: England - Switzerland 1-0 (0-0)
England: Pauline Cope-Boanas, Becky Easton (68 Vicky Exley), Julie Fletcher, Mo Marley, Danielle Murphy, Sammy Britton (73 Katie Sarah Chapman), Karen Burke, Gillian Coultard, Sue Smith, Marieanne Spacey, Karen Walker (80 Rachel Yankey).   Coach: Hope Powell
Switzerland: Kathrin Lehmann, Katja Aeschlimann, Mirjam Berz, Sandra de Pol, Meret Wenger, Karin Hofstetter (68 Janine Levitt-Helmlinger), Beatrice Mettler (73' Evelyn Zimmermann), Christa Meyer (81 Sylvie Orlando-Gaillard), Sandra Sommer, Manuela Zürcher, Anouk Chatton-Macheret.   Coach: Simon Steiner
Goal: Sue Smith (55)
Referee: Anri Saarivainio Hänninen (Finland)   Attendance: 5,900.

151. 04.06.2000   EURO 2001 Qualifiers
Melløs Stadion, Moss: Norway - England 8-0 (4-0)
Norway: Bente Nordby, Gøril Kringen (46 Kristin Bekkevold Sørum), Bente Kvitland, Brit Sandaune, Anne Tønnessen, Solveig Gulbrandsen, Unni Lehn (65 Margunn Humlestøl Haugenes), Dagny Mellgren Haugland, Anita Rapp-Ødegaard (65 Monica Knudsen), Hege Riise, Marianne Iren Pettersen.   Coach: Per Mathias Høgmo
England: Rachel Brown-Finnis, Katie Sarah Chapman *(YC)*, Becky Easton, Julie Fletcher, Mo Marley, Sammy Britton, Karen Burke, Vicky Exley (65 Danielle Murphy), Sue Smith, Kelly Jayne Smith (75 Tara Proctor), Rachel Yankey.   Coach: Hope Powell
Goals: Dagny Mellgren Haugland (6, 60), Anita Rapp-Ødegaard (17, 61), Marianne Iren Pettersen (33, 71, 81), Solveig Gulbrandsen (42),
Referee: Maria Jose Alcantara Negrin (Spain)   Attendance: 1,278.

152. 16.08.2000   Stade Vélodrome, Marseille: France - England 1-0 (1-0)
France: Sandrine Roux (46 Céline Marty), Natacha Brandy (46 Peggy Provost), Corinne Diacre, Aline Riéra Ubiergo, Sonia Bompastor (81 Nelly Guilbert), Sandrine Soubeyrand, Gaëlle Blouin (72 Stéphanie Mugeret-Béghé), Sarah M'Barek, Françoise Jézéquel (46 Candie Herbert), Mélanie Briche (46 Angélique Roujas), Anne Zenoni (61 Hoda Lattaf).
Coach: Elisabeth Loisel
England: Leanne Hall (46 Layla Young), Sammy Britton, Mo Marley (56 Faye White), Katie Sarah Chapman (68 Casey Stoney), Julie Fletcher (46 Rachel Unitt), Karen Burke (69 Claire Utley), Becky Easton, Tara Proctor (56 Vicky Exley), Sue Smith, Karen Walker (46 Marianne Spacey), Rachel Yankey *(YC)* (46 Angela Banks).   Coach: Hope Powell
Goal: Anne Zenoni (5)
Referee: Katriina Elovirta (Finland)   Attendance: 5,000.

153. 28.09.2000   Brisbane Road, London: England - Finland 2-1 (2-1)
Goals: Karen Burke (15), Angela Banks (..) / Heidi Kackur (4)

154. 30.10.2000   EURO 2001 Play-offs
                  Kolos Stadium, Boryspil: Ukraine - England 1-2 (0-0)
Ukraine: Veronika Shulha, Oxana Andruschenko, Viktoriya Izhko *(YC)*, Tetyana Verezoubova, Tetyana Chorna, Yuliya Karpenkova, Svitlana Stasyuk (73 Galina Mikhailenko), Natalia Zinchenko, Nadia Mischenko, Lyudmyla Pekur *(YC)*, Inesa Titova (70 Nataliya Zhdanova, 82 Nataliya Ignatovich).   Coach: Anatoliy Piskovets
England: Rachel Brown-Finnis, Angela Banks (46 Kelly Jayne Smith), Katie Sarah Chapman, Becky Easton, Julie Fletcher *(YC)*, Mo Marley, Sammy Britton (80 Faye White), Karen Burke, Tara Proctor, Sue Smith, Marieanne Spacey (76 Karen Walker).   Coach: Hope Powell
Goals: Natalia Zinchenko (90) / Kelly Jayne Smith (58), Karen Walker (84)
Referee: Bente Ovedie Skogvang (Norway)   Attendance: 2,000.

155. 28.11.2000   EURO 2001 Play-offs
                  Brisbane Road, London: England - Ukraine 2-0 (0-0)
England: Pauline Cope-Boanas, Angela Banks (88 Karen Walker), Katie Sarah Chapman (90 Faye White), Becky Easton, Mo Marley, Danielle Murphy, Rachel Unitt, Tara Proctor, Sue Smith, Kelly Jayne Smith, Marieanne Spacey (70 Rachel Yankey).   Coach: Hope Powell
Ukraine: Veronika Shulha, Oxana Andruschenko (46 Oxana Rezvin), Olena Mazureko, Tetyana Verezoubova, Tetyana Chorna *(YC)*, Vera Djatel, Galina Ivanova (59 Lyudmyla Lemeshko), Yuliya Karpenkova, Natalia Zinchenko, Svitlana Frishko (72 Nataliya Zhdanova), Nadia Mischenko.   Coach: Anatoliy Piskovets
Goals: Sue Smith (62), Rachel Yankey (78)
Referee: Sabrina Rinaldi (Italy)   Attendance: 7,102.

156. 22.03.2001   Kenilworth Road, Luton: England - Spain 4-2
Goals: Kelly Smith, Sue Smith (3x) / *Unknown*

157. 27.05.2001   Reebok Stadium, Bolton: England - Scotland 1-0 (1-0)
England: Pauline Cope-Boanas, Danielle Murphy, Mo Marley (20 Faye White), Katie Sarah Chapman, Rachel Unitt (46 Julie Fletcher), Karen Burke, Becky Easton, Vicky Exley (46 Sammy Britton), Smith (46 Marieanne Spacey), Angela Banks (46 Karen Walker), Rachel Yankey.   Coach: Hope Powell
Scotland: Gemma Fay, Rhonda Jones, Stacey Cook, Michelle Barr, Smith, Amanda Burns (86 Denise Brolly), Grant, Penglase, James, Gilmour (64 Bruce), Julie Fleeting.
Goal: Angela Banks (43)
Referee: C.Richards (Wales)   Attendance: 3,004.

158. 24.06.2001   EURO 2001 Germany Group A
                  Ernst-Abbe-Sportfeld, Jena: Russia - England 1-1 (0-1)
Russia: Svetlana Petko, Marina Bourakova, Elena Zikhareva, Natalia Karaseva *(YC)*, Galina Komarova, Tatyana Egorova, Irina Grigorieva (63 Tatiana Skotnikova), Alexandra Svetlitskaya (85 Oksana Shmachkova), Elena Fomina, Natalia Barbashina, Olga Letyuskova (57 Olga Kremleva).   Coach: Iouri Bystritsky
England: Pauline Cope-Boanas, Angela Banks (62 Kelly Jayne Smith), Katie Sarah Chapman, Becky Easton (83 Sammy Britton), Mo Marley, Danielle Murphy, Rachel Unitt (70 Julie Fletcher), Karen Burke, Tara Proctor, Sue Smith, Marieanne Spacey.   Coach: Hope Powell
Goals: Alexandra Svetlitskaya (62) / Angela Banks (45)
Referee: Rita Ruiz Tacoronte (Spain)   Attendance: 1,253.

159. 27.06.2001   EURO 2001 Germany Group A
                  Ernst-Abbe Sportfeld, Jena: Sweden - England 4-0 (2-0)
Sweden: Caroline Jönsson, Sofia Eriksson, Hanna Marklund, Jane Törnqvist, Anna Karolina Walfridsson Westberg, Malin Lovén (79 Linda Fagerström), Kristin Bengtsson (71 Therese Sjögran), Hanna Ljungberg, Malin Moström, Tina Nordlund-Lovesan, Elin Fryborg (53 Victoria Sandell Svensson).   Coach: Marika Domanski-Lyfors
England: Pauline Cope Boanas, Angela Banks, Katie Sarah Chapman, Becky Easton (52 Kelly Jayne Smith *(YC)*), Mo Marley, Danielle Murphy, Rachel Unitt, Sammy Britton, Karen Burke, Tara Proctor (66 Marieanne Spacey), Sue Smith (46 Rachel Yankey *(YC)*).
Coach: Hope Powell
Goals: Kristin Bengtsson (2), Jane Törnqvist (27), Hanna Ljungberg (74), Sofia Eriksson (82)
Referee: Claudine Brohet (Belgium)   Attendance: 1,000.

160. 30.06.2001   EURO 2001 Germany Group A
                  Ernst-Abbe-Sportfeld, Jena: England - Germany 0-3 (0-0)
England: Pauline Cope-Boanas, Katie Sarah Chapman, Danielle Murphy, Rachel Unitt (65 Julie Fletcher), Faye White, Sammy Britton (75 Vicky Exley), Karen Burke, Tara Proctor, Sue Smith, Kelly Jayne Smith (90 Angela Banks), Karen Walker.   Coach: Hope Powell
Germany: Silke Rottenberg, Stephanie Ann (Steffi) Jones, Doris Fitschen, Sandra Minnert, Ariane Hingst, Pia Wunderlich (76 Linda Bresonik), Bettina Wiegmann *(YC)*, Renate Lingor, Sandra Smisek (46 Petra Wimbersky *(YC)*), Birgit Prinz, Claudia Müller (46 Martina Müller).
Coach: Tina Theune-Meyer
Goals: Petra Wimbersky (57), Bettina Wiegmann (65), Renate Lingor (67)
Referee: Bente Ovedie Skogvang (Norway)   Attendance: 11,312.

Kelly Smith missed a penalty kick (89)

161. 23.08.2001   Sixfields Stadium, Northampton: England - Denmark 0-3 (0-2)
England: Coach: Hope Powell
Denmark: Heidi Elgaard Johansen, Gitte Andersen (59 Mitzi Ann Møller), Julie H.Andersson, Lene Terp (84 Gitte Kousgaard Pedersen), Christina Bonde, Julie Rudahl Bukh (67 Cathrine Paaske Sørensen), Nadia Kjældgaard, Anja Møller, Katrine Søndergaard Pedersen (75' Jeanette Johansen), Mette Jokumsen (46 Lene R.Jensen), Merete Pedersen (46 Janne Madsen). Coach: Poul Højmose
Goals: Mette Jokumsen (10), Merete Pedersen (22), Lene R.Jensen (87)
Attendance: 2,902.

162. 27.09.2001   FIFA World Cup Qualifiers
Auestadion, Kassel: Germany - England 3-1 (3-0)
Germany: Silke Rottenberg, Ariane Hingst, Sandra Minnert, Kerstin Stegemann, Nia Künzer, Renate Lingor, Navina Omilade-Keller, Pia Wunderlich (55 Petra Wimbersky), Martina Müller (67 Verena Hagedorn), Birgit Prinz, Sandra Smisek.   Coach: Tia Theune-Meyer
England: Pauline Cope-Boanas, Katie Sarah Chapman, Danielle Murphy (69 Kirsty Pealling), Rachel Unitt, Faye White, Sammy Britton *(YC)*, Karen Burke (46 Karen Yankey), Tara Proctor, Sue Smith *(YC)* (69 Amanda Barr), Kelly Jayne Smith *(YC)*, Karen Walker.
Coach: Hope Powell
Goals: Martina Müller (4), Sandra Smisek (7, 11) / Rachel Yankey (48)
Referee: Vibeke Karlsen-Gabrielsen (Norway)   Attendance: 7,720.

163. 04.11.2001   FIFA World Cup Qualifiers
Blundell Park, Grimsby Town: England - Netherlands 0-0
England: Pauline Cope-Boanas, Katie Sarah Chapman, Julie Fletcher, Danielle Murphy (81 Kirsty Pealling), Faye White, Sammy Britton (72 Vicky Exley), Karen Burke, Tara Proctor, Kelly Jayne Smith, Karen Walker, Rachel Yankey (65 Angela Banks).   Coach: Hope Powell
Netherlands: Marleen Wissink, Marloes de Boer, Daphne Koster, Hanneke Mensink, Sandra van Tol *(YC)* (85 Marlous van Petersen-Eijben), Lisanne Goudena, Annemieke Kiesel-Griffioen, Sandra Muller, Miranda Noom, Nicole Delies, Lisette Tromp (63 Ilona Stouthamer). Coach: Frans de Kat
Referee: Katriina Elovirta (Finland)   Attendance: 4,130.

164. 24.11.2001   FIFA World Cup Qualifiers
Complexo Desportivo da Gafanha, Gafanha da Nazaré: Portugal - England 1-1 (1-1)
Portugal: CARLA CRISTINA Trindade Aco Correia, Anabela Fernanda Pinto Silva "BÉ", CARLA Susana Anunciacao MONTEIRO, Adriana PAULA MESQUITA Gouveia da Silva, MÓNICA Sofia Matos Ribeiro (46 SUSANA Queimado LOURIDO), OLÍVIA Maria Silva Marinho, MARIA JOÃO Fernandes Clemente Lopes XAVIER, PAULA CRISTINA Dias Santos, PATRÍCIA Alexandra Pimentel Sequeira (62 SÓNIA Cristina Peixoto Teixeira Silva), CARLA Sofia Basilio COUTO, ANABELA Loureiro Santos (75 EDITE Christiana Fernandes).   Coach: NUNO Preto Rebelo Cristovão ALMEIDA
England: Pauline Cope-Boanas, Katie Sarah Chapman, Julie Fletcher, Rachel Unitt, Faye White, Sammy Britton (69 Fara Williams), Karen Burke, Tara Proctor, Sue Smith *(YC)* (82 Aran Embleton), Karen Walker, Rachel Yankey.   Coach: Hope Powell
Goals: ANABELA Loureiro Santos (6) / Karen Walker (38)
Referee: Claudine Brohet (Belgium)   Attendance: 1,500.

165. 25.01.2002   La Manga Stadium, La Manga (Spain): England - Sweden 0-5 (0-3)
England: Pauline Cope-Boanas (Leanne Hall), Kirsty Pealling, Faye White (Casey Stoney), Katie Sarah Chapman, Julie Fletcher (Rachel Unitt), Karen Burke (Karen Walker), Vicky Exley, Sammy Britton (Carly Hunt), Rachel Yankey, Angela Banks, Kelly Jayne Smith. Coach: Hope Powell
Sweden: Hedvig Lindahl, Hanna Marklund (Victoria Sandell), Kristin Bengtsson, Malin Mostrőm (Ulrika Björn), Salina Olsson (Therese Lundin), Malin Lovén, Hanna Ljungberg (Anna Maria Carlsson), Linda Fagerström (Sara Mattsson), Therese Sjögran, Frida Östberg, Sara Call.   Coach: Marika Domanski-Lyfors
Goals: Malin Mostrőm (8), Therese Sjögran (18), Hanna Ljungberg (26), Salina Olsson (47), Malin Lovén (65)
Referee: Paloma Quintero Silas (Spain)   Attendance: 125.

166. 24.02.2002 FIFA World Cup 2003 Qualifiers
             Fratton Park, Portsmouth: England - Portugal 3-0 (1-0)
England: Pauline Cope-Boanas, Katie Sarah Chapman, Kirsty Pealling, Rachel Unitt, Faye White (90 Casey Stoney), Sammy Britton, Karen Burke, Fara Williams, Kelly Jayne Smith, Karen Walker, Rachel Yankey.   Coach: Hope Powell
Portugal: LUISA Maria Gonçalves de Castro, CARLA Susana Anunciacao MONTEIRO *(YC)*, Anabela Fernanda Pinto Silva "BÉ", ANA RITA Andrade Gomes, OLÍVIA Maria Silva Marinho, MÓNICA Sofia Matos Ribeiro *(YC)*, MARIA JOÃO Fernandes Clemente Lopes XAVIER (66 SANDRA Cristina Castro SILVA), PAULA CRISTINA Dias Santos, PATRÍCIA Alexandra Pimentel Sequeira, CARLA Sofia Basilio COUTO (87 Adriana PAULA MESQUITA Gouveia da Silva), SÓNIA Cristina Peixoto Teixeira Silva (87 ANA Maria Crispim GROSSO).   Coach: NUNO Preto Rebelo Cristovão ALMEIDA
Goals: Fara Williams (20), Kelly Smith (58, 60)
Referee: Anri Saarivainio Hänninen (Finland)   Attendance: 8,821.

167. 01.03.2002   Algarve Cup
         Estádio Municipal de Albufeira, Albufeira (Portugal): England - Norway 1-3 (1-2)
England: Rachel Brown-Finnis, Angela Banks, Amanda Barr, Julie Fletcher, Carly Hunt, Mary Rose Phillip, Casey Stoney, Rachel Unitt (77 Rachel Yankey), Vicky Exley, Rachel McArthur, Una Obiose Kriston Nwatjei (46 Karen Burke).   Coach: Hope Powell
Norway: Bente Nordby, Bente Kvitland (85), Brit Sandaune, Ane Stangeland Horpestad, Anne Tønnessen, Solveig Gulbrandsen (63 Monica Knudsen), Unni Lehn, Anita Rapp-Ødegaard (75 Ingrid Camilla Fosse Sæthre), Hege Riise, Trine Bjerke Rønning (46 Linda Ørmen), Dagny Mellgren Haugland.   Coach: Åge Steen
Goals: Angela Banks (18) /
Dagny Mellgren Haugland (8), Anne Tønnessen (33), Hege Riise (79)
Referee: Martina Storch-Schäfer (Germany)   Attendance: 200.

168. 03.03.2002   Algarve Cup
Sports Complex Nora, Ferreiras (Portugal): England - USA 0-2 (0-0)
England: Rachel Brown-Finnis (46 Leanne Hall), Rachel McArthur (86 Mary Rose Phillip), Faye White, Katie Sarah Chapman, Julie Fletcher (69 Rachel Unitt *(YC71)*), Karen Burke, Fara Williams (64 Sammy Britton), Vicky Exley (85 Carly Hunt), Rachel Yankey, Karen Walker, Angela Banks.   Coach: Hope Powell
USA: Loraine Ming (Lorrie) Fair (46 Kylie Bivens *(YC90+2)*), Catherine Anne Whitehill, Shannon MacMillan (70 Heather Ann O'Reilly), Aly Wagner, Julie Foudy, Kristine Marie Lilly, Joy Fawcett-Biefield, Tiffeny Milbrett (88 Devvyn Hawkins), Hope Solo, Danielle Slaton (60 Kate Markgraf), Danielle Fotopoulos-Garrett (46 Kelly Wilson).
Coach: April Heinrichs
Goals: Shannon MacMillan (58), Kelly Wilson (75)
Referee: Jillanta Proctor (Canada)   Attendance: 500.

169. 05.03.2002   Algarve Cup
Estádio Municipal, Lagos (Portugal): England - Sweden 3-6 (0-3)
England: Pauline Cope, Casey Stoney, Rachel Unitt, Faye White, Katie Sarah Chapman, Karen Burke, Sammy Britton, Fara Williams, Rachel Yankey, Angela Banks, Karen Walker.
Coach: Hope Powell
Sweden: Sofia Lundgren, Hanna Marklund, Sara Mattsson-Larsson, Karolina Walfridsson Westberg, Linda Fagerström, Malin Lovén-Andersson (76 Hanna Ljungberg), Malin Moström, Frida Östberg, Therese Sjögran, Elin Flyborg (76 Ulrika Björn), Victoria Sandell Svensson (62 Anna Sjöström Amcoff).   Coach: Marika Domanski-Lyfors
Goals: Karen Walker (47, 53), Amanda Barr (88) / Therese Sjögran (7, 41), Elin Flyborg (8), Hanna Ljungberg (69), Ulrika Björn (79, 89)
Referee: Jillanta Proctor (Canada)

170. 07.03.2002   Algarve Cup Place Nine
Estádio Municipal, Quarteira (Portugal): England - Scotland 4-1 (3-1)
England: Coach: Hope Powell
Scotland: Gemma Fay, Kerr, Stacey Cook, Michelle Barr, Smith, Joanne Love, Penglase (86 Pauline Hamill), James (89 Campbell), Julie Fleeting (65 Gilmour), Debbie McWinnie, McLean (80 Robertson). Coach: Vera Pauw
Goals: Karen Walker (10), Vicky Exley (42), Fara Williams (57), Karen Burke (71) / Stacey Cook (24)
Referee: Tonje Nordby (Norway)

171. 23.03.2002   FIFA World Cup 2003 Qualifiers
Sportpark Zuiderpark WIK, The Hague: Netherlands - England 1-4 (0-2)
Netherlands: Martine van Pelt, Cindy Burger, Daphne Koster *(YC,YC61)*, Hanneke Mensink, Jeanette van der Laan, Lisanne Goudena, Annemieke Kiesel-Griffioen, Gilanne Louwaars, Miranda Noom, Nicole Delies, Shirley Smith (73 Dyanne Bito).   Coach: Frans de Kat
England: Pauline Cope-Boanas, Katie Sarah Chapman, Casey Stoney, Rachel Unitt, Faye White (52 Mary Rose Phillip), Sammy Britton, Karen Burke, Vicky Exley, Kelly Jayne Smith *(YC60)* (90 Amanda Barr), Karen Walker *(YC44)*, Rachel Yankey (71 Fara Williams).
Coach: Hope Powell
Goals: Annemieke Kiesel-Griffioen (55) / Katie Sarah Chapman (16), Karen Burke (24), Kelly Jayne Smith (73), Karen Walker (89)
Referee: Ausra Kance-Tvarijonaite (Lithuania)   Attendance: 4,311.

Sent-off: Daphne Koster (61)

172. 19.05.2002   FIFA World Cup 2003 Qualifiers
Selhurst Park Stadium, London: England - Germany 0-1 (0-1)
England: Pauline Cope-Boanas (35 Leanne Hall), Angela Banks (46 Amanda Barr), Katie Sarah Chapman, Mary Rose Phillip, Casey Stoney, Rachel Unitt, Faye White, Karen Burke, Vicky Exley, Karen Walker, Rachel Yankey (84 Julie Fletcher).   Coach: Hope Powell
Germany: Silke Rottenberg, Sandra Minnert, Kerstin Stegemann, Stefanie Gottschlich, Nia Künzer, Renate Lingor (68 Verena Hagedorn), Navina Omilade-Keller, Bettina Wiegmann, Pia Wunderlich, Inka Grings (80 Conny Pohlers), Birgit Prinz (53 Jana Schadrack).
Coach: Tia Theune-Meyer
Goal: Stefanie Gottschlich (40)
Referee: Sabrina Rinaldi (Italy)   Attendance: 14,107.

173. 23.07.2002   Carrow Road, Norwich: England - Nigeria 0-1
Attendance: 8,000.

174. 16.09.2002   FIFA World Cup 2003 Relegation (Play-offs Semi-finals)
Laugardalsvöllur Stadion, Reykjavik: Iceland - England 2-2 (1-1)
Iceland: Thora Björg Helgadóttir, Gudrun Soley Gunnarsdóttir, Rósa Júlia Steinthórsdóttir, Elín Jóna Thorsteinsdóttir, Edda Gardarsdóttir, Asthildur Helgadóttir, Erla Hendriksdóttir (90 Laufey Olafsdóttir), Gudlaug Jónsdóttir, Katrin Jónsdóttir, Margrét Rannveig Ólafsdóttir, Andrea Olga Færseth.   Coach: Jörundur Áki Sveinsson
England: Rachel Brown-Finnis, Mary Rose Phillip, Casey Stoney, Rachel Unitt, Faye White, Sammy Britton, Karen Burke, Vicky Exley, Rachel Yankey, Amanda Barr (75 Una Obiose Kriston Nwatjei), Karen Walker *(YC)*.   Coach: Hope Powell
Goals: Andrea Olga Færseth (42), Erla Hendriksdóttir (56) / Karen Walker (44, 88)
Referee: Katerina Elorvita (Finland)   Attendance: 2,974.

175. 22.09.2002   FIFA World Cup 2003 Relegation (Play-offs Semi-finals)
St Andrews Park, Birmingham City: England - Iceland 1-0 (0-0)
England: Pauline Cope-Boanas, Mary Rose Phillip, Casey Stoney, Rachel Unitt, Faye White, Sammy Britton (69 Fara Williams), Karen Burke (46 Kristy Moore), Vicky Exley, Rachel Yankey (81 Sue Smith), Amanda Barr *(YC)*, Jodie Handley.   Coach: Hope Powell
Iceland: Thora Björg Helgadóttir, Rósa Júlia Steinthórsdóttir, Elín Jóna Thorsteinsdóttir, Edda Gardarsdóttir, Asthildur Helgadóttir, Erla Hendriksdóttir, Gudlaug Jónsdóttir, Katrin Jónsdóttir, Laufey Olafsdóttir (88 Ásgerdur Hildur Ingibergsdóttir), Margrét Rannveig Ólafsdóttir, Andrea Olga Færseth.   Coach: Jörundur Áki Sveinsson
Goal: Amanda Barr (87)
Referee: Ingrid Jonsson (Sweden)   Attendance: 7,019.

176. 17.10.2002   FIFA World Cup 2003 Play-off for Final Tournament
Selhurst Park Stadium, London: England - France 0-1 (0-0)
England: Pauline Cope-Boanas, Mary Rose Philipp, Casey Stoney, Rachel Unitt, Faye White *(YC41)*, Sammy Britton (66 Vicky Exley), Karen Burke (78 Kristy Moore), Fara Williams, Rachel Yankey (46 Sue Smith), Amanda Barr, Karen Walker.   Coach: Hope Powell
France: Céline Marty, Sonia Bompastor, Corinne Diacre, Peggy Provost, Aline Riéra Ubiergo, Sandrine Soubeyrand, Sabrina Viguier, Stéphanie Mugneret-Béghé, Elodie Woock, Hoda Laalami-Lattaf (82 Séverine Lecouflé), Marinette Pichon.   Coach: Elisabeth Loisel
Goal: Marinette Pichon (75)
Referee: Vibeke Karlsen-Gabrielsen (Norway)   Attendance: 6,252.

177. 16.11.2002   FIFA World Cup 2003 Play-off for Final Tournament
                   Stade Geoffoy-Guichard, Saint-Étienne: France - England 1-0 (0-0)
France: Céline Marty, Sonia Bompastor, Corinne Diacre, Peggy Provost, Aline Riéra Ubiergo, Sandrine Soubeyrand, Sabrina Viguier, Marie-Ange Kramo (78 Emmanuelle Sykora), Stéphanie Mugneret-Béghé (90+1 Laura Georges), Elodie Woock, Marinette Pichon.
Coach: Elisabeth Loisel
England: Pauline Cope-Boanas, Mary Rose Philipp, Casey Stoney, Rachel Unitt, Sammy Britton, Rachel McArthur *(YC38)*, Fara Williams (84 Vicky Exley), Rachel Yankey (75 Sue Smith), Amanda Barr *(YC31)* (56 Karen Burke), Karen Walker, Kristy Moore.
Coach: Hope Powell
Goal: Corinne Diacre (54)
Referee: Nicole Pétignat (Switzerland)   Attendance: 23,680.

178. 25.02.2003   Stadio dei Pini, Viareggio: Italy - England 1-0 (1-0)
Italy: Comin (46 Brunozzi), Tesse (52 Masia), Perelli, Plachi (90+3 Serra), Boni (61 Deiana), Zorri, Conti, Turrino, Panico, Guarino, Gazzoli.   Coach: Carolina Morace
England: Rachel Brown-Finnis, Rachel McArthur (62 Laura Bassett), Leanne Champ, Hunt, Casey Stoney, Mary Rose Phillip, Jodie Handley, Vicy Exley (52 McDougall), Karen Walker (71 Walker), Fara Williams, Smith (71 Rachel Yankey).   Coach: Hope Powell
Goal: Placchi (36)
Referee: Anna De Toni (Italy)

179. 17.05.2003   Legion Field, Birmingham, Alabama: USA - England 6-0 (3-0)
USA: LaKeysia Beene (46 Siri Mullinix), Cat Reddick, Joy Fawcett (46 Kate Sorbero), Brandi Chastain (46 Heather Mitts), Christie Pearce, Julie Foudy (46 Tiffany Roberts), Kristine Lilly, Aly Wagner (46 Angela Hucles), Cindy Parlow (58 Abby Wambach), Shannon MacMillan (46 Tiffeny Milbrett), Mia Hamm.   Coach: April Heinrichs
England: Pauline Cope-Boanas, Leanne Champ *(YC54)* (59 Kirsty Pealling), Rachel Unitt, Casey Stoney, Mary Rose Phillip, Rachel McArthur (73 Kelly McDougall), Kristy Moore (46 Jody Handley), Vicky Exley, Sammy Britton *(YC19)*, Karen Walker (59' Amanda Barr), Rachel Yankey.   Coach: Hope Powell
Goals: Mia Hamm (30), Cindy Parlow (42, 45, 50, 55), Tiffany Milbrett (68)
Referee: Kari Seitz (USA)   Attendance: 12,102.

Mia Hamm missed a penalty kick.

180. 19.05.2003   Soccerplexe Catalogna, Lachine, Quebec: Canada - England 4-0 (2-0)
Canada: Taryn Swiatek, Breanna Boyd, Sharolta Nonen, Diana Matheson (68 Véronique Maranda), Brittany Timko Baxter, Kristina Kiss (79 Sasha Andrews), Kara Lang, Charmaine Hooper (67 Amber Allen), Andrea Neil (75 Melanie Booth), Candace Chapman, Randee Hermus (79 Carmelina Moscato).   Coach: Even Pellerud
England: Rachel Brown-Finnis, Kirsty Pealling, Rachel Unitt (74 Leanne Champ), Kelly McDougall *(YC)*, Laura Bassett, Mary Rose Philipp, Kristy Moore (46 Jody Handley), Rachel McArthur (46 Sammy Britton *(YC)*), Carmain Walker, Amanda Barr (66 Ellen Maggs), Sue Smith.   Coach: Hope Powell
Goals: Andrea Neil (20, 36), Kara Lang (68, 72)
Attendance: 2,000.

181. 22.05.2003   Frank Clair Stadium, Ottawa: Canada - England 4-0 (3-0)
Canada: Karina Le Blanc, Randee Hermus (76 Sasha Andrews), Charmaine Hooper (68 Amber Allen), Brittany Timko *(YC40)* (84 Veronique Maranda), Breanna Boyd, Kristina Kiss (63 Diana Matheson), Andrea Neil, Christine Latham, Sharolta Nonen, Candace Chapman (80 Melanie Booth), Kara Lang.   Coach: Even Pellerud
England: Rachel Brown-Finnis (46 Pauline Cope-Boanas), Casey Stoney, Rachel Unitt, Sammy Britton (87 Alexa Hunn), Laura Bassett, Mary Rose Philipp, Jody Handley (87 Kristy Moore), Vicky Exley, Carmain Walker *(YC43)*, Kelly McDougall (46 Karen Walker), Rachel Yankey.   Coach: Hope Powell
Goals: Andrea Neil (8, 21), Christine Latham (17), Kara Lang (79)
Attendance: 17,242.

182. 04.09.2003   Turf Moor, Burnley: England - Australia 1-0 (1-0)
England: Rachel Brown-Finnis, Leanne Champ, Rachel Unitt, Katie Sarah Chapman, Casey Stoney, Mary Rose Phillip, Kristy Moore (46 Jody Handley), Vicky Exley (60 Rachel McArthur), Carmaine Walker (70 Kelly McDougall), Kelly Jayne Smith (46 Amanda Barr), Rachel Yankey (67 Sue Smith).   Coach: Hope Powell
Australia: Cassandra Kell, Gillian Foster (57 Pam Grant), Sasha Wainwright, Cheryl Salisbury, Rhian Davies (89 Hayley Crawford), Kelly Golebiowski (71 April Mann), Joanne Peters, Heather Garriock, Karla Reuter, Tal Matilda Karp (61 Bryony Duus), Danielle Small (71 Taryn Rockall).   Coach: Adrian Santrac
Goal: Rachel Yankey (1)
Attendance: 4,349.

183. 11.09.2003   Böllenfalltor Stadion, Darmstadt: Germany - England 4-0 (3-0)
Germany: Silke Rottenberg, Linda Bresonik (33 Sonja Fuss), Kerstin Stegemann, Sandra Minnert, Steffi Jones (64 Nia Künzer), Ariane Hingst (64 Stefanie Gottschlich), Bettina Wiegmann, Renate Lingor (64 Pia Wunderlich), Kerstin Garefrekes (64 Sandra Smisek), Birgit Prinz (74 Conny Pohlers), Maren Meinert (74 Martina Müller).   Coach: Tia Theune
England: Pauline Cope-Boanas, Rachel Unitt (87 Corinne Yorston), Mary Rose Phillip, Leanne Champ, Casey Stoney, Rachel Yankey, Kelly McDougall (72 Kelly Jayne Smith), Fara Williams (82 Vicky Exley), Katie Sarah Chapman, Karen Walker (81 Amanda Barr), Sue Smith (62 Karen Burke).   Coach: Hope Powell
Goals: Birgit Prinz (8, 16), Renate Lingor (35 pen), Bettina Wiegmann (73)
Referee: Miriam Dietz (Germany)   Attendance: 5,870.

184. 21.10.2003   "Kryoia Soveto", Moscow: Russia - England 2-2 (0-1)
Russia: Svetlana Petko (46 Maria Pigaleva), N.Digaj, E.Stepanenko, E.Denchschik (58 Olga Sergaeva), V.Stroukova, Elena Morozova, Elena Fomina, Tatiana Skotnikova, Elena Danilova, Natalia Barbashina (69 N.Perzeva), Elena Terexova.
England: Rachel Brown-Finnis (46 Pauline Cope-Boanas), Leanne Champ, Faye White (46 Casey Stoney), Mary Rose Phillip, Rachel Unitt, Jody Handley, Katie Sarah Chapman *(YC32)*, Fara Williams (68 Vicky Exley), Rachel Yankey (46 Sue Smith), Kelly Jayne Smith (46 Kelly McDougall), Amanda Barr (81 Ellen Maggs).   Coach: Hope Powell
Goals: Elena Danilova (60), Elena Terexova (82) / Jody Handley (27), Amanda Barr (52)
Attendance: 200.

185. 13.11.2003   Deepdale Stadium, Preston: England - Scotland 5-0 (3-0)
England: Rachel Brown-Finnis, Leanne Champ (66 Casey Stoney), Rachel Unitt, Katie Sarah Chapman, Faye White, Mary Rose Phillip, Jody Handley (56 Kristy Moore), Fara Williams, Amanda Barr, Kelly Jayne Smith, Rachel Yankey.   Coach: Hope Powell
Scotland: Gemma Fay (46 Claire Johnstone), Suzy Robertson, Stacey Cook, Megan Sneddon, Michelle Barr, Julie Ferguson (35 Suzanne Grant), Joanne Love, Amanda Burns, Kirsty McBride, Julie Fleeting, Debbie McWinnie.
Goals: Amanda Barr (14), Faye White (32, 48), Leanne Champ (43), Claire Johnstone (86 og)
Referee: Trevor Parks (England)   Attendance: 6,779.

186. 19.02.2004   Fratton Park, Portsmouth: England - Denmark 2-0 (0-0)
England: Pauline Cope-Boanas, Casey Stoney, Rachel Unitt (57 Corinne Yorston), Katie Sarah Chapman, Faye White, Mary Rose Phillip, Jody Handley, Fara Williams, Ellen Maggs (46 Kristy Moore), Kelly Jayne Smith, Rachel Yankey.   Coach: Hope Powell
Denmark: Tine Cederkvist Viskær, Bettina Falk Hansen, Gitte Andersen, Katrine Søndergaard Pedersen, Louise Hansen, Julie Rydahl Bukh, Janni Lund Johansen, Anne Dot Eggers Nielsen, Mariann Gajhede Knudsen, Signe Højen Andersen (76 Marie S.Herping), Lene R.Jensen.
Coach: Poul Højmose
Goals: Kristy Moore (72), Kelly Jayne Smith (84 pen)
(Other sources report the first goal as an own goal from Tine Cederkvist Viskær)
Referee: Wendy Toms (England)   Attendance: 8,157.

187. 22.04.2004   Madejski Stadium, Reading: England - Nigeria 0-3 (0-1)
England: Leanne Hall, Casey Stoney, Fay White, Mary Rose Phillip, Rachel Unitt, Jody Handley (59 Amanda Barr), Katie Sarah Chapman (72 Rachel McArthur), Fara Williams, Kelly Jayne Smith, Rachel Yankey (72 Sue Smith), Kristy Moore.   Coach: Hope Powell
Nigeria: Precious Dede (90 Ogechi Onyinanya), Felicia Eze (78 Akudo Sabi), Florence Omagbemi, Yinka Kudaisi, Faith Ikidi, Vera Okolo, Maureen Mmadu (78 Effionwan Ekpo), Mercy Akide (83 Ajumatt Ameh), Rita Nwadike (90 Gift Otuwe), Nkechi Egbe (61 Stella Mbachu), Perpetual Nkwocha (88 Blessing Igbojionu).   Coach: Ismaila Mabo
Goals: Rita Nwadike (24), Perpetual Nkwocha (65, 85)
Attendance: 4,089.

188. 14.05.2004   London Road, Peterborough: England - Iceland 1-0 (1-0)
England: Leanne Hall, Kristy Pealling (46 Laura Bassett), Rachel Unitt (46 Leanne Champ), Katie Sarah Chapman (46 Vicky Exley), Casey Stoney, Mary Rose Phillip (46 Anita Asanta), Kristy Moore (46 Sue Smith), Fara Williams, Amanda Barr (46 Carmaine Walker), Kelly Jayne Smith, Rachel Yankey (46 Jody Handley).   Coach: Hope Powell
Iceland: Thóra Björg Helgadóttir, Gudrún Sóley Gunnarsdóttir, Olga Færseth, Edda Gardarsdóttir (78 Dóra Stefánsdóttir), Björg Ásta Thórdardóttir, Laufey Ólafsdóttir, Hólmfrídur Magnúsdóttir (83 Dóra María Lárusdóttir), Erla Henriksdóttir, Margrét Lára Vidarsdóttir, Íris Andrésdóttir (46 Málfrídur Erna Sigurdardóttir), Erna Björk Sigurdardóttir (64 Rakel Logadóttir).   Coach: Helena Olafsdóttir
Goal: Fara Williams (40)
Attendance: 2,762.

189. 19.08.2004   Memorial Stadium, Bristol: England - Russia 1-2 (0-0)
England: Leanne Hall, Leanne Champ, Casey Stoney, Mary Rose Phillip, Rachel Unitt, Jody Handley (63 Sue Smith), Kelly McDougall (63 Vicky Exley), Katie Sarah Chapman, Fara Williams, Rachel Yankey, Carmaine Walker (46 Kristy Moore).   Coach: Hope Powell
Russia: Svetlana Petko (46 Maria Pigaleva), Natalia Karaseva, Olga Sergaeva (79 Tatiana Skotnikova), Marina Kolomiets, Tatiana Zaitseva, Irina Voskressenskaya, Tatiana Egorova, Elena Fomina (46 Irina Grigorieva), Lina Rabakh (46 Galina Komarova), Larissa Savina (46 Olga Letiouchova), Olga Kremleva (46 Natalia Barbachina).   Coach: Yury Bystritsky
Goals: Fara Williams (67) / Natalia Barbachina (70, 90+1)
Referee: Hilda McDermott (Republic of Ireland)   Attendance: 1,439.

190. 18.09.2004   Sportpark De Wending, Heerhugowaard: Netherlands - England 1-2 (1-1)
Netherlands: Marleen Wissink, Manoe Meulen (74 Marloes de Boer), Daphne Koster, Petra Hogewoning, Esther Scheenaard, Gilanne Louwaars (16 Sylvia Smit), Marjan Brouwer, Annemieke Kiesel, Lisanne Vermeulen (66 Sandra Muller), Monique van Veen, Manon Melis.   Coach: Remy Reynierse
England: Leanne Hall, Rachel Unitt, Lindsay Johnson, Casey Stoney, Laura Bassett (46 Alex Scott), Vicky Exley, Katie Sarah Chapman, Fara Williams (46 Kelly McDougall), Sue Smith, Jody Handley (78 Jo Potter), Eniola Aluko (60 Amanda Barr).   Coach: Hope Powell
Goals: Sylvia Smit (37) / Vicky Exley (45+3), Amanda Barr (64)
Referee: Harry van Hatten (Netherlands)

191. 22.09.2004   Sportpark De Kuil, Tuitjenhorn: Netherlands - England 0-1 (0-0)
Netherlands: Martine van Pelt, Manoe Meulen, Daphne Koster, Petra Hogewoning, Esther Scheenaard, Marieke Ran (78 Renee de Vries), Marjan Brouwer (64 Anouk Hoogendijk), Annemieke Kiesel, Sandra Muller (73 Lisanne Vermeulen), Sylvia Smit (64 Cindy Burger), Manon Melis.   Choach: Remy Reynierse
England: Siobhan Rebecca Chamberlain (46 Leanne Hall), Alex Scott (46 Leanne Champ), Mary Ross Phillip, Lindsay Johnson (46 Anita Asante), Rachel Unitt, Vicky Exley (46 Rachel McArthur), Katie Sarah Chapman, Fara Williams, Eniola Aluko (46 Jo Potter), Kristy Moore (66 Ellen Maggs), Rachel Yankey.   Coach: Hope Powell
Goal: Rachel Unitt (66)
Referee: Fred Gerritsen (Netherlands)   Attendance: 800.

192. 17.02.2005   National Hockey Stadium, Milton Keynes: England - Italy 4-1 (3-0)
England: Josephine Fletcher, Alex Scott, Faye White, Mary Rose Phillip, Rachel Unitt, Jody Handley (46 Karen Carney), Fara Williams, Katie Sarah Chapman, Rachel Yankey (64 Sue Smith), Emily Westwood, Amanda Barr (46 Eniola Aluko).   Coach: Hope Powell
Italy: Carla Brunozzi, Damiana Deiana, Elena Ficarelli, Viviana Schiavi, Tatiana Zorri, Elisa Camporese, Sara Di Filippo, Piera Maglio (46 Melania Gabbiadini), Ilaria Pasqui, Patrizia Panico, Valentina Boni (46 Valentina Lanzieri).   Coach: Carolina Morace
Goals: Fara Williams (9), Jody Handley (24), Amanda Barr (36), Karen Carney (64) / Damiana Deiana (79)
Attendance: 6,546.

193. 09.03.2005   Algarve Cup
Estádio Municipal, Paderne (Portugal): Northern Ireland - England 0-4 (0-1)
Northern Ireland: Christine Drain, Aine McGovern, Sara Booth, Ashley Hutton, Kellie-Ann Leyland, Elaine Roden, Lynsey Patterson, Kimberley Turner (43 Lisa O'Neill), Gail Macklin (76 Rachel Furness), Wendy Bailie, Sarah McFadden.   Coach: Alfie Wylie
England: Karen Bardsley, Lindsay Johnson, Alex Scott, Casey Stoney, Rachel Unitt, Anita Asante, Karen Carney, Vicky Exley, Rachel McArthur, Eniola Aluko, Sue Smith.
Coach: Hope Powell
Goals: Karen Carney (32), Vicky Exley (53, 89), Rachel McArthur (56)

194. 11.03.2005   Algarve Cup
Estádio São Luís, Faro (Portugal): Portugal - England 0-4 (0-2)
Portugal: CARLA CRISTINA Aco Correia, SUSANA Queimado LOURIDO (57 PAULA CRISTINA Dias Santos *(YC)*), CÁTIA Teresa RELÍQUIAS (88 DULCE COSTA), INÊS Inacio Sabido BORGES (88 SÓNIA Maria Moreira BARBOSA), TÂNIA Alexandra Araujo PINTO (57 Anna Carolina "KIKAS" – Macedo Rolim Marques), HELGA Maria Pereira PORTUGAL Barata Lima, Ana RITA Moreira CARNEIRO (88 SÓNIA Patricia Pereira MATIAS), SÍLVIA Maria Nunes BRUNHEIRA, LILIANA Maria Pereira MARTINS (88 Daniele Ferreira Costa Veloso "DANI"), EDITE Christiana FERNANDES *(YC)*, CARLA COUTO.   Coach: JOSÉ AUGUSTO Pinto de Almeida
England: Josephine Fletcher, Alex Scott *(YC)*, Casey Stoney *(YC)*, Rachel Unitt, Katie Sarah Chapman, Mary Rose Phillip, Emily Westwood, Fara Williams *(YC)*, Rachel Yankey, Amanda Barr, Jody Handley (71 Karen Carney).   Coach: Hope Powell
Goals: Casey Stoney (10), Rachel Yankey (30, 90), Amanda Barr (77)
Referee: Eun Ah Hong (South Korea)

195. 13.03.2005   Algarve Cup
Estádio Municipal, Lagos (Portugal): Mexico - England 0-5 (0-2)
Mexico: JENNIFER Marie MOLINA Shea, ELIZABETH Patricia GOMEZ Randall, RUBI Marlene SANDOVAL, Mónica González, MARIA DE JESÚS CASTILLO Nicacio, JESSICA ROMERO (63 LUZ DEL ROSARIO Soto Saucedo), MÓNICA Christine González CABALES, FÁTIMA LEYVA Morán (77 ALEXANDREA Rebecca MENDOZA), JUANA EVELYN LÓPEZ Luna (69 CHRISTINE Yvette NIEVA), PATRICIA PÉREZ Pena (81 MARIA de LOURDES "LULU" GORDILLO Maradiaga), MÓNICA VERGARA Rubio (51 REBECCA JUAREZ Bazan), TERESA Guadalupe WORBIS (46' LETICIA Connie VILLALPANDO),   Coach: LEONARDO CUELLAR Rivera
England: Josephine Fletcher, Alex Scott (69 Lindsay Johnson), Faye White (46 Casey Stoney), Mary Rose Phillip, Rachel Unitt, Jody Handley, Fara Williams, Katie Sarah Chapman (75 Rachel McArthur), Rachel Yankey (75 Sue Smith), Emily Westwood (63 Vicky Exley), Amanda Barr (63 Eniola Aluko).   Coach: Hope Powell
Goals: Fara Williams (2, 68), Jody Handley (34), Rachel Yankey (52), Sue Smith (78)
Referee: Bentla D'Coth (India)

196. 15.03.2005   Algarve Cup 7th Place Match
   Complexo Desportivo Arsénio Catuna, Guia (Portugal): CHINA V ENGLAND 0-0
China: XIAO Zhen, ZHAN Yanru, LIU Huana, LI Jie, SUN Hongxia, ZHAN Ying, REN Liping, SHI Mengyu (55 PAN Lina), QU Feifei (55 PU Wei), ZHAO Xiaoyan ZHANG Tong (65 JI Ting), HAN Duan (65 ZHANG Ouying). Coach: WANG Haiming
England: Jo Fletcher, Alex Scott, Rachel Unitt, Lindsay Johnson, Mary Rose Phillip, Jody Handley, Fara Williams, Katie Sarah Chapman, Rachel Yankey, Emily Westwood, Amanda Barr. Coach: Hope Powell

Penalties: LI Jie 1-0, Alex Scott missed, Unknown 2-0, Rachel Unitt 2-1, Unknown 3-1, Mary Rose Phillip 3-2, Unknown 4-2, Fara Williams 4-3, Unknown 5-3

China won 5-3 on penalties following extra time. The Chinese penalty scorers are not known.

197. 21.04.2005   Prenton Park, Tranmere: England - Scotland 2-1 (1-1)
England: Jo Fletcher, Alex Scott, Faye White, Mary Rose Phillip, Rachel Unitt, Fara Williams, Emily Westwood, Katie Sarah Chapman (46 Anita Asante), Jody Handley (Karen Carney), Amanda Barr (Eniola Aluko), Rachel Yankey.   Coach: Hope Powell
Scotland: Gemma Fay, Rhonda Jones, Kerr, Ifeoma Dieke, Stacey Cook, Sneddon, Joanne Love (Burns), Suzanne Grant (N..Grant), Julie Fleeting, Julie Smith, Susanne Malone (Ferguson). Coach: Anna Signeul
Goals: Amada Barr (27), Julie Smith (90+4 og) / Julie Fleeting (44)
Attendance: 6,000.

Amanda Barr missed a penalty kick (47)

198. 06.05.2005   Oakwell Ground, Barnsley: England - Norway 1-0 (1-0)
England: Jo Fletcher, Alex Scott, Rachel Unitt, Anita Asante, Faye White, Casey Stoney (58 Karen Carney), Mary Philip, Ga Williams, Amanda Barr, Emily Westwood (72 Kelly Jayne Smith), Rachel Yankey. Coach: Hope Powell
Norway: Bente Dalum Nordby, Marianne Paulsen (72 Elisabeth Wahlin), Gunhild Bentzen Følstad, Marit Helene Fiane Grødum, Sire Kristine Nordby, Trine Rønning (68 Ingvild Stensland), Solveig Ingersdatter Gulbrandsen, Lise Klaveness, Unni Lehn (72 Marie Knutsen), Stine Frantzen Schultz, Dagny Mellgren Haugland (75 Tonje Hansen Boork).
Goal: Anita Asante (34)
Referee: Evans (England)   Attendance: 5,000.

199. 26.05.2005   Bescot Stadium, Walsall: England - Czech Republic 4-1 (0-1)
England: Jo Fletcher (46 Rachel Brown-Finnis), Alex Scott, Faye White (76 Lindsay Johnson), Mary Rose Phillip, Rachel Unitt, Katie Sarah Chapman (74 Vicky Exley), Emily Westwood (46 Kelly Jayne Smith), Fara Williams, Jody Handley (46 Eniola Aluko), Amanda Barr, Rachel Yankey.   Coach: Hope Powell
Czech Republic: Zuzana Pincová (57 Marcela Zborilová), Veronika Hoferková, Petra Bertholdová, Dagmar Urbancová, Katerina Hejlová (68 Irena Martínková), Lucie Martínková (61 Iveta Stojkovicová), Blanka Penicková, Eva Smeralová (74 Martina Danielová), Alexandra Mouchová, Pavlína Scasná, Gabriela Chlumecká (79 Iva Mocová).   Coach: Dusan Zovinec.
Goals: Rachel Unitt (65, 73), Kelly Jayne Smith (69), Eniola Aluko (77) /
Gabriela Chlumecká (16)
Referee: Alan G.Wiley (England)   Attendance: 6,869.

200.　05.06.2005　　EURO 2005 England Group A
　　　　　　　　City of Manchester Stadium, Manchester: England - Finland 3-2 (2-0)
England: Jo Fletcher, Mary Rose Phillip, Alex Scott, Rachel Unitt, Faye White (85 Lindsay Johnson), Karen Carney, Katie Sarah Chapman, Fara Williams, Rachel Yankey, Amanda Barr (73 Eniola Aluko), Kelly Jayne Smith (46 Emily Westwood).　Coach: Hope Powell
Finland: Satu Kunnas, Petra Paulina Vaelma, Sanna Valkonen, Tiina Sofia Salmén, Eveliina Sarapää, Jessica Carola Julin, Anne Mäkinen, Anna-Kaisa Rantanen, Laura Österberg Kalmari, Heidi Kackur *(YC)* (81 Sanna Talonen), Jessica Thorn (74 Minna Mustonen).
Coach: Michael Käld
Goals: Sanna Valkonen (18 og), Amanda Barr (40), Karen Carney (90) / Anna-Kaisa Rantanen (56), Laura Österberg Kalmari (89)
Referee: Gyöngyi Krisztina Gaál (Hungary)　Attendance: 29,092.

201.　08.06.2005　　EURO 2005 England Group A
　　　　　　　　Ewood Park, Blackburn: Denmark - England 2-1 (0-0)
Denmark: Tine Cederkvist Viskær, Bettina Falk-Hansen, Katrine Søndergaard Pedersen, Gitte Andersen, Mariann Gajhede Knudsen, Louise Hansen, Cathrine Paaske Sørensen, Anne Dot Eggers Nielsen (71 Tanja Mejer Christensen), Nanna Mølbach Johansen (57 Lene Revsbeck Jensen), Merete Pedersen, Johanna Baltensperger Rasmussen.　Coach: Peter Bonde
England: Jo Fletcher, Mary Rose Phillip, Alex Scott, Rachel Unitt, Faye White, Karen Carney, Katie Sarah Chapman *(YC)*, Fara Williams *(YC)*, Rachel Yankey, Amanda Barr (64 Eniola Aluko), Kelly Jayne Smith *(YC)* (46 Vicky Exley).　Coach: Hope Powell
Goals: Merete Pedersen (80), Cathrine Paaske Sørensen (88) / Fara Williams (52 pen)
Referee: Alexandra Sasa Ihringová (Slovakia)　Attendance: 14,695.

202.　11.06.2005　　EURO 2005 England Group A
　　　　　　　　Ewood Park, Blackburn: England - Sweden 0-1 (0-1)
England: Rachel Brown-Finnis, Mary Rose Phillip, Alex Scott, Rachel Unitt, Faye White, Karen Carney (69 Amanda Barr), Katie Sarah Chapman, Fara Williams, Rachel Yankey *(YC)*, Eniola Aluko, Kelly Jayne Smith *(YC)*.　Coach: Hope Powell
Sweden: Hedvig Lindahl, Sara Margareta Larsson (Mattsson), Jane Törnqvist *(YC45)*, Hanna Marklund, Kristin Bengtsson (78 Karolina Walfridsson Westberg), Hanna Ljungberg, Malin Moström *(YC28)*, Caroline Seger *(YC5)* (54 Frida Östberg), Therese Sjögran, Anna Sjöström Amcoff, Victoria Sandell Svensson (90 Josefine Öqvist).　Coach: Marika Domanski-Lyfors
Goal: Anna Sjöström Amcoff (3)
Referee: Nicole Petignat (Switzerland)　Attendance: 25,694.

203.　01.09.2005　　FIFA World Cup 2007 Qualifiers
　　　　　　　　Erti Glas, Amstetten: Austria - England 1-4 (1-2)
Austria: Bianca Reischer *(YC)*, Katherina Pregartbauer, Natascha Celouch, Melanie Fischer (78 Susanne Just), Maria Gstöttner, Cäcilia Metzler, Sonja Spieler, Gertrud Stallinger, Katrin Walzl (70 Marion Gröbner), Nina Aigner, Nina Burger (82 Irene Fuhrmann).
Coach: Ernst Weber
England: Rachel Brown-Finnis, Mary Rose Phillip, Alex Scott (61 Casey Stoney), Rachel Unitt, Faye White *(YC)*, Karen Carney, Katie Sarah Chapman, Fara Williams *(YC)*, Amanda Barr, Jo Potter (46 Sue Smith), Kelly Jayne Smith (66 Emily Westwood).
Coach: Hope Powell
Goals: Natascha Celouch (21) / Fara Williams (23 pen), Kelly Jayne Smith (35), Amanda Barr (56), Sue Smith (90+2)
Referee: Ausra Kance-Tvarijonaite (Lithuania)　Attendance: 1,700.

204. 27.10.2005   FIFA World Cup 2007 Qualifiers
Tapolca Stadium, Tapolca: Hungary - England 0-13 (0-7)
Hungary: Melinda Szvorda, Monika Bango (60 Krisztina Kanta *(YC)*), Rita Méry (18 Cecilia Gaspár), Aranka Paraoanu, Éva Sümegi, Agnes Czuder, Angela Hummel-Smutczer (78 Anita Padár), Anita Szekér, Gabriella Tóth, Réka Jakab, Györgyi Sebestyén.   Coach: Andras Telek
England: Rachel Brown-Finnis (74 Siobhan Rebecca Chamberlain), Lindsay Johnson, Mary Rose Phillip, Alex Scott, Casey Stoney, Rachel Unitt, Katie Sarah Chapman, Fara Williams, Rachel Yankey (46 Jo Potter), Eniola Aluko (63 Jody Handley), Kelly Jayne Smith.
Coach: Hope Powell
Goals: Kelly Jayne Smith (3, 43, 80), Rachel Yankey (5), Eliona Aluko (12, 50), Alex Scott (15, 38), Katie Sarah Chapman (30), Fara Williams (61, 88 pen), Jo Potter (75 pen), Jody Handley (79)
Referee: Dagmar Damkova (Czech Republic)   Attendance: 350.

205. 17.11.2005   FIFA World Cup 2007 Qualifiers
Oosterenk Stadion, Zwolle: Netherlands - England 0-1 (0-0)
Netherlands: Marleen Wissink, Dyanne Bito, Marloes de Boer *(YC55)*, Dionne Anna Johanna Demarteau, Petra Marieka Jacoba Hogewoning, Elisabeth Migchelsen, Annemieke Kiesel-Griffioen, Gilanne Louwaars, Nicole Delies (69 Sylvia Smit), Manon Melis, Shirley Smith (46 Kirsten Johanna Maria van de Ven).   Coach: Vera Pauw
England: Rachel Brown-Finnis, Mary Rose Phillip, Casey Stoney, Rachel Unitt, Faye White *(YC38)*, Karen Carney (59 Jo Potter), Vicky Exley (82 Anita Asante), Fara Williams, Rachel Yankey, Eniola Aluko (46 Amanda Barr), Kelly Jayne Smith.   Coach: Hope Powell
Goal: Fara Williams (55 pen)
Referee: Christine Frai (Germany)   Attendance: 2,319.

206. 07.02.2006   GSZ Stadium, Larnaca (Cyprus): Sweden - England 0-0
Sweden: Hedvig Lindahl, Frida Östberg, Sara Mattsson (79 Karolina Walfridsson Westberg), Stina Segerström, Caroline Näfver, Linda Fagerström *(YC54)* (62 Johanna Almgren), Caroline Seger *(YC30)*, Therese Sjögran, Lotta Schelin, Therese Lundin (66 Salina Olsson), Victoria Sandell.   Coach: Thomas Dennerby
England: Rachel Brown-Finnis, Mary Rose Phillip, Casey Stoney, Rachel Unitt, Anita Asante (86 Jo Potter), Katie Sarah Chapman, Vicky Exley, Fara Williams, Eniola Aluko (74 Amanda Barr), Karen Carney (66 Jody Handley), Rachel Yankey (66 Sue Smith).   Coach: Hope Powell
Attendance: 400.

207. 09.02.2006   Dasaki Stadium, Achna (Cyprus): Sweden - England 1-1 (1-0)
Sweden: Sofia Lundgren, Maria Bergkvist, Sara Mattsson (46 Stina Segerström), Karolina Walfridsson Westberg, Anna Paulsson (73 Frida Östberg), Maria Karlsson (73 Caroline Näfver), Nilla Fischer (38 Caroline Seger), Salina Olsson, Johanna Almgren, Victoria Sandell (46 Lotta Schelin), Maria Aronsson.   Coach: Thomas Dennerby
England: Rachel Brown-Finnis, Lindsay Johnson, Rachel Unitt, Anita Asante, Katie Sarah Chapman, Mary Rose Phillip, Karen Carney, Fara Williams, Amanda Barr (63 Casey Stoney), Kelly Jayne Smith (82 Eniola Aluko), Jo Potter.   Coach: Hope Powell
Goals: Maria Aronsson (5) / Rachel Unitt (64)
Attendance: 175.

208. 09.03.2006   Carrow Road, Norwich: England - Iceland 1-0 (0-0)
England: Rachel Brown-Finnis (46 Siobhan Rebecca Chamberlain), Casey Stoney (46 Lindsay Johnson), Rachel Unitt, Anita Asante, Katie Sarah Chapman, Mary Rose Phillip, Karen Carney, Fara Williams, Eniola Aluko (60 Alex Scott), Kelly Jayne Smith, Rachel Yankey (67 Jo Potter).   Coach: Hope Powell
Iceland: Thora Helgasdottir, Gundrun Gunnarsdottir, Olga Færseth (54 Erla Arnadottir), Edda Gardarsdottir (84 Harpa Thorsteinsdottir), Katrin Jonsdottir, Dora Stefansdottir, Olina Vidarsdottir, Margaret Vidarsdottir, Dora Larusdottir, Gudlaug Jonsdottir, Holmfridur Magnusdottir (62 Greta Samuelsdottir).
Goal: Karen Carney (79)
Referee: Alexandra (Sasa) Ihringova (England)   Attendance: 9,616.

209. 26.03.2006   FIFA World Cup 2007 Qualifiers
            Ewood Park, Blackburn: England - France 0-0
England: Rachel Brown-Finnis, Mary Rose Phillip, Casey Stoney, Rachel Unitt, Anita Asante (87 Vicky Exley), Karen Carney, Katie Sarah Chapman, Fara Williams, Rachel Yankey, Eniola Aluko (79 Alex Scott), Kelly Jayne Smith.   Coach: Hope Powell
France: Sarah Bouhaddi, Sonia Bompastor *(YC63)*, Anne-Laure Casseleux, Laura Georges, Peggy Provost, Sandrine Soubeyrand, Sabrina Viguier, Camille Abily *(YC15)*, Elise Bussaglia (86 Amélie Coquet), Hoda Laalami-Lattaf (57 Marinette Pichon), Laëtitia Tonazzi.
Coach: Elisabeth Loisel
Referee: Bente Ovedie Skogvang (Norway)   Attendance: 12,164.

210. 20.04.2006   FIFA World Cup 2007 Qualifiers
            Gulligham's Priestfield Stadium, Gillingham: England - Austria 4-0 (1-0)
England: Rachel Brown-Finnis, Lindsay Johnson, Mary Rose Phillip, Rachel Unitt, Fay White, Karen Carney, Katie Sarah Chapman, Fara Williams *(YC)*, Rachel Yankey (84 Sue Smith), Amanda Barr (59 Jody Handley), Kelly Jayne Smith.   Coach: Hope Powell
Austria: Bianca Reischer, Susanna Gahleitner, Susanne Just, Natascha Celouch, Melanie Fischer (89 Susanne Maria Koch), Marlies Hanschitz *(YC)*, Birgitt Schalkhammer-Hufnagl, Sonja Spieler, Katrin Walzl (78 Maria Gstöttner), Nina Aigner (87 Katharina Pregartbauer), Nina Burger.   Coach: Ernst Weber
Goals: Karen Carney (36), Fara Williams (85), Sue Smith (87), Jody Handley (90+2)
Referee: Snjezana Focic (Croatia)   Attendance: 8,068.

211. 11.05.2006   FIFA World Cup 2007 Qualifiers
            St Mary's, Southampton: England - Hungary 2-0 (1-0)
England: Rachel Brown-Finnis, Lindsay Johnson (69 Casey Stoney), Mary Rose Phillip, Rachel Unitt, Faye White, Anita Asante, Karen Carney (57 Alex Scott *(YC)*), Vicky Exley, Jody Handley (54 Lianne Sanderson), Jo Potter, Sue Smith.   Coach: Hope Powell
Hungary: Melinda Szvorda, Krisztina Kanta, Aranka Paraoanu *(YC)*, Éva Sümegi, Agnes Czuder (86 Judit Fenyvesi), Timea Gal, Cecilia Gaspár, Angela Hummel-Smutczer, Anita Padár (76 Rita Méry), Anett Nagy-Dombai, Györgyi Sebestyén (51 Anita Szekér).
Coach: Andras Telek
Goals: Vicky Exley (40), Alex Scott (90+1)
Referee: Lena Arwedahl (Sweden)   Attendance: 8,817.

212. 31.08.2006 FIFA World Cup 2007 Qualifiers
The Valley, London: England - Netherlands 4-0 (2-0)
England: Rachel Brown-Finnis, Mary Rose Phillip, Alex Scott, Rachel Unitt, Anita Asante, Karen Carney, Katie Sarah Chapman, Fara Williams, Rachel Yankey (74 Sue Smith), Eniola Aluko (85 Jody Handley), Kelly Jayne Smith (82 Jill Scott). Coach: Hope Powell
Netherlands: Marleen Wissink, Dyanne Bito, Marloes de Boer, Dionne Anna Johanna Demarteau, Petra Marieka Jacoba Hogewoning, Elisabeth Migchelsen, Sherida Spitse (55 Anouk Hoogendijk), Manon Melis, Sylvia Smit, Karin Stevens (81 Nicole Delies), Claudia van den Heiligenberg (65 Nangila Naomi van Eyck). Coach: Vera Pauw
Goals: Kelly Jayne Smith (9, 24 pen, 50), Rachel Yankey (67)
Referee: Floarea Cristina Babadac-Ionescu (Romania)   Attendance: 7,931.

213. 30.09.2006 FIFA World Cup 2007 Qualifiers
Stade de la Route de Lorient, Rennes: France - England 1-1 (0-0)
France: Sarah Bouhaddi, Sonia Bompastor, Anne-Laure Casseleux (86 Ludivine Diguelman), Sandrine Dusang, Laura Georges, Laure Lepailleur, Sandrine Soubeyrand, Elise Bussaglia (74 Elodie Thomis), Hoda Laatami-Lattaf, Marinette Pichon, Laëtitia Tonazzi (81 Camille Abily). Coach: Elisabeth Loisel
England: Rachel Brown-Finnis *(YC85)*, Mary Rose Phillip, Alex Scott, Rachel Unitt (46 Casey Stoney), Anita Asante *(YC29)*, Karen Carney *(YC78)* (90 Lindsay Johnson), Katie Sarah Chapman, Fara Williams, Rachel Yankey (77 Sue Smith), Eliona Aluko, Kelly Jayne Smith. Coach: Hope Powell
Goals: Ludivine Diguelman (88) / Hoda Laatami-Lattaf (63 og)
Referee: Jenny Palmqvist (Sweden)   Attendance: 19,215.

214. 25.10.2006 Städtisches Waldstadion, Aalen: Germany - England 5-1 (2-1)
Germany: Ulrike Schmetz, Kerstin Stegemann (73 Babett Peter), Sandra Minnert (85 Bianca Rech), Annike Krahn, Ariane Hingst, Isabell Bachor (46 Célia Sasic), Renate Lingor (68 Martina Müller), Kerstin Garefrekes, Britta Carlson (46 Petra Wimbersky), Sandra Smisek, Birgit Prinz (83 Conny Pohlers). Coach: Silvia Neid
England: Rachel Brown-Finnis (56' Siobhan Rebecca Chamberlain), Alex Scott, Casey Stoney, Fara Williams (77 Eliona Aluko), Anita Asante, Mary Rose Phillip, Karen Carney (46 Lindsay Johnson), Vicky Exley, Jody Handley, Kelly Jayne Smith (61 Jill Scott), Rachel Yankey (68 Susan (Sue) Smith).   Coach: Hope Powell
Goals: Kerstin Stegemann (29), Sandra Smisek (37), Birgit Prinz (66), Martina Müller (75), Célia Sasic (86) / Jill Scott (26)
Referee: Christine Baitinger (Germany)   Attendance: 11,161.

215. 26.01.2007 Four Nations Tournament
Guangdong Olympic Stadium, Guangzhou (China): China - England 2-0 (2-0)
China: ZHANG Yanru (84 HAN Wenxia), WENG Xinzhi (76 LIU Huana), LIE Jie, PU Wie, ZHOU Gaoping, YUE Min, ZHANG Ying, QU Feifel (71 LOU Xiaoxu), SHI Mengyu (65 ZHANG Tong), HAN Duan (80 MA Xiaoxu), LIU Sa.
England: Siobhan Rebecca Chamberlain, Alex Scott, Casey Stoney (87 Rachel Unitt), Katie Sarah Chapman, Anita Asante, Mary Rose Phillip, Karen Carney (46 Lindsay Johnson), Fara Williams, Jody Handley (73 Lianne Sanderson), Kelly Jayne Smith (62 Emily Westwood), Sue Smith.   Coach: Hope Powell
Goals: ZHANG Ying (16), HAN Duan (45)

216. 28.01.2007   Four Nation Tournament
   Guangdong Olympic Stadium, Guangzhou (China): England - USA 1-1 (0-1)
England: Rachel Brown-Finnis, Alex Scott, Casey Stoney, Anita Asante, Emily Westwood (79 Rachel Unitt), Katie Sarah Chapman (83 Vicky Exley), Fara Williams, Kelly Jayne Smith, Karen Carney, Eniola Aluko (59 Jill Scott), Rachel Yankey. Coach: Hope Powell
USA: Brianna Scurry, Heather Mitts, Lori Chalupny, Cat Whitehill, Kathryn Markgraf (60 Stefanie Lopez), Leslie Osborne, Marci Miller (46 Carli Lloyd), Angela Hucles (60 Yael Averbuch), Natasha Kai (78 Joanna Lohman), Casey Noguiera (46 Lindsay Tarpley), Heather O'Reilly.
Goals: Alex Scott (47) / Heather O'Reilly (17)
Referee: Bibiana Steinhaus (Germany)   Attendance: 3,000.

217. 30.01.2007   Four Nations Tournament
   Guangdong Olympic Stadium, Guangzhou (China): Germany - England 0-0
Germany: Stephanie Ulrich, Kerstin Stegemann, Annike Krahn, Ariane Hingst, Fatmire Alushi (46 Babett Peter), Jennifer Zietz (46 Linda Bresonik), Célia Sasic, Britta Carlson (46 Navina Omilade-Keller), Petra Wimbersky (60 Conny Pohlers), Sandra Smisek (46 Martina Müller), Anja Mittag. Coach: Silvia Neid
England: Rachel Brown-Finnis, Alex Scott, Rachel Unitt, Jill Scott (66 Vicky Exley), Mary Rose Phillip (29 Anita Asante), Emily Westwood, Fara Williams (55 Katie Sarah Chapman), Kelly Jayne Smith, Karen Carney (46 Lindsay Johnson), Eniola Aluko (46 Lianne Sanderson), Rachel Yankey. Coach: Hope Powell
Referee: Da-Su Ping (China)   Attendance: 2,500.

218. 08.03.2007   National Hockey Stadium, Milton Keynes: England - Russia 6-0 (4-0)
England: Rachel Brown-Finnis, Alex Scott (57 Lindsay Johnson), Casey Stoney, Katie Sarah Chapman (86 Vicky Exley), Anita Asante (86 Laura Bassett), Emily Westwood (73 Steph Houghton), Karen Carney, Fara Williams (73 Jill Scott), Eniola Aluko (46 Jody Handley), Kelly Jayne Smith, Rachel Yankey. Coach: Hope Powell
Russia: Maria Pigaleva, Oxana Shmatchkova, Ksenia Tsybutovich, Olga Sergaeva (69 Anna Kozhnikova), Maria Dyachkova, Natalia Barbashina (46 Natalia Mokshanova), Elena Morozova, Olga Petrova (46 Olga Kremleva), Olesya Kurochkina (57 Svetlana Tsidikova), Valentina Savchenkova, Elena Fomina (46 Tatiana Skotnikova).
Goals: Alex Scott (10), Eniola Aluko (15), Karen Carney (24), Kelly Jayne Smith (43), Rachel Yankey (..), Casey Stoney (80).
Referee: Sasa Ihringgova (England)   Attendance: 5,421.

219. 11.03.2007   Adams Park Stadium, High Wycombe: England - Scotland 1-0 (1-0)
England: Siobhan Rebecca Chamberlain (46 Carly Telford), Steph Houghton, Rachel Unitt (78 Corinne Yorston), Jill Scott, Laura Bassett, Mary Rose Phillip, Alex Scott (78 Lindsay Johnson), Fara Williams, Lianne Sanderson (58 Amanda Barr), Kelly Jayne Smith (46 Katie Sarah Chapman), Sue Smith (58 Jo Potter). Coach: Hope Powell
Scotland: Gemma Fay, Rhonda Jones, Leanne Ross (84 Jayne Sommerville Cameron), Ifeoma Dieke, Amy McDonald, Joanne Love, Amanda Burns, Kirsty McBride (81 Denise Brolly), Megan Sneddon (57 Kim Little), Julie Fleeting, Pauline Hamill (66 Suzanne Mulvey). Coach: Anna Signeul
Goal: Fara Williams (30)
Referee: M.P.Russel (England)   Attendance: 2,066.

220. 14.03.2007   County Ground, Swindon: England - Netherlands 0-1 (0-0)
England: Rachel Brown-Finnis, Anita Asante, Emily Westwood, Casey Stoney, Alex Scott, Katie Sarah Chapman, Karen Carney (79 Steph Houghton), Fara Williams, Kelly Jayne Smith, Eniola Aluko, Rachel Yankey (69 Jo Potter). Coach: Hope Powell
Netherlands: Loes Geurts, Elisabeth Migchelsen, Petra Hogewoning, Marloes de Boer, Dyanne Bito, Anouk Hoogendijk, Linda Bos (62 Karin Legemate), Sherida Spitse, Jessica Torny (89 Claudia van den Heiligenberg), Sylvia Smit, Manon Melis. Coach: Vera Pauw
Goal: Manon Melis (78)
Referee: Amy Rayner (England)   Attendance: 6,000.

221. 13.05.2007   EURO 2009 Qualifiers
                  Priestfield, Gillingham: England - Northern Ireland 4-0 (0-0)
England: Rachel Brown-Finnis, Steph Houghton (78 Amanda Barr), Mary Rose Phillip, Alex Scott, Rachel Unitt, Anita Asante, Katie Sarah Chapman, Fara Williams, Lianne Sanderson (78 Karen Carney), Kelly Jayne Smith *(YC)* (74 Faye White), Sue Smith. Coach: Hope Powell
Northern Ireland: Emma Higgins, Stacey Hall (80 Clare Carson), Ashley Hutton *(YC)*, Kellie-Ann Leyland, Julie Nelson, Kelly Baillie, Rebecca Corish, Una Harkin, Kimberly (Kim) Turner (90+1 Lynsey Patterson), Sarah McFadden, Helen McKenna (56 Laura Giltespie). Coach: Alfie Wylie
Goals: Kelly Jayne Smith (52), Una Harkin (66 og), Katie Sarah Chapman (73), Lianne Sanderson (77)
Referee: Ann-Helen Rosenberg Østervold (Norway)   Attendance: 3,944.

222. 17.05.2007   Roots Hall Stadium, Southend: England - Iceland 4-0
England: Rachel Brown-Finnis, Alex Scott (46 Lindsay Johnson), Casey Stoney, Katie Sarah Chapman (79 Steph Houghton), Anita Asante, Mary Rose Phillip (46 Faye White), Karen Carney (69 Sue Smith), Fara Williams (46 Jill Scott), Jody Handley, Kelly Jayne Smith (84 Lianne Sanderson), Rachel Yankey (46 Jo Potter). Coach: Hope Powell
Iceland: Thore Helgadottir, Gudrunseley Gunnarsdottir, Grete Mjoll Sanuelsdottir, Edda Gardarsdottir (77 Olina Gudbjörg Vidarsdottir), Asta Arnadottir (62 Gudny Björk Odinsdottir), Sif Atladottir (81 Gudny Petrina Thorsdottir), Rakel Logadottir (86 Anna Björg Björnsdottir), Katrin Jonsdottir, Margret Lara Vidarsdottir, Dora Maria Larusdottir, Eria Steina Arnardottir (53 Katrin Omarsdottir).
Goals: Rachel Yankey (23), Katie Sarah Chapman (30, ..), Kelly Jayne Smith
Referee: Wendy Toms (England)   Attendance: 7,606.

Kelly Jayne Smith missed a penalty kick.

223. 26.08.2007   Macau Olympic Stadium, Macau: China - England 1-0 (1-0)
China: HAN Wenxia, PU Wei, LI Jie (46 WANG Kun), BI Yan, MA Xiaoxu (73 LIU Sa), HAN Duan Zhang Uuying, XIE Caixia, ZHANG Tong (55 PAN Lina), LIU Yali, QU Feifel (55 SONG Xiaoli), ZHOU Gaoping (58 ZHANG Ying).
England: Rachel Brown-Finnis (80 Siobhan Rebecca Chamberlain), Alex Scott, Casey Stoney, Katie Sarah Chapman, Anita Asante (37 Faye White), Mary Rose Phillip, Karen Carney, Fara Williams, Eniola Aluko, Kelly Jayne Smith, Rachel Yankey (70 Sue Smith).
Coach: Hope Powell
Goal: ZHANG Tong (44)

224. 11.09.2007   FIFA World Cup 2007 China Group A
Hongkou Stadium, Shanghai: Japan - England 2-2 (0-0)
Japan: Miho Fukumoto, Hiromi Isozaki (86 Yūki Nagasato), Yukari Kinga (46 Kozue Andō), Azusa Iwashimizu, Rumi Utsugi, Tomomi Miyamoto (71 Ayumi Hara), Tomoe Sakai, Aya Miyama, Eriko Arakawa, Homare Sawa, Shinobu Ohno.   Coach: Hiroshi Ohashi
England: Rachel Brown-Finnis, Alex Scott (89 Lindsay Johnson), Casey Stoney, Faye White, Mary Rose Phillip, Katie Sarah Chapman, Fara Williams, Kelly Jayne Smith, Karen Carney, Eniola Aluko (74 Jill Scott), Rachel Yankey.   Coach: Hope Powell
Goals: Aya Miyama (55, 90+5) / Kelly Jayne Smith (81, 84)
Referee: Kari Seitz (USA)   Attendance: 27,146.

225. 14.09.2007   FIFA World Cup 2007 China Group A
Hongkou Stadium, Shanghai: England - Germany 0-0
England: Rachel Brown-Finnis, Alex Scott, Casey Stoney, Faye White, Mary Rose Phillip, Katie Sarah Chapman, Fara Williams, Kelly Jayne Smith, Anita Asante, Jill Scott, Karen Carney (57 Rachel Yankey).   Coach: Hope Powell
Germany: Nadine Angerer, Kerstin Stegemann, Annike Krahn, Linda Bresonik, Ariane Hingst, Melanie Behringer (62 Fatmire Alushi), Renate Lingor, Simone Laudehr, Kerstin Garefrekes, Sandra Smisek, Birgit Prinz.   Coach: Silvia Neid
Referee: Jenny Palmqvist (Sweden)   Attendance: 27,730.

226. 17.09.2007   FIFA World Cup 2007 China Group A
Chengdu Sports Center, Chengdu: England - Argentina 6-1 (2-0)
England: Rachel Brown-Finnis, Alex Scott (68 Sue Smith), Casey Stoney, Faye White, Mary Rose Phillip, Fara Williams, Kelly Jayne Smith (80 Jody Handley), Anita Asante, Jill Scott, Eniola Aluko (80 Vicky Exley), Rachel Yankey.   Coach: Hope Powell
Argentina: Romina Ferro, Eva Nadia González, Gabriela Patricia Chávez, Clarisa Belén Huber (52 Valeria Cotelo), Catalina Pérez, Maria Florencia Quiñones (76 Mariela del Carmen Coronel), Florencia Mandrile, Fabiana Gisella Vallejos, María Belén Potassa, Analía Soledad Almeida (62 Natalia Gatti), Mercedes Pereyra.   Coach: José Carlos Borrello
Goals: Eva Nadia González (9 og), Jill Scott (10), Fara Williams (50 pen), Kelly Jayne Smith (64, 77), Vicky Exley (90 pen) / Eva Nadia González (60)
Referee: Dianne Ferreira-James (Guyana)   Attendance: 30,730.

Sent-off: Catalina Pérez (49)

227. 22.09.2007   FIFA World Cup 2007 China Quarter-finals
Olympic Sports Centre, Tianjin: USA - England 3-0 (0-0)
USA: Hope Solo, Christie Rampone, Cat Whitehill, Stephanie Cox, Kate Markgraf, Shannon Boxx (82 Carli Lloyd), Heather O'Reilly, Leslie Osborne, Kristine Lilly, Lori Chalupny, Abby Wambach (86 Natasha Kai).   Coach: Greg Ryan
England: Rachel Brown-Finnis, Alex Scott, Casey Stoney, Faye White, Mary Rose Phillip (80 Lianne Sanderson), Katie Sarah Chapman, Kelly Jayne Smith, Anita Asante, Jill Scott, Karen Carney, Eniola Aluko (46 Rachel Yankey).   Coach: Hope Powell
Goals: Abby Wambach (48), Shannon Boxx (57), Kristine Lilly (60)
Referee: Jenny Palmqvist (Sweden)   Attendance: 29,586.

228. 27.10.2007   EURO 2009 Qualifiers
    Bescot Stadium, Walsall: England - Belarus 4-0 (2-0)
England: Rachel Brown-Finnis, Mary Rose Phillip, Alex Scott *(YC)*, Casey Stoney, Anita Asante, Karen Carney (46 Sue Smith), Katie Sarah Chapman (61 Jill Scott), Fara Williams, Rachel Yankey, Eniola Aluko, Kelly Jayne Smith (55 Lianne Sanderson).
Coach: Hope Powell
Belarus: Svetlana Novikova, Svetlana Astasheva, Viktoria Krylova, Olga Radko (75 Elena Shevchuk), Svetlana Ryzhova, Oksana Shpak, Lyudmila Kuznetsova (58 Iryna Kazeeva), Olga Novikova, Natallia Ryzhevich, Alesia Davydovich, Irina Chukisova (52 Marina Lis).
Coach: Uladzimir Kasakouski
Goals: Alex Scott (10, 64), Kelly Jayne Smith (32), Eniola Aluko (48)
Referee: Marylin Remy (France)   Attendance: 8,632.

229. 25.11.2007   EURO 2009 Qualifiers
    Greenhous Meadow, Shrewsbury: England - Spain 1-0 (0-0)
England: Rachel Brown-Finnis, Alex Scott, Casey Stoney, Jill Scott, Faye White, Anita Asante, Karen Carney, Fara Williams, Eniola Aluko (55 Lianne Sanderson), Kelly Jayne Smith, Rachel Yankey.   Coach: Hope Powell
Spain: AINHOA TIRAPU de Goñi, MARTA TORREJÓN Moya, NOELIA AYBAR "RIVA", MELISA NICOLAU Martín, ITZIAR GURRUTXAGA Bengoetxea (74 MARÍA PAZ Vilas Dono), LAURA DEL RÍO García, VANESA Carlota Gimbert Acosta, SANDRA VILANOVA Tous, IRAIA ITURREGI Sustatxa (70 RUTH GARCÍA García), GURUTZE FERNÁNDEZ Callejo "GURU" (63 MARIA JOSÉ PÉREZ González), ERIKA Vázquez Morales.
Coach: IGNACIO QUEREDA Laviña
Goal: Karen Carney (64)
Referee: Claudine Brohet (Belgium)   Attendance: 8,753.

230. 12.02.2008   Dasaki Stadium, Achna (Cyprus): Sweden - England 2-0 (1-0)
Sweden: Hedvig Lindahl, Anna Paulsson, Sara Mattsson, Stina Segerström, Sara Thunebro, Nilla Fischer (77 Linda Sembrant), Frida Nordin (65 Madelaine Edlund), Frida Östberg (77 Maria Karlsson), Lisa Dahlkvist, Lotta Schelin, Jessica Landström (65 Maria Nordbrandt).
Coach: Thomas Dennerby
England: Siobhan Rebecca Chamberlain, Alex Scott (80 Jody Handley), Faye White (80 Laura Bassett), Mary Rose Phillip, Casey Stoney (82 Rachel Unitt), Anita Asante, Jill Scott (40 Eniola Aluko), Fara Williams, Karen Carney (46 Sue Smith, 69 Lindsay Johnson), Kelly Jayne Smith (62' Emily Westwood), Rachel Yankey.   Coach: Hope Powell
Goals: Lotta Schelin (44, 79)
Referee: Dimitros Chrisostomou (Cyprus)   Attendance: 60.

231. 14.02.2008   Larnaca (Cyprus): England - Norway 2-1 (0-0)
England: Siobhan Rebecca Chamberlain (71 Kay Hawke), Alex Scott, Casey Stoney, Anita Asante, Faye White, Karen Carney *(YC25)*, Mary Phillip, Ga Williams, Lianne Sanderson (71 Eniola Aluke), Kelly Smith, Rachel Yankey *(YC70)*.   Coach: Hope Powell
Norway: Christine Colombo Nilsen, Ane Stangeland Horpestad, Gunhild Bentzen Følstad, Siri Kristine Nordby, Runa Vikestad, Ingvild Stensland, Marie Knutsen, Solveig Ingersdatter Gulbrandsen, Lindy Melissa Løvbræk Wiik, Kristin Lie, Lene Glesåen Storløkken.
Goals: Ga Williams (47), Kelly Smith (64) / Ingvild Stensland (53)
Referee: Sofia Karagiergi (Cyprus)   Attendance: 50.

232. 06.03.2008   EURO 2009 Qualifiers
            Mourneview Park, Lurgan: Northern Ireland - England 0-2 (0-1)
Northern Ireland: Emma Higgins, Sarah Booth (66 Rebecca Corish), Ashley Hutton, Aine McGovern, Kelly Bailie, Julie Nelson, Una Harkin, Kim Turner, Demi Vance, Helen McKenna, Sarah McFadden (83 Amy McCann). Coach: Alfie Wylie
England: Siobhan Rebecca Chamberlain, Mary Rose Phillip, Alex Scott (71 Lindsay Johnson), Casey Stoney, Anita Asante, Faye White, Karen Carney, Jill Scott, Fara Williams, Kelly Jayne Smith *(YC)*, Rachel Yankey. Coach: Hope Powell
Goals: Fara Williams (19), Faye White (84)
Referee: Silvia Tea Spinelli (Italy)

233. 20.03.2008   EURO 2009 Qualifiers
            Keepmoat Stadium, Doncaster: England - Czech Republic 0-0
England: Siobhan Rebecca Chamberlain, Mary Rose Phillip (46 Lindsay Johnson), Alex Scott, Casey Stoney, Anita Asante, Faye White, Karen Carney, Emily Westwood, Fara Williams, Lianne Sanderson (46 Eniola Aluko), Rachel Yankey.   Coach: Hope Powell
Czech Republic: Marcela Zborilová, Petra Bertholdová, Lucie Heroldová, Irena Martínková *(YC)*, Veronika Pincová *(YC)*, Lucie Kladrubská (69 Veronika Hoferková), Blanka Penicková (88 Adéla Pivonková), Eva Knavova-Smeralova *(YC)*, Kamila Veselá, Katerina Dosková, Lucie Martínková.   Coach: Dusan Zovinec
Referee: Eva Ödlund (Sweden)

234. 08.05.2008   EURO 2009 Qualifiers
            Darida Stadium, Minsk: Belarus - England 1-6 (1-4)
Belarus: Svetlana Novikova, Svetlana Astasheva (73 Olga Manzhuk), Elena Shevtsova, Oksana Shpak, Alina Vasilyeva *(YC)*, Nina Akhrymuk, Olga Novikova, Natallia Ryzhevich, Alesia Baranava (81 Svetlana Znaidenova), Iryna Kazeeva, Marina Lis (71 Tatsiana Kiose). Coach: Uladzimir Kasakouski
England: Siobhan Rebecca Chamberlain, Alex Scott (46 Jody Handley), Casey Stoney *(YC)*, Faye White, Anita Asante, Karen Carney (46 Lindsay Johnson), Jill Scott, Fara Williams, Lianne Sanderson, Kelly Jayne Smith (72 Laura Bassett), Rachel Yankey.
Coach: Hope Powell
Goals: Natallia Ryzhevich (30) / Jill Scott (1), Fara Williams (7, 25, 87), Lianne Sanderson (44), Faye White (90)
Referee: Cristina Dorcioman (Romania)

235. 17.07.2008   Generali Sportpark, Unterhaching: Germany - England 3-0 (1-0)
Germany: Nadine Angerer, Kerstin Stegemann (70 Babett Peter), Annike Krahn (46 Saskia Bartusiak), Ariane Hingst, Fatmire Alushi (46 Melanie Behringer), Renate Lingor (70 Célia Sasic), Simone Laudehr, Kerstin Garefrekes (70 Conny Pohlers), Linda Bresonik, Sandra Smisek (46 Anja Mittag), Birgit Prinz.   Coach: Silvia Neid
England: Rachel Brown-Finnis, Alex Scott (60 Lindsay Johnson), Faye White, Casey Stoney, Anita Asante, Rachel Yankey, Fara Williams, Jill Scott, Kelly Jayne Smith, Lianne Sanderson (65 Emily Westwood), Karen Carney. Coach: Hope Powell
Goals: Sandra Smisek (15), Birgit Prinz (55), Melanie Behringer (71 pen)
Referee: Christine Baitinger (Germany)   Attendance: 9,185.

236. 28.09.2008   EURO 2009 Qualifiers
          Dolicek Stadion, Prague: Czech Republic - England 1-5 (1-0)
Czech Republic: Marcela Zborilová, Petra Bertholdová, Lucie Heroldová *(YC)*, Veronika Pincová, Eva Knavova-Smeralova (20 Lucie Kladrubská), Blanka Penicková (57 Petra Divisová), Adéla Pivonková, Pavlína Scasná, Katerina Dosková, Iva Mocová (72 Veronika Hoferková), Markéta Ringelová.   Coach: Dusan Zovinec
England: Rachel Brown-Finnis, Lindsay Johnson, Alex Scott, Casey Stoney (83 Rachel Unitt), Anita Asante, Karen Carney, Jill Scott, Fara Williams, Rachel Yankey (65 Sue Smith), Lianne Sanderson (46 Emily Westwood), Kelly Jayne Smith.   Coach: Hope Powell
Goals: Katerina Dosková (28) / Emily Westwood (61), Kelly Jayne Smith (79, 86), Karen Carney (81), Jill Scott (83)
Referee: Christine Baitinger (Germany)

237. 02.10.2008   EURO 2009 Qualifiers
          Estadio Ruta de la Plata, Zamora: Spain - England 2-2 (2-0)
Spain: AINHOA TIRAPU de Goñi, MARTA TORREJÓN Moya, LAURA DEL RÍO García, MELISA NICOLAU Martín, VANESA Carlota Gimbert Acosta, Verónica "VERO" Boquete Giadans, SONIA Bermúdez Tribano (70 SANDRA VILANOVA Tous), Sonia Vesga Ruiz "BURGOS", Silvia MESEGUER Bellido (86 MARIA JOSÉ PÉREZ González), ADRIANA Martín Santamaría, ERIKA Vázquez Morales (58 Ana María Romero Moreno "WILLY").   Coach: IGNACIO QUEREDA Laviña
England: Rachel Brown-Finnis, Lindsay Johnson, Alex Scott, Casey Stoney, Anita Asante, Karen Carney, Jill Scott, Fara Williams *(YC)*, Rachel Yankey (82 Sue Smith), Eniola Aluko (46 Emily Westwood), Kelly Jayne Smith.   Coach: Hope Powell
Goals: Verónica "VERO" Boquete Giadans (8), SONIA Bermúdez Tribano (42) / Karen Carney (54), Kelly Jayne Smith (76)
Referee: Jenny Palmqvist (Sweden)

238. 09.02.2009   Alpha Sports Centre, Larnaca (Cyprus): Finland - England 2-2 (2-2)
Goals: Leena Puranen, Anne Mäkinen 43) / Kelly Jayne Smith (2 pen), Lianne Sanderson (4)

239. 11.02.2009   Alpha Sports Centre, Larnaca (Cyprus): England - Finland 4-1 (3-0)
Goals: Faye White (40), Emily Westwood, Kelly Jayne Smith (pen), Rachel Yankey (65) /
Unknown

240. 05.03.2009   Cyprus Cup
          GSZ Stadium, Larnaca (Cyprus): South Africa - England 0-6 (0-3)
South Africa: Mukondi Mulaudzi, Simphiwe Dludlu, Janine Van Wyk (46 Emily Magotlhe), Hlengiwe Ngwane, Lena Mosebo, Busisiwe Ndimeni, Kylie-Ann Louw (46 Chantelle Esau), Mpho Rammala, Nompumelelo Nyandeni *(YC,YC70)*, Sebata Molatelo (46 Amanda Dlamini), Noko Matlou.
England: Siobhan Rebecca Chamberlain, Alex Scott, Casey Stoney, Anita Asante, Steph Houghton, Fara Williams, Jill Scott (46 Katie Sarah Chapman), Kelly Jayne Smith (46 Emily Westwood, 72 Danielle Buet), Karen Carney (62 Jessica (Jess) Clarke), Lianne Sanderson (74 Eniola Aluko), Sue Smith (46 Rachel Yankey).   Coach: Hope Powell
Goals: Fara Williams (18), Lianne Sanderson (19), Kelly Jayne Smith (42), Steph Houghton (54), Katie Sarah Chapman (87, 90+1)

241. 07.03.2009   Cyprus Cup
Municipal 'Tasos Markou' Stadium, Paralimni (Cyprus): England - France 2-2 (1-1)
England: Rachel Brown-Finnis, Anita Asante, Steph Houghton, Lindsay Johnson (46 Alex Scott), Casey Stoney, Karen Carney *(YC81)*, Jill Scott, Emily Westwood (68 Katie Sarah Chapman), Fara Williams, Kelly Jayne Smith *(YC54)* (56 Eniola Aluko), Sue Smith.
Coach: Hope Powell
France: Sarah Bouhaddi, Delphine Blanc (57 Caroline Pizzala), Laura Georges, Sabrina Viguier, Ludivine Diguelman, Elodie Thomis, Corine Petit-Franco, Sandrine Soubeyrand, Elise Bussaglia (46 Eugénie Le Sommer), Louisa Necib-Cadamuro (73 Gaëtane Thiney), Candie Herbert (73 Laëtitia Tonazzi).   Coach: Bruno Bini
Goals: Karen Carney (28), Casey Stoney (76) / Corine Petit-Franco (15), Élodie Thomis (72)
Referee: Andreas Kantis Georgiou (Cyprus)   Attendance: 40.

242. 10.03.2009   Cyprus Cup
GSZ Stadium, Larnaca (Cyprus): Scotland - England 0-3 (0-1)
Scotland: Gemma Fay, Rhonda Jones (85 Frankie-Fantom Brown), Jennifer Beattie (78 Kirsty McBride), Ifeoma Dieke (85 Hollie Thomson), Leanne Ross, Joanne Love, Kim Little, Megan Sneddon (85 Amy McDonald), Suzanne Grant, Pauline Hamill (46 Jane Ross), Rachel Corsie.
Coach: Anna Signeul
England: Siobhan Rebecca Chamberlain, Lindsay Johnson, Alex Scott, Rachel Unitt, Corinne Yonston, Danielle Josephine Buet, Katie Sarah Chapman, Jess Clarke, Emily Westwood, Rachel Yankey, Eniola Aluko (82 Lianne Sanderson).   Coach: Hope Powell
Goals: Eliona Aluko (40), Emily Westwood (66), Jess Clarke (83)
Attendance: 200.

243. 12.03.2009   Cyprus Cup
GSP Stadium, Nicosia (Cyprus): England - Canada 3-1 (3-1)
England: Rachel Brown-Finnis, Anita Asante, Steph Houghton, Alex Scott, Casey Stoney, Karen Carney, Jill Scott (63 Katie Sarah Chapman), Fara Williams, Lianne Sanderson (68 Eniola Aluko), Kelly Jayne Smith, Sue Smith.   Coach: Hope Powell
Canada: Melanie Booth, Martina Franko (46 Sarah Andrews), Emily Jane Zurrer, Brittany Baxter-Timko, Kaylyn Mckenzie Kyle (59 Amy Walsh), Diana Beverly Matheson, Kelly Parker, Chelsea Stewart (46 Marie Eve Nault), Melissa Palma Julie Tancredi (68 Amy Vermeulen), Christine Margaret Sinclair.   Coach: Carolina Morace
Goals: Lianne Sanderson (32), Kelly Jayne Smith (40), Fara Williams (45) / Christine Margaret Sinclair (14)
Attendance: 50.

244. 23.04.2009   Prostad Stadium, Shrewsbury: England - Norway 3-0 (2-0)
England: Rachel Brown, Alex Scott, Casey Stoney, Fara Williams, Lindsay Johnson, Karen Carney, Jill Scott *(YC)*, Eniola Aluko (66 Katie Chapman), Anita Asante, Kelly Smith, Sue Smith (79 Jess Clarke).   Coach: Hope Powell
Norway: Caroline Knutsen, Trine Rønning, Hedda Strand Gardsjord (80 Camilla Engrønningen Huse), Maren Nævdal Mjelde, Toril Hetland Akerhaugen, Ingvild Stensland *(YC)*, Solveig Ingersdatter Gulbrandsen, Lene Glesåen Storløkken (60 Anneli Giske), Isabell Lehn Herlovsen (60 Lindy Melissa Løvbræk Wiik), Ingvild Landvik Isaksen, Kristin Lie (60 Elise Hove Thorsnes).
Goals: Fara Williams (19, 81), Lindsay Johnson (40)
Referee: Alexandra (Sasa) Ihringova (England)   Attendance: 4,468.

245. 16.07.2009 Weston Homes Community Stadium, Colchester: England - Iceland 0-2 (0-1)
England: Siobhan Rebecca Chamberlain (46 Carly Telford), Rachel Unitt, Corinne Yorston (65 Dunia Susi), Faye White, Laura Bassett, Danielle Buet, Jess Clarke (79 Gemma Davison), Jill Scott (65 Rachel Williams), Emily Westwood, Eniola Aluko, Rachel Yankey.
Coach: Hope Powell
Iceland: Thóra Björg Helgadóttir, Gudrún Sóley Gunnarsdóttir, Ólína Gudbjörg Vidarsdóttir *(YC77)*, Katrin Jonsdottir, Edda Gardarsdóttir, Dora Maria Larusdottir (82 Erla Steina Arnardóttir), Dora Stefansdottir (69 Katrin Omarsdottir), Holmfridur Magnusdóttir, Erna Björk Sigurdardóttir, Sara Björk Gunnarsdóttir, Margrét Lára Vidarsdóttir.
Goals: Holmfridur Magnúsdóttir (24), Margrét Lára Vidarsdóttir (81)
Referee: Amy Rayner (England)   Attendance: 4,170.

246. 22.07.2009   County Ground Stadium, Swindon: England - Denmark 1-0 (0-0)
England: Karen Bardsley, Alex Scott, Casey Stoney, Katie Chapman, Lindsay Johnson, Anita Asante, Karen Carney, Jill Scott (90 Emily Westwood), Lianne Sanderson (46 Jody Handley), Fara Williams, Sue Smith. Coach: Hope Powell
Denmark: Heidi Elgaard Johansen (46 Tine Cederkvist Viskær), Line Røddik Hansen, Marie Bjerg, Mette V.Jensen, Sanne Troelsgaard (89 Marianne Løth Pedersen), Ditte Larsen, Katrine Søndergaard Pedersen, Nanna Christiansen (88 Janne Madsen), Maiken With Pape (46 Lene Jensen), Nadia Nadim, Katrine Veje (73 Tina K.Rasmussen). Coach: Kenneth Heiner-Møller
Goal: Jody Handley (87)
Referee: Simon Hooper (England)   Attendance: 4,177.

247. 25.08.2009   EURO 2009 Finland Group C
          Lahti Stadium, Lahti: England - Italy 1-2 (1-0)
England: Rachel Brown-Finnis, Alex Scott, Casey Stoney *(RC28)*, Faye White, Fara Williams *(YC)*, Anita Asante (73 Rachel Unitt), Katie Sarah Chapman, Jill Scott, Karen Carney, Eniola Aluko (46 Kelly Jayne Smith), Sue Smith (85 Lianne Sanderson). Coach: Hope Powell
Italy: Anna Maria Picarelli, Sara Gama, Roberta D'Adda, Elisabeth Tona, Viviana Schiavi, Alessia Tuttino, Tatiana Zorri, Carolina Pini (77 Alia Guagni), Giulia Domenichetti (53 Alice Parisi), Melania Gabbiadini (90 Raffaella Manieri), Patrizia Panico. Coach: Pietro Ghedin
Goals: Fara Williams (38 pen) / Patrizia Panico (56), Alessia Tuttuno (81)
Referee: Bibiana Steinhaus (Germany)   Attendance: 2,950.

Sent-off: Casey Stoney (28)

248. 28.08.2009   EURO 2009 Finland Group C
          Finnair Stadium, Helsinki: England - Russia 3-2 (3-2)
England: Rachel Brown-Finnis, Alex Scott, Lindsay Johnson, Faye White, Rachel Unitt, Fara Williams, Katie Sarah Chapman, Karen Carney, Eniola Aluko, Kelly Jayne Smith, Sue Smith (66 Jess Clarke). Coach: Hope Powell
Russia: Elena Kochneva, Oksana Shmachkova, Olga Poryadina (90 Nadezhda Myskiv), Natalia Pertseva, Ksenia Tsybutovich, Tatiana Skotnikova, Valentina Savchenkova, Elena Fomina (76 Natalia Barbashina), Elena Morozova, Olesya Kurochkina, Elena Danilova (43 Olga Petrova). Coach: Igor Shalimov
Goals: Karen Carney (24), Eniola Aluko (31), Kelly Jayne Smith (42) /
Ksenia Tsybutovich (2), Olesya Kurochkina (22)
Referee: Dagmar Damková (Czech Republic)   Attendance: 1,462.

249. 31.08.2009   EURO 2009 Finland Group C
Veritas Stadion, Turku: Sweden - England 1-1 (1-1)
Sweden: Helvig Lindahl, Charlotte Rohlin, Stina Segerström, Anna Paulson, Sara Thunebro, Caroline Seger, Kosovare Asllani *(YC64)* (67 Lina Nilsson), Therese Sjögran *(YC27)*, Lisa Dahlkvist (60 Jessica Landström), Lotta Schelin (90 Sara Lindén), Victoria Sandell Svensson.
Coach: Thomas Dennerby
England: Rachel Brown-Finnis, Lindsay Johnson, Alex Scott, Casey Stoney, Faye White, Karen Carney, Katie Sarah Chapman, Fara Williams, Eniola Aluko (65 Emily Westwood), Kelly Jayne Smith, Sue Smith (90 Jess Clarke).   Coach: Hope Powell
Goals: Victoria Sandell Svensson (40 pen) / Faye White (28)
Referee: Kateryna Monzul (Ukraine)   Attendance: 6,142.

250. 03.09.2009   EURO 2009 Finland Quarter-finals
Veritas Stadion, Turku: Finland - England 2-3 (0-1)
Finland: Tinja-Riikka Korpela, Petra Pauliina Vaelma, Tiina Sofia Salmén, Tuija Annika Hyyrynen, Maija Saari, Jessica Carola Julin (72 Anna Westerlund), Anne Mäkinen, Essi Katriina Sainio (52 Annica Sjölund), Laura Österberg Kalmari, Linda Sällström, Sanna Talonen (75 Susanna Lehtinen).   Coach: Michael Käld
England: Rachel Brown-Finnis, Anita Asante, Lindsay Johnson (68 Laura Bassett), Casey Stoney, Faye White (41 Jill Scott), Karen Carney, Katie Sarah Chapman, Fara Williams, Eniola Aluko, Kelly Jayne Smith, Sue Smith.   Coach: Hope Powell
Goals: Annica Sjölund (65), Linda Sällström (79) / Eniola Aluko (14, 67), Fara Williams (49)
Referee: Dagmar Damková (Czech Republic)   Attendance: 7,247.

251. 06.09.2009   EURO 2009 Finland Semi-finals
Ratina Stadion, Tampere: England - Netherlands 2-1 (0-0,1-1)
England: Rachel Brown-Finnis, Anita Asante, Jess Clarke (91 Jill Scott), Lindsay Johnson, Alex Scott, Casey Stoney, Katie Sarah Chapman, Fara Williams, Eniola Aluko (70 Lianne Sanderson), Kelly Jayne Smith, Sue Smith (46 Karen Carney).   Coach: Hope Powell
Netherlands: Loes Geurts, Dyanne Bito (117 Marloes de Boer), Daphne Koster, Manoe Meulen, Petra Marieka Jacoba Hogewoning, Anouk Hoogendijk, Annemieke Kiesel-Griffioen, Marlous Pieëte (86 Kirsten Johanna Maria van de Ven), Manon Melis, Karin Stevens (120 Shanice Janice van de Sanden), Sylvia Smit. Coach: Vera Pauw
Goals: Kelly Jayne Smith (61), Jill Scott (116) / Marlous Pieëte (64)
Referee: Gyöngyi Krisztina Gaál (Hungary)   Attendance: 4,621.

England won after extra-time.

252. 10.09.2009   EURO 2009 Finland Final
Helsingin Olympiastadion, Helsinki: England - Germany 2-6 (1-2)
England: Rachel Brown-Finnis, Anita Asante, Alex Scott, Casey Stoney *(YC)*, Faye White, Karen Carney, Katie Sarah Chapman (86 Emily Westwood), Jill Scott, Fara Williams, Kelly Jayne Smith, Eniola Aluko (81 Lianne Sanderson).   Coach: Hope Powell
Germany: Nadine Angerer, Saskia Bartusiak, Babett Peter, Annike Krahn, Linda Bresonik, Kerstin Garefrekes (83 Fatmire "Lira" Alushi-Bajramaj), Kim Kulig-Soyah, Simone Laudehr, Melanie Behringer (60 Célia Sasic-Okoyino da Mbabi), Inka Grings, Birgit Prinz.
Coach: Silvia Neid
Goals: Karen Carney (24), Kelly Jayne Smith (55) /
Birgit Prinz (20, 76), Melanie Behringer (23), Kim Kulig-Soyah (50), Inka Grings (62, 73)
Referee: Dagmar Damková (Czech Republic)   Attendance: 15,877.

253. 25.10.2009   FIFA World Cup 2011 Qualifiers
Bloomfield Road, Blackpool: England - Malta 8-0 (4-0)
England: Karen Bardsley, Laura Bassett, Jess Clarke, Alex Scott, Rachel Unitt, Faye White (58 Lindsay Johnson), Danielle Josephine Buet, Jill Scott, Fara Williams (68 Emily Westwood), Lianne Sanderson (54 Jody Handley), Sue Smith.   Coach: Hope Powell
Malta: Sharon Costantino, Rebecca Chircop *(YC)* (64 Kathleen Saliba), Rebecca D'Agostino, Natasha Pace *(YC,YC57)*, Charlene Zammit, Rachel Cuschieri, Mandy Debono (85 Chantal Marie Fenech), Kimberly Parnis, Dorianne Theuma, Catherine Camilleri (51 Marisa Deguara), Ylenia Carabott *(YC)*.   Coach: Pierre Brincat
Goals: Faye White (8), Fara Williams (21, 39, 66), Jessica Clarke (37, 76), Emily Westwood (78), Rachel Unitt (87)
Referee: Florence Guillemin (France)   Attendance: 3,681.

Sent-off: Natasha Pace (57)

254. 26.11.2009   FIFA World Cup 2011 Qualifiers
Buca Arena, Izmir: Turkey - England 0-3 (0-0)
Turkey: Duygu Yilmaz, Feride Bakir, Yeliz Demir, Çigdem Belci, Cansu Yag (87 Helga Nadire Inan Ertürk), Seval Kiraç (83 Ayse Gürbüz), Fatma Kara, Bilgin Defterli, Eylül Elgalp, Filiz Koç-Heilmann (70 Reyhan Seker), Lütfiye Ercimen.   Coach: Hamdi Aslan
England: Karen Bardsley, Laura Bassett, Jess Clarke (74 Lianne Sanderson), Alex Scott, Rachel Unitt, Faye White, Dani Buet (60 Karen Carney), Emily Westwood, Fara Williams, Jody Handley (83 Natasha Dowie), Sue Smith.   Coach: Hope Powell
Goals: Alex Scott (77), Lianne Sanderson (81), Rachel Unitt (85)
Referee: Sandra Braz Bastos (Portugal)

255. 24.02.2010   Cyprus Cup
Larnaca (Cyprus): England - South Africa 1-0 (1-0)
England: Rachel Brown-Finnis (46 Siobhan Rebecca Chamberlain), Dunia Susi, Casey Stoney, Dani Buet (58 Laura Bassett), Faye White (67 Rachel Unitt), Lindsay Johnson, Jess Clarke (76 Rachel Yankey), Jill Scott, Emily Westwood, Jody Handley, Sue Smith.   Coach: Hope Powell
South Africa:
Goal: Jill Scott (5)

256. 27.02.2010   Cyprus Cup
Alpha Sports Centre, Larnaca (Cyprus): Canada - England 1-0 (1-0)
Canada: Karina Chenelle LeBlanc, Candace-Marie Chapman (71 Cindy Walsh), Marie Eve Nault, Rhian Emilie Wilkinson, Emily Jane Zurrer, Diana Beverly Matheson, Carmelina Moscato, Kelly Parker, Christine Marie Katarina Julien, Jodi Ann Robinsson (65 Desiree Rose Marie Scott), Christine Margaret Sinclair.   Coach: Carolina Morace
England: Karen Bardsley, Laura Bassett (59 Dunia Susi), Jess Clarke, Alex Scott, Casey Stoney, Rachel Unitt, Faye White, Jill Scott, Fara Williams, Rachel Yankey, Lianne Sanderson (59 Emily Westwood).   Coach: Hope Powell
Goal: Christine Marie Katarina Julien (10)
Attendance: 150.

257. 01.03.2010   Cyprus Cup
GSP Stadium, Nicosia (Cyprus): Switzerland - England 2-2 (1-0)
Switzerland: Marisa Brunner, Danique Stein, Marie Andrea Egli, Caroline Abbé, Rahel Graf, Noémie Beney *(YC30)*, Vanessa Bürki (85 Jehona Mehmeti), Sandy Maendly (61 Daniela Regula Schwarz), Lara Dickenmann, Martina Moser (90 Selina Kuster), Ramona Bachmann (90 Ana-Maria Crnogorcevic).   Coach: Béatrice von Siebenthal
England: Siobhan Rebecca Chamberlain, Lindsay Johnson, Alex Scott, Casey Stoney, Dunia Susi (80 Jess Clarke), Rachel Unitt, Dani Buet, Jill Scott, Emily Westwood (73 Kelly Jayne Smith), Jody Handley (46 Lianne Sanderson), Sue Smith.   Coach: Hope Powell
Goals: Lara Dickenmann (27, 85) / Casey Stoney (56), Lianne Sanderson (76)
Referee: Katalin Anna Kulscar (Hungary)   Attendance: 50.

258. 03.03.2010   Cyprus Cup fifth place
GSP Stadium, Nicosia (Cyprus): Italy - England 2-3 (1-1)
Italy: Sara Penzo, Sara Gama, Viviana Schiavi, Laura Neboli, Raffaella Manieri, Giulia Domenichetti (46 Alice Parisi), Tatiana Zorri (37 Marta Carissimi), Alessia Turrino, Carolina Pini, Silvia Fuselli (62 Pamela Conti), Elisa Camporese.   Coach: Pietro Ghedin
England: Rachel Brown-Finnis (68 Karen Bardsley), Dunia Susi, Faye White, Casey Stoney, Rachel Unitt, Laura Bassett, Jill Scott, Sue Smith (46 Lianne Sanderson), Alex Scott, Jess Clarke, Rachel Yankey.   Coach: Hope Powell
Goals: Rachel Brown-Finnis (43 og), Elisa Camporese (64) /
Alex Scott (8, 58), Faye White (90+2)

259. 25.03.2010   FIFA World Cup 2011 Qualifiers
Loftus Road, London: England - Austria 3-0 (1-0)
England: Karen Bardsley, Alex Scott, Casey Stoney, Dunia Susi (62 Ellen White), Rachel Unitt (85 Claire Rafferty), Faye White, Katie Sarah Chapman, Fara Williams, Rachel Yankey (85 Sue Smith), Eniola Aluko, Lianne Sanderson.   Coach: Hope Powell
Austria: Jasmin Pfeiler, Kathrin Entner, Susanna Gahleitner, Susanna Höller, Marion Gröbner *(YC)* (63 Nina Burger), Marlies Hanschitz, Nadine Prohaska, Sarah Puntigam (89 Susanna Koch), Daniela Tasch, Carina Wenninger, Nina Aigner.   Coach: Johannes Uhlig
Goals: Lianne Sanderson (16), Eniola Aluko (67), Ellen White (90)
Referee: Caroline De Boeck (Belgium)   Attendance: 3,980.

260. 01.04.2010   FIFA World Cup 2011 Qualifiers
The Den Stadium, London-Millwall: England - Spain 1-0 (1-0)
England: Rachel Brown-Finnis, Jess Clarke *(YC)*, Alex Scott, Casey Stoney, Rachel Unitt, Faye White, Katie Sarah Chapman, Fara Williams, Rachel Yankey (84 Sue Smith), Eniola Aluko (69 Ellen White), Kelly Jayne Smith (59 Jill Scott).   Coach: Hope Powell
Spain: AINHOA TIRAPU de Goñi, MARTA TORREJÓN Moya *(YC)*, Sonia Vesga Ruiz "BURGOS" *(YC)*, RUTH GARCÍA García, SONIA Bermúdez Tribano (66 MARIA JOSÉ PÉREZ González), Verónica "VERO" Boquete Giadans, ADRIANA Martín Santamaría, SANDRA VILANOVA Tous (80 Silvia MESEGUER Bellido), Ana Maria "ANI" Escribano, AMAIA OLABARRIETA Elordui, Elisabeth "ELI" Ibarra Rabancho (74 Ana María Romero Moreno "WILLY").   Coach: IGNACIO QUEREDA Laviña
Goal: Katie Sarah Chapman (30)
Referee: Christina Westrum Pedersen (Norway)   Attendance: 5,041.

261. 20.05.2010   FIFA World Cup 2011 Qualifiers
           Centenary Stadium, Ta'Qali: Malta - England 0-6 (0-3)
Malta: Sharon Costantino, Rebecca Chircop, Rebecca D'Agostino, Natasha Pace, Corissa Vella (63 Mandy Debono), Rachel Cuschieri, Chantal Marie Fenech (90+2 Kathleen Saliba), Kimberly Parnis, Dorianne Theuma, Ylenia Carabott, Gabriella Zahra (71 Emma Xuereb).
Coach: Pierre Brincat
England: Rachel Brown-Finnis, Jess Clarke, Claire Rafferty, Alex Scott (46 Dunia Susi), Casey Stoney, Faye White (74 Natasha Dowie), Katie Sarah Chapman, Fara Williams, Rachel Yankey (64 Karen Carney), Ellen White, Kelly Jayne Smith.   Coach: Hope Powell
Goals: Faye White (7), Kelly Jayne Smith (15), Fara Williams (29, 82), Jess Clarke (56), Ellen White (67)
Referee: Marte Sørø (Norway)   Attendance: 50.

262. 19.06.2010   FIFA World Cup 2011 Qualifiers
           Estadio El Montecillo, Aranda de Duero: Spain - England 2-2 (1-0)
Spain: AINHOA TIRAPU de Goñi, MARTA TORREJÓN Moya (46 AMAIA OLABARRIETA Elordui), Sonia Vesga Ruiz "BURGOS", MÍRIAM DIÉGUEZ de Oña *(YC)*, RUTH GARCÍA García, SONIA Bermúdez Tribano (81 María Victoria "VICKY" LOSADA Gómez), Verónica "VERO" Boquete Giadans, ADRIANA Martín Santamaría, SANDRA VILANOVA Tous, Elisabeth "ELI" Ibarra Rabancho, ERIKA Vázquez Morales (63 Silvia MESEGUER Bellido).   Coach: IGNACIO QUEREDA Laviña
England: Rachel Brown-Finnis, Alex Scott, Casey Stoney, Rachel Unitt, Faye White, Karen Carney, Katie Sarah Chapman *(YC)*, Fara Williams, Rachel Yankey (46 Jill Scott), Eniola Aluko (74 Ellen White), Kelly Jayne Smith.   Coach: Hope Powell
Goals: ADRIANA Martín Santamaría (16), SONIA Bermúdez Tribano (67) / Rachel Unitt (78), Faye White (88)
Referee: Jenny Palmqvist (Sweden)   Attendance: 2,800.

263. 29.07.2010   FIFA World Cup 2011 Qualifiers
           Bescot Stadium, Walsall: England - Turkey 3-0 (1-0)
England: Rachel Brown-Finnis, Jess Clarke (77 Dunia Susi), Alex Scott, Casey Stoney, Rachel Unitt, Faye White, Katie Sarah Chapman, Jill Scott, Fara Williams (77 Laura Bassett), Rachel Yankey, Eniola Aluko (46 Ellen White).   Coach: Hope Powell
Turkey: Duygu Yilmaz, Feride Bakir, Çigdem Belci, Cansu Yag, Seval Kiraç, Melisa Dilber Ertürk, Seyma Erenli (59 Basak Ersoy), Esra Erol (66 Fatma Kara), Eylül Elgalp (90 Zübeyde Kaya), Leyla Güngör, Gülcan Koca *(YC)*.   Coach: Hamdi Aslan
Goals: Rachel Yankey (23), Ellen White (62), Jess Clarke (78)
Referee: Floarea Cristina Babadac-Ionescu (Romania)   Attendance: 5,457.

264. 21.08.2010   FIFA World Cup 2011 Qualifiers
           Sepp-Doll-Stadion, Krems an der Donau: Austria - England 0-4 (0-3)
Austria: Jasmin Pfeiler, Kathrin Entner, Susanna Höller, Laura Feiersinger (66 Virginia Kirchberger), Marion Gröbner (46 Sarah Puntigam), Isabella Grössinger, Jennifer Pöltl, Nadine Prohaska, Sonja Spieler, Carina Wenninger (46 Nina Burger), Lisa Marie Makas.
Coach: Ernst Weber
England: Rachel Brown-Finnis, Alex Scott, Casey Stoney, Rachel Unitt, Faye White (46 Sophie Bradley-Auckland), Karen Carney, Katie Sarah Chapman (60 Steph Houghton), Jill Scott, Fara Williams, Rachel Yankey, Kelly Jayne Smith (46 Ellen White).
Coach: Hope Powell
Goals: Kelly Jayne Smith (7, 30), Alex Scott (40), Ellen White (80)
Referee: Kirsi Katja Maria Heikkinen (Finland)   Attendance: 1,500.

265. 12.09.2010   FIFA World Cup 2011 Qualifiers Decider 1. Round
Greenhous Meadow, Shrewsbury: England - Switzerland 2-0 (2-0)
England: Rachel Brown-Finnis, Alex Scott, Casey Stoney, Rachel Unitt *(YC89)*, Faye White, Katie Sarah Chapman, Jill Scott *(YC53)*, Fara Williams *(YC90+3)*, Rachel Yankey (90 Jess Clarke), Eniola Aluko, Kelly Jayne Smith.   Coach: Hope Powell
Switzerland: Marisa Brunner, Caroline Abbé, Noémie Beney (80 Selina Kuster), Marina Keller *(YC19)*, Lara Dickenmann, Rahel Graf *(YC89)*, Sandy Maendly, Martina Moser (63 Isabelle Meyer), Nicole Corinne Remund, Selina Zumbühl, Ramona Bachmann (76 Ana-Maria Crnogorcevic).   Coach: Béatrice von Siebenthal
Goals: Fara Williams (44), Kelly Jayne Smith (45+2)
Referee: Claudine Brohet (Belgium)   Attendance: 4,119.

266. 16.09.2010   FIFA World Cup 2011 Qualifiers Decider 1. Round
Niedermatten, Wohlen: Switzerland - England 2-3 (1-2)
Switzerland: Marisa Brunner, Caroline Abbé, Noémie Beney (71 Martina Moser), Marina Keller *(YC82)*, Ana-Maria Crnogorcevic, Lara Dickenmann, Rahel Graf, Sandy Maendly (58 Selina Kuster), Nicole Corinne Remund (58 Isabelle Meyer), Selina Zumbühl, Ramona Bachmann.   Coach: Béatrice von Siebenthal
England: Rachel Brown-Finnis *(RC41)*, Alex Scott, Casey Stoney, Rachel Unitt, Faye White *(YC77)*, Katie Sarah Chapman, Jill Scott, Fara Williams, Rachel Yankey (78 Jess Clarke), Eniola Aluko (42 Siobhan Rebecca Chamberlain *goalkeeper*), Kelly Jayne Smith (88 Ellen White).   Coach: Hope Powell
Goals: Ramona Bachmann (41), Selina Zumbühl (65) /
Kelly Jayne Smith (32), Eniola Aluko (34), Fara Williams (50 pen)
Referee: Cristina Dorcioman (Romania)   Attendance: 1,800.

Kelly Jayne Smith missed a penalty kick (9)

Sent-off: Rachel Brown-Finnis (41)

267. 19.10.2010   Peace Queen Cup
Suwon Civil Stadium, Suwon (South Korea): South Korea - England 0-0
South Korea: JUN Min-Kyung, YU Ji-Eun, SHIM Seo-Yeon, HONH Kyung-Suk, LEE Eun-Mi, KIM Soo-Yun, KIM Na-Rae (55 CHA Yun-Hee), KWON Hah-Nul, JEON Ga-EUL, JI So-Yun (70 KWON Eun-Som), PARK Hee-Young *(YC37)* (75' YOO Young-A).
Coach: CHOI In-Cheul
England: Rachel Brown, Alex Scott, Sophie Bradley, Casey Stoney, Claire Rafferty, Jess Clarke (73 Eniola Aluko), Jill Scott, Fara Williams *(YC24)*, Steph Houghton, Rachel Yankey, Kelly Jayne Smith (60 Ellen White).   Coach: Hope Powell
Attendance: 9,764.

268. 21.10.2010   Peace Queen Cup
Suwon Civil Stadium, Suwon (South Korea): New Zealand - England 0-0
New Zealand: Jenny Bindon, Ria Percival, Rebecca Smith, Abby Erceg, Anna Green (55 Betsy Hassett), Hayley Moorwood, Katie Hoyle, Ali Riley, Rosie White (86 Emma Kete), Amber Hearn, Hannah Wilkinson (55 Sarah Gregorius).
England: Karen Bardsley, Dunia Susi (78 Ellen White), Alex Scott, Faye White, Rachel Unitt, Jess Clarke, Laura Bassett, Lindsay Johnson, Anita Asante, Kelly Jayne Smith (85' Fara Williams), Eniola Aluko (87 Rachel Yankey).   Coach: Hope Powell

269. 02.03.2011   Cyprus Cup
Larnaca (Cyprus): England - Italy 2-0 (2-0)
England: Karen Bardsley, Dunia Susi (81 Sue Smith), Faye White, Casey Stoney, Rachel Unitt, Anita Asante, Steph Houghton, Jess Clarke (66 Alex Scott), Kelly Jayne Smith *(YC)*, Rachel Yankey, Ellen White.   Coach: Hope Powell
Italy: Anna Maria Picarelli, Roberta D'Adda, Elisabetta Tona, Laura Neboli, Sara Gama, Alessia Tuttino, Carolina Pini (90 Alia Guagni), Giulia Domenichetti *(YC)*, Pamela Conti (80 Evelyn Vicchiarello), Elisa Camporese (68 Marta Carissimi), Patrizia Panico (64 Ilaria Mauro). Coach: Pietro Ghedin
Goals: Ellen White (3), Kelly Jayne Smith (38 pen)

270. 04.03.2011   Cyprus Cup
GSP Stadium, Nicosia (Cyprus): England - Scotland 0-2 (0-1)
England: Siobhan Rebecca Chamberlain, Lindsay Johnson, Alex Scott, Casey Stoney, Rachel Unitt, Laura Bassett, Jill Scott, Sue Smith, Fara Williams, Eniola Aluko, Jess Clarke (68 Dunia Susi). Coach: Hope Powell
Scotland: Shannon Lynn, Frankie-Fantom Brown, Ifeoma Dieke, Leanne Ross (70 Christie Murray), Jennifer Beattie, Rachel Corsie, Emma Fernon, Kim Little, Joanne Love (85 Rhonda Jones), Megan Sneddon, Hayley Lauder.   Coach: Anna Signeul
Goals: Kim Little (26), Jennifer Beattie (53)
Referee: Katalin Anna Kulcsar (Hungary)

271. 07.03.2011   Cyprus Cup
GSP Stadium, Nicosia (Cyprus): Canada - England 2-0 (1-0)
Canada: Erin McLeod, Melanie Booth (66 Marie Eve Nault), Candace-Marie Chapman, Chelsea Stewart (46 Brittany Baxter-Timko), Rhian Emilie Wilkinson, Emily Jane Zurrer, Diana Beverly Matheson, Carmelina Moscato, Sophie Diana Schmidt (84 Kaylyn Mckenzie Kyle), Desiree Rose Marie Scott (65 Robyn Gayle), Christine Margaret Sinclair (86 Christina Marie Katarina Julien). Coach: Carolina Morace
England: Karen Bardsley, Sophie Bradley-Auckland (73 Casey Stoney), Alex Scott, Dunia Susi, Faye White, Anita Asante, Steph Houghton, Fara Williams, Kelly Jayne Smith, Ellen White, Rachel Yankey. Coach: Hope Powell
Goals: Christine Margaret Sinclair (45), Brittany Baxter-Timko (55)
Referee: Ausra Kance-Tvarijonaite (Lithuania)   Attendance: 30.

272. 09.03.2011   Cyprus Cup 5th Place Match
Stade Dhasaki, Achnas (Cyprus): England - South Korea 2-0 (1-0)
England: Karen Bardsley (46 Siobhan Rebecca Chamberlain), Lindsay Johnson, Casey Stoney, Dunia Susi (46 Alex Scott), Rachel Unitt (59 Steph Houghton), Laura Bassett, Jill Scott, Sue Smith, Eniola Aluko, Jess Clarke (62 Ellen White), Kelly Jayne Smith. Coach: Hope Powell
South Korea: JUN Min-Kyung, LEE Eun-Mi, SHIM Seo-Yeon, YU Ji-Eun, KIM Na-Rae, KWON Hah-Nul (58 JEON Ga-Eun), LEE Hyun-Young (58 YOO Young-A), LEE Sea-Eun (78 JUNG Won-Jung), JI So-Yun, PARK Hee-Young (84 LEE Jin-Hwa), PARK Hee-Young (69 YEO Min-Ji).   Coach: CHOI In-Chul
Goals: Sue Smith (14, 80)

273. 02.04.2011   Matchroom Stadium, London: England - USA 2-1 (2-1)
England: Karen Bardsley, Alex Scott, Casey Stoney, Faye White (68 Sophie Bradley-Auckland), Rachel Unitt, Jill Scott, Fara Williams, Jess Clarke, Kelly Smith, Rachel Yankey (75 Karen Carney), Ellen White.   Coach: Hope Powell
USA: Nicole Barnhart (46 Hope Solo), Ali Krieger, Christie Rampone, Rachel Buehler, Amy Le Peilbet (46 Stephanie Cox), Heather O'Reilly, Shannon Boxx, Carli Lloyd, Megan Rapinoe (70 Tobin Heath), Amy Rodriguez (70 Alex Morgan), Abby Wambach (62 Lauren Cheney).   Coach: Pia Sundhage
Goals: Jess Clarke (8), Rachel Yankey (26) / Megan Rapinoe (39)
Referee: Sian Massey (England)   Attendance: 5,801.

274. 17.05.2011   Kassam Stadium, Oxford: England - Sweden 2-0 (0-0)
England: Karen Bardsley (78 Siobhan Rebecca Chamberlain), Alex Scott, Rachel Unitt (46 Eniola Aluko), Anita Asante (46 Karen Carney), Sophie Bradley-Auckland, Casey Stoney (87 Fern Whelan), Jess Clarke, Jill Scott, Ellen White (46 Steph Houghton), Kelly Jayne Smith (46 Claire Rafferty), Rachel Yankey.   Coach: Hope Powell
Sweden: Hedvig Lindahl, Charlotte Rohlin, Linda Sembrant, Annica Svensson, Caroline Seger, Sara Thunebro, Lotta Schelin, Jessica Landström, Therese Sjögran (80 Johanna Almgren), Linda Nordin (63 Sofia Jakobsson), Maria Hammarström Liljesson (65 Elin Ekblom Bak).   Coach: Thomas Dennerby
Goals: Jill Scott (47), Karen Carney (70 pen)
Referee: Sarah Garratt (England)   Attendance: 5,167.

275. 23.06.2011   Volkswagen Arena, Wolfsburg (Germany): Australia - England 2-0 (2-0)
Goals: *Unknown* (15), *Unknown* (28)

276. 27.06.2011   FIFA World Cup 2011 Germany Group B
           Volkswagen Arena, Wolfsburg: Mexico - England 1-1 (1-1)
Mexico: CECILIA Aurora SANTIAGO Cisneros, Rubi MARLENE SANDOVAL Nungaray, ALINA Lisa GARCIAMENDEZ-Rowold, NATALIE Raquel Nuño VINTI, TERESA Guadalupe Aguilar WORBIS, DINORA Lizeth GARZA Rodríguez (85 TERESA NOYOLA Bayardo), Lydia NAYELI RANGEL Hernández, LUZ Del Rosario SAUCEDO Soto, MARIBEL DOMÍNGUEZ Castelan (75 Daniel Mahon), MÓNICA OCAMPO Medina, Sandra STEPHANY MAYOR Gutiérrez.   Coach: LEONARDO CUÉLLAR Rivera
England: Karen Bardsley, Alex Scott, Rachel Unitt, Faye White (82 Sophie Bradley-Auckland), Casey Stoney, Jill Scott, Fara Williams, Rachel Yankey, Kelly Jayne Smith, Karen Carney (71 Ellen White), Eniola Aluko.   Coach: Hope Powell
Goals: Mónica Ocampo Medina (33) / Fara Williams (21)
Referee: Silvia Elizabeth Reyes Juárez (Peru)   Attendance: 18,702.

277. 01.07.2011   FIFA World Cup 2011 Germany Group B
           Glücksgas-Stadion, Dresden: New Zealand - England 1-2 (1-0)
New Zealand: Jenny Bindon, Ria Percival (71 Rosie White), Anna Green, Abby Erceg, Rebecca Smith, Ali Riley, Katie Bowen (46 Hayley Bowden), Katie Duncan, Betsy Hassett, Amber Hearn, Sarah Gregorius (90 Hannah Wilkinson).   Coach: John Herdman
England: Karen Bardsley, Alex Scott, Rachel Unitt, Faye White (86 Sophie Bradley-Auckland), Casey Stoney, Jill Scott, Fara Williams, Rachel Yankey (65 Jess Clarke), Ellen White, Kelly Jayne Smith, Eniola Aluko (46 Karen Carney).   Coach: Hope Powell
Goals: Sarah Gregorius (18) / Jill Scott (63), Jess Clarke (81)
Referee: Therese Raissa Neguel Damgoua (Cameroon)   Attendance: 19,110.

278. 05.07.2011   FIFA World Cup 2011 Germany Group B
SGL Arena, Augsburg: England - Japan 2-0 (1-0)
England: Karen Bardsley, Alex Scott, Rachel Unitt, Casey Stoney, Sophie Bradley-Auckland, Jill Scott, Jess Clarke (46 Rachel Yankey), Anita Asante, Ellen White (90 Laura Bassett), Kelly Jayne Smith (62 Eniola Aluko), Karen Carney. Coach: Hope Powell
Japan: Ayumi Kaihori, Yukari Kinga, Azusa Iwashimizu, Saki Kumagai, Aya Sameshima, Mizuho Sakaguchi (75 Mana Iwabuchi), Aya Miyama, Homare Sawa, Kozue Andō (56 Karina Maruyama), Shinobu Ohno (82 Nahomi Kawasumi), Yūki Nagasato. Coach: Norio Sasaki
Goals: Ellen White (14), Rachel Yankey (66)
Referee: Carol-Anne Chénard (Canada)   Attendance: 20,777.

279. 09.07.2011   FIFA World Cup 2011 Germany Quarter-finals
BayArena, Leverkusen: England - France 1-1 (0-0,1-1)
England: Karen Bardsley *(YC87)*, Alex Scott (81 Steph Houghton), Rachel Unitt (81 Claire Rafferty), Faye White, Casey Stoney, Jill Scott *(YC90)*, Fara Williams *(YC5)*, Rachel Yankey (84 Anita Asante), Ellen White *(YC77)*, Kelly Jayne Smith, Karen Carney.
Coach: Hope Powell
France: Céline Deville, Laura Georges, Sonia Bompastor, Laure Lepailleur, Sabrina Viguier, Sandrine Soubeyrand (67 Élodie Thomis), Camille Abily, Louisa Necib-Cadamuro (79 Sandrine Brétigny, 106 Eugénie Le Sommer), Élise Bussaglia, Gaëtane Thiney, Marie-Laure Delie. Coach: Bruno Bini
Goals: Jill Scott (59) / Élise Bussaglia (88)
Referee: Jenny Palmqvist (Sweden)   Attendance: 26,395.

Penalties: Camille Abily (missed), 1-0 Kelly Jayne Smith, 1-1 Élise Bussaglia, 2-1 Karen Carney, 2-2 Gaëtane Thiney, 3-2 Casey Stoney, 3-3 Sonia Bompastor, Claire Rafferty (missed), 3-4 Eugénie Le Sommer, Faye White (missed)

France won 4-3 on penalties following extra-time.

280. 17.09.2011   EURO 2013 Qualifiers
Omladinski, Belgrade: Serbia - England 2-2 (0-2)
Serbia: Milena Vukovic, Marina Nesic, Lidija Stojkanovic, Indira Ilic (83 Danijela Trajkovic), Jovana Sretenovic (39 Marija Radojicic), Danka Podovac, Milena Pesic, Vesna Smiljkovic, Violeta Slovic, Mirela Tenkov (78 Zorica Karadzic), Jovana Damnjanovic.
Coach: Suzana Stanojevic
England: Rachel Brown-Finnis, Sophie Bradley-Auckland, Casey Stoney, Dunia Susi, Rachel Unitt, Laura Bassett, Jill Scott, Karen Carney, Natasha Dowie (46 Rachel Williams), Ellen White, Rachel Yankey. Coach: Hope Powell
Goals: Danka Podovac (55), Vesna Smiljkovic (90+4) /
Rachel Yankey (6), Violeta Slovic (19 og)
Referee: Sandra Braz Bastos (Portugal)   Attendance: 500.

281. 22.09.2011   EURO 2013 Qualifiers
The County Ground, Swindon: England - Slovenia 4-0 (2-0)
England: Karen Bardsley, Sophie Bradley-Auckland (76 Fern Whelan), Alex Scott, Casey Stoney, Rachel Unitt, Steph Houghton, Fara Williams, Karen Carney, Jess Clarke (90 Dani Buet), Ellen White, Rachel Yankey (81 Rachel Williams). Coach: Hope Powell
Slovenia: Lucija Mori, Manja Benak *(YC)*, Snezana Malesevic, Anja Milenkovic *(YC)*, Ines Spelic, Tjasa Tibaut, Urska Zganec (73 Stasa Spur), Mateja Zver, Natalija Golob (57 Fata Salkunic), Lucija Grad, Tanja Vrabel (80 Anja Levacic). Coach: Darko Zizek
Goals: Rachel Yankey (1), Ellen White (5), Steph Houghton (56), Rachel Williams (88)
Referee: Karolina Radzik-Johan (Poland)   Attendance: 3,878.

282. 27.10.2011   EURO 2013 Qualifiers
                MAC3PARK Stadion, Zwolle: Netherlands - England 0-0
Netherlands: Loes Geurts *(YC50)*, Dyanne Bito, Daphne Koster, Mandy van den Berg, Anouk Hoogendijk, Sherida Spitse, Kirsten Johanna Maria van de Ven, Lieke Elisabeth Petronella Martens (69 Chantal de Ridder), Manon Melis, Sylvia Smit, Claudia van den Heiligenberg.
Coach: Roger Reijners
England: Karen Bardsley, Sophie Bradley-Auckland, Alex Scott, Casey Stoney, Rachel Unitt, Jill Scott, Fara Williams *(YC70)*, Rachel Williams, Karen Carney, Jess Clarke (46 Steph Houghton), Ellen White. Coach: Hope Powell
Referee: Bibiana Steinhaus (Germany)   Attendance: 8,800.

Fara Williams missed a penalty kick (50)

283. 23.11.2011   EURO 2013 Qualifiers
                Keepmoat Stadium, Doncaster: England - Serbia 2-0 (1-0)
England: Karen Bardsley, Sophie Bradley-Auckland, Alex Scott, Casey Stoney, Rachel Unitt, Jill Scott, Fara Williams (77 Steph Houghton), Karen Carney *(YC)*, Jess Clarke, Ellen White (87 Rachel Williams), Rachel Yankey (70 Kelly Jayne Smith). Coach: Hope Powell
Serbia: Milena Vukovic, Violeta Slovic, Lidija Stojkanovic *(YC)*, Milena Pesic (73 Marija Ilic), Danka Podovac, Jovana Damnjanovic, Marija Radojicic, Aleksandra Savanovic, Vesna Smiljkovic, Jovana Sretenovic (65 Indira Ilic), Danijela Trajkovic. Coach: Suzana Stanojevic
Goals: Karen Carney (41), Ellen White (51)
Referee: Natalia Avdonchenko (Russia)   Attendance: 4,112.

284. 28.02.2012   Cyprus Cup
                GSP Stadium, Nicosia (Cyprus): Finland - England 1-3 (1-1)
Finland: Minna Meriluoto, Tuija Annika Hyyrynen, Maija Saari, Emmi Alanen, Annika Elina Kukkonen (80 Maiju Ruotsalainen), Katri Mattson (Nokso-Koivisto) (80 Tiina Saario), Pernilla Sofie Nordlund, Essi Katriina Sainio, Anna Westerlund, Linda Sällstrom, Marianna Tolvanen. Coach: Andrée Jeglertz
England: Siobhan Rebecca Chamberlain, Laura Bassett, Steph Houghton *(YC)*, Alex Scott, Casey Stoney, Jade Moore, Sue Smith *(YC)* (83 Jess Clarke), Fara Williams, Karen Carney, Kelly Jayne Smith *(YC)*, Ellen White (71 Rachel Williams). Coach: Hope Powell
Goals: Marianna Tolvanen (8) / Kelly Jayne Smith (36 pen, 88 pen), Karen Carney (50)

285. 01.03.2012   Cyprus Cup
                Neo GSZ Stadium, Larnaca (Cyprus): Switzerland - England 0-1 (0-0)
Switzerland: Marisa Brunner, Marina Keller, Marie Andrea Egli, Caroline Abbé, Sandra Betschart (75 Valérie Gillioz *(YC89)*), Vanessa Bürki, Sandy Maendly, Martina Moser, Selina Kuster, Lara Dickenmann, Ana-Maria Crnogorcevic (70 Jehona Mehmeti).
Coach: Martina Voss-Tecklenburg
England: Rachel Brown-Finnis (64 Siobhan Rebecca Chamberlain), Sophie Bradley-Auckland (32 Steph Houghton), Rachel Unitt, Fern Whelan (16 Casey Stoney), Jess Clarke, Jill Scott, Sue Smith (64 Jade Moore), Fara Williams, Rachel Williams, Karen Carney (64 Ellen White), Dunia Susi. Coach: Hope Powell
Goal: Fara Williams (77)
Referee: Kirsi Katja Maria Heikkinen (Finland)   Attendance: 20.

286. 04.03.2012   Cyprus Cup
Stade Dhasaki Achnas, Achnas (Cyprus): England - France 0-3 (0-1)
England: Karen Bardsley (72 Carly Telford), Laura Bassett, Steph Houghton, Alex Scott, Casey Stoney, Anita Asante (46 Fara Williams), Jess Clarke, Jill Scott, Karen Carney, Kelly Jayne Smith (57 Rachel Williams *(YC61)*), Ellen White.   Coach: Hope Powell
France: Sarah Bouhaddi (87 Laëtitia Philippe), Sonia Bompastor, Ophélie Meilleroux, Corinne Petit-Franco, Wendie Renard *(YC76)*, Camille Abily, Elise Bussaglia *(YC53)*, Louisa Necib-Cadamuro, Gaëtane Thiney *(YC47)* (84 Laure Boulleau *(YC90+3)*), Marie-Laure Delie (73 Elodie Thomis), Eugénie Le Sommer (87 Camille Catala).   Coach: Bruno Bini
Goals: Louisa Necib-Cadamuro (11), Marie-Laure Delie (49), Gaëtane Thiney (80)
Referee: Kirsi Katja Maria Heikkinen (Finland)   Attendance: 30.

287. 06.03.2012   Cyprus Cup Third Place Match
Municipal 'Tasos Markou' Stadium, Paralimni (Cyprus): England - Italy 1-3 (1-0)
England: Rachel Brown-Finnis (60 Siobhan Rebecca Chamberlain), Laura Bassett, Steph Houghton (46 Jill Scott), Alex Scott, Casey Stoney, Rachel Unitt, Jade Moore, Sue Smith, Fara Williams, Rachel Williams (59 Ellen White), Dunia Susi (69 Karen Carney).
Coach: Hope Powell
Italy: Anna Maria Picarelli, Alia Guagni, Raffaella Manieri, Laura Neboli, Elisabeth Tona, Elisa Camporese (46 Pamela Conti), Giulia Domenichetti, Alessia Turrino, Melania Gabbiadini, Sandy Iannella (70 Roberta D'Adda), Patrizia Panico.   Coach: Pietro Ghedin
Goals: Jade Moore (26) / Patrizia Panico (59), Pamela Conti (64), Melania Gabbaidini (86)

288. 31.03.2012   EURO 2013 Qualifiers
Town stadium, Vrbovec: Croatia - England 0-6 (0-5)
Croatia: Nicole Vuk, Allison Lee Scurich, Ana Petrovic, Sandra Zigic, Maja Joscak, Iva Landeka, Izabela Lojna *(YC)*, Barbara Peric (64 Andrea Martic), Martina Salek (46 Dusanka Juko), Katarina Kolar (33 Mateja Bulut), Andreja Valusek *(YC)*.   Coach: Dean Klafuric
England: Karen Bardsley, Alex Scott, Rachel Unitt, Laura Bassett, Steph Houghton *(YC)*, Jill Scott, Fara Williams (46 Jade Moore), Rachel Williams, Karen Carney (46 Anita Asante), Jess Clarke, Ellen White *(YC)* (62 Eniola Aluko).   Coach: Hope Powell
Goals: Rachel Williams (4), Jess Clarke (15), Rachel Unitt (18), Ellen White (35), Steph Houghton (45, 68)
Referee: Petra Pavlikova (Slovakia)   Attendance: 1,000.

289. 17.06.2012   EURO 2013 Qualifiers
Salford City Stadium, Salford: England - Netherlands 1-0 (0-0)
England: Rachel Brown-Finnis, Sophie Bradley-Auckland, Alex Scott, Casey Stoney, Steph Houghton, Jill Scott, Fara Williams, Rachel Williams (46 Ellen White), Eniola Aluko, Karen Carney (72 Anita Asante), Rachel Yankey.   Coach: Hope Powell
Netherlands: Loes Geurts, Dyanne Bito, Maayke Heuver (73 Marije Brummel), Daphne Koster, Mandy van den Berg (86 Leonne Suzanne Stentler), Anouk Hoogendijk, Marlous Pieëte (74 Sylvia Smit), Sherida Spitse, Lieke Elisabeth Petronella Martens, Manon Melis, Claudia van den Heiligenberg.   Coach: Roger Reijners
Goal: Rachel Yankey (67)
Referee: Jenny Palmqvist (Sweden)   Attendance: 5,505.

290. 21.06.2012 EURO 2013 Qualifiers
Ob Jezeru Stadium, Velenje: Slovenia - England 0-4 (0-2)
Slovenia: Sonja Cevnik, Manja Benak, Kaja Jerina, Anja Milenkovic, Andreja Niki (46 Tanja Vrabel), Anisa Rola, Dominika Conc (54 Pamela Begic), Urska Zganec, Kaja Erzen *(YC)*, Lucija Grad, Fata Salkunic (80 Anja Levacic). Coach: Damir Rob
England: Rachel Brown-Finnis, Sophie Bradley-Auckland, Alex Scott, Casey Stoney, Anita Asante, Steph Houghton (61 Claire Rafferty), Jill Scott, Fara Williams (70 Rachel Williams), Eniola Aluko, Ellen White *(YC)* (46 Karen Carney), Rachel Yankey. Coach: Hope Powell
Goals: Jill Scott (29, 43), Karen Carney (54), Rachel Williams (85)
Referee: Katalin Anna Kulcsár (Hungary) Attendance: 800.

291. 19.09.2012 EURO 2013 Qualifiers
Bescot Stadium, Walsall: England - Croatia 3-0 (1-0)
England: Karen Bardsley, Sophie Bradley-Auckland, Alex Scott *(YC)*, Casey Stoney (87 Claire Rafferty), Anita Asante, Steph Houghton, Jill Scott, Fara Williams, Eniola Aluko, Karen Carney, Rachel Yankey (79 Toni Duggan). Coach: Hope Powell
Croatia: Doris Bacic, Dragica Cepernic (76 Izabela Lojna), Helenna Hercigonja-Moulton, Allison Lee Scurich, Gabrijela Gaiser, Ana Jelencic (68 Martina Salek), Maja Joscak, Iva Landeka, Katarina Kolar, Andrea Martic, Kristina Sundov (85 Monika Conjar).
Coach: Dean Klafuric
Goals: Jill Scott (21), Enila Aluko (47), Casey Stoney (80)
Referee: Esther Azzopardi Farrugia (Malta) Attendance: 5,821.

292. 20.10.2012 Stade Charléty, Paris: France - England 2-2 (0-2)
France: Sarah Bouhaddi *(YC33)*, Corine Petit-Franco, Laura Georges, Ophélie Meilleroux, Laure Boulleau, Sandrine Soubeyrand (46 Camille Catala), Camille Abily, Gaëtane Thiney (46 Elodie Thoms, 90 Kheira Hamraoui), Louisa Necib-Cadamuro, Marie-Laure Delie, Eugénie Le Sommer. Coach: Bruno Bini
England: Karen Bardsley (70 Siobhan Rebecca Chamberlain), Steph Houghton, Sophie Bradley (79 Laura Bassett), Casey Stoney, Alex Scott, Anita Asante, Jill Scott, Karen Carney, Eniola Aluko (46 Fara Williams), Rachel Yankey (46 Toni Duggan), Ellen White (79 Susi Dunia). Coach: Hope Powell
Goals: Marie-Laure Delie (59, 82) / Steph Houghton (34), Jill Scott (39)
Referee: Silvia Tea Spinelli (Italy) Attendance: 5,919.

293. 06.03.2013 Cyprus Cup
GSP Stadium, Nicosia (Cyprus): Italy - England 2-4 (2-3)
Italy: Chiara Marchitelli, Roberta D'Adda (85 Daniela Stracchi), Sara Gama (77 Federica Di Criscio), Raffaella Manieri (85 Giorgia Motta), Elisabeth Tona, Elisa Camporese, Pamela Conti (58 Marta Carissimi), Alice Parisi *(YC)*, Alessia Turrino, Sandy Iannella (68 Cristiana Girelli), Patrizia Panico. Coach: Antonio Cabrini
England: Karen Bardsley, Laura Bassett, Sophie Bradley-Auckland (46 Fara Williams), Steph Houghton, Alex Scott, Anita Asante, Jess Clarke (80 Karen Carney), Jordan Nobbs, Rachel Yankey (68 Ellen White), Eniola Aluko (68 Toni Duggan), Kelly Jayne Smith (79 Jill Scott). Coach: Hope Powell
Goals: Elisa Camporese (17, 27) /
Jordan Nobbs (7), Steph Houghton (29), Jess Clarke (33), Ellen White (83)
Referee: Rhona Daly (Republic of Ireland)

294. 08.03.2013   Cyprus Cup
GSZ Stadium, Larnaca (Cyprus): Scotland - England 4-4 (1-2)
Scotland: Gemma Fay, Frankie-Fantom Brown, Rhonda Jones, Eilish McSorley (69 Leanne Ross), Jennifer Beattie, Kim Little, Joanne Love (73 Emma Mitchell), Jane Ross, Megan Sneddon, Leanne Crichton, Lisa Evans.   Coach: Anna Signeul
England: Rachel Brown-Finnis, Steph Houghton, Alex Scott, Casey Stoney (28 Anita Asante), Rachel Unitt, Fara Williams *(YC)*, Rachel Williams, Karen Carney (46 Kelly Jayne Smith), Toni Duggan (78 Eniola Aluko), Dunia Susi, Ellen White.   Coach: Hope Powell
Goals: Lisa Evans (18), Jane Ross (48), Kim Little (53), Emma Mitchell (82) / Ellen White (40), Toni Duggan (45+1), Rachel Williams (73), Kelly Jayne Smith (77)

295. 11.03.2013   Cyprus Cup
GSZ Stadium, Nicosia (Cyprus): New Zealand - England 1-3 (1-0)
New Zealand: Erin Nayler, Abby May Erzeg, Anna Green, Alexandra Lowe Riley (74 Holly Patterson), Rebekah Ashley Stott, Betsy Doon Hasset, Katie Cherie Hoyle-Duncan *(YC)*, Hayley Rose Moorwood-Bowden (77 Rosemary Eleanor Florence Whit), Sarah Joelle Gregorius, Amber Liarnie Rose Hearn, Hannah Lilian Wilkinson (60 Helen Collins).
Coach: Tony Readings
England: Siobhan Rebecca Chamberlain, Sophie Bradley-Auckland (66 Laura Bassett), Steph Houghton (46 Anita Asante), Alex Scott, Casey Stoney (46 Rachel Unitt), Jess Clarke (69 Ellen White), Jordan Nobbs, Jill Scott, Rachel Yankey (79 Toni Duggan), Eniola Aluko, Karen Carney (46 Fara Williams).   Coach: Hope Powell
Goals: Amber Liarnie Rose Hearn (7) / Ellen White (71), Eniola Aluko (72), Toni Duggan (90)

296. 13.03.2013   Cyprus Cup Final
GSP Stadium, Nicosia (Cyprus): Canada - England 0-1 (0-0)
Canada: Erin McLeod, Kadeisha Buchanan *(YC)*, Carmelina Moscato *(YC)* (79 Emily Jane Zurrer), Lauren Sesseleman, Rhian Emilie Wilkinson (82 Robyn Gayle), Diana Beverly Matheson, Sophie Diana Schmidt (40' Kaylyn Mckenzie Kyle *(YC)*), Desiree Rose Marie Scott, Jonelle Filigno (82 Ashley Lawrence), Adriana Kristina Leon (60 Christina Marie Katarina Julien), Christine Margaret Sinclair.   Coach: John Herdman
England: Karen Bardsley, Sophie Bradley-Auckland (46 Jordan Nobbs), Steph Houghton (46 Dunia Susi), Alex Scott, Casey Stoney (69 Laura Bassett), Anita Asante, Jill Scott, Fara Williams *(YC)*, Rachel Yankey, Eniola Aluko (46 Karen Carney, 59 Jess Clarke), Ellen White (71 Rachel Williams).   Coach: Hope Powell
Goal: Rachel Yankey (70)
Referee: Rhona Daly (Republic of Ireland)   Attendance: 200.

297. 07.04.2013   New York Stadium, Rotherham: England - Canada 1-0 (0-0)
England: Karen Bardsley (59 Rachel Brown-Finnis), Alex Scott, Steph Houghton, Anita Asante (59 Jordan Nobbs), Sophie Bradley-Auckland, Casey Stoney, Eniola Aluko (69 Toni Duggan), Jill Scott, Ellen White, Fara Williams, Rachel Yankey (82 Jess Clarke).
Coach: Hope Powell
Canada: Erin McLeod, Cameron, Carmelina Moscato, Kaylyn Mckenzie Kyle, Rhian Emilie Wilkinson, Diana Beverly Matheson, Desiree Rose Marie Scott, Christine Margaret Sinclair, Sophie Diana Schmidt, Kadeisha Buchanan, Sjoman.
Goal: Ellen White
Attendance: 4,875.

298. 26.06.2013   Pirelli Stadium, Burton: England - Japan 1-1 (1-0)
England: Karen Bardsley, Dunia Susi (67 Lucy Bronze), Sophie Bradley-Auckland, Laura Bassett (67 Jade Moore *(YC)*), Alex Scott, Jill Scott (83 Jordan Nobbs), Anita Asante, Eniola Aluko (83 Lincoln), Fara Williams *(YC)*, Rachel Yankey, Ellen White (83' Toni Duggan).
Coach: Hope Powell
Japan: Kaihori, Ariyoshi, Iwashimizu, Osafune (89 Tanaka), Utsugi (64 Kamionobe), Ando (46 Nakajima), Sakaguchi, Kumagai, Nahomi Kawasumi (87 Maruyama), Ohno (87 Iwabichi), Ogimi.
Goals: Eniola Aluko (41) / Nahomi Kawasumi (76)
Referee: L.Andersson (Sweden)

299. 04.07.2013   Skarsjövallen, Ljungskile: Sweden - England 4-1 (2-1)
Sweden: Kristin Hammarström, Charlotte Rohlin, Nilla Fischer (75 Amanda Ilestedt), Sara Thunebro, Lotta Schelin (75 Jenny Hjohlman), Kosovare Asllani (74 Emmelie Konradsson), Antonia Göransson (46 Therese Sjögran), Josefine Örqvist (46 Sofia Jakobsson), Caroline Seger, Jessica Samuelsson, Marie Hammarström Liljesson (46 Lisa Dahlkvist).
Coach: Pia Sundhage
England: Karen Bardsley (46 Rachel Brown-Finnis), Alex Scott, Steph Houghton (46 Dunis Suai), Jill Scott (63 Jordan Nobbs), Sophie Bradley-Auckland, Casey Stoney (46 Laura Bassett), Eniola Aluko, Anita Asante, Ellen White (46 Toni Duggan), Fara Williams, Rachel Yankey (46 Karen Carney).   Coach: Hope Powell
Goals: Antonia Göransson (30), Lotta Schelin (33, 68), Caroline Seger (51) / Ellen White (13)
Referee: Christine Baitinger (Germany)   Attendance: 4,524.

300. 12.07.2013   EURO 2013 Sweden Group C
          Linköping Arena, Linköping: England - Spain 2-3 (1-1)
England: Karen Bardsley, Laura Bassett *(YC)*, Steph Houghton, Alex Scott, Casey Stoney, Anita Asante, Jill Scott, Fara Williams, Rachel Yankey (90+1 Jess Clarke), Eniola Aluko (72 Karen Carney), Ellen White.   Coach: Hope Powell
Spain: AINHOA Tirapu de Goñi, RUTH Garcia Garcia, MARTA TORREJÓN Moya, IRENE Paredes Hernández *(YC)*, Silvia MESEGUER Bellido, Elisabeth IBARRA Rabancho, Jennifer "JENNI" HERMOSO Fuentes, SONIA Bermúdez Tribano (74 ALEXIA Putellas Segura), Verónica "VERO" BOQUETE Giadans, ADRIANA MARTÍN Santamaría, NAGORE CALDERÓN Rodríguez *(YC)* (61 María Victoria "VICKY" LOSADA Gómez).
Coach: IGNACIO QUEREDA Laviña
Goals: Eniola Aluko (8), Laura Bassett (89) / Verónica "VERO" BOQUETE Giadans (4), Jennifer "JENNI" HERMOSO Fuentes (85), ALEXIA Putellas Segura (90+3)
Referee: Kateryna Monzul (Ukraine)   Attendance: 5,190.

301. 15.07.2013   EURO 2013 Sweden Group C
          Linköping Arena, Linköping: England - Russia 1-1 (0-1)
England: Karen Bardsley, Laura Bassett, Steph Houghton (64 Toni Duggan), Alex Scott, Casey Stoney, Anita Asante, Jill Scott, Fara Williams *(YC)*, Rachel Yankey (17 Karen Carney), Eniola Aluko (78 Kelly Jayne Smith), Ellen White.   Coach: Hope Powell
Russia: Elvira Todua, Valentina Savchenkova (84 Maria Dyachkova), Anastasia Kostyukova, Elena Medved-Semenchenko, Ksenia Tsybutovich, Olga Petrova, Elena Terekhova (90+3 Olesya Kurochkina), Alla Sidorovskaya-Rogova, Elena Morozova, Ekaterina Sochneva, Nelli Korovkina (90 Natalia Shlyapina-Mokshanova).   Coach: Sergei Lavrentyev
Goals: Toni Duggan (90+2) / Nelli Korovkina (38)
Referee: Bibiana Steinhaus (Germany)   Attendance: 3,629.

302. 18.07.2013   EURO 2013 Sweden Group C
            Linköping Arena, Linköping: France - England 3-0 (1-0)
France: Céline Deville, Sabrina Delannoy, Jessica Houara d'Hommeaux, Corine Petit-Franco, Wendie Renard, Amandine Henry (61 Camille Catala), Louisa Necib-Cadamuro, Sandrine Soubeyrand (46 Camille Abily), Gaëtane Thiney (46 Élise Bussaglia), Eugénie Le Sommer, Élodie Thomis. Coach: Bruno Bini
England: Karen Bardsley, Sophie Bradley-Auckland, Steph Houghton, Alex Scott, Casey Stoney, Anita Asante (46 Jill Scott), Karen Carney (73 Jess Clarke), Fara Williams *(YC76)*, Eniola Aluko (60 Kelly Jayne Smith), Toni Duggan, Ellen White. Coach: Hope Powell
Goals: Eugénie Le Sommer (9), Louisa Necib-Cadamuro (62), Wendie Renard (64)
Referee: Kirsi Katja Maria Heikkinen (Finland)   Attendance: 7,332.

303. 21.09.2013   FIFA World Cup 2015 Qualifiers
            Goldsands Stadium, Bournemouth: England - Belarus 6-0 (4-0)
England: Rachel Brown-Finnis, Sophie Bradley-Auckland, Lucy Bronze, Alex Scott, Casey Stoney, Karen Carney (63 Jill Scott), Jordan Nobbs, Fara Williams (72 Jade Moore), Eniola Aluko, Toni Duggan (56 Natasha Dowie), Ellen White. Coach: Brent Hills
Belarus: Olga Savostyan, Svetlana Astashova (85 Yulia Denisenko), Oksana Shpak, Alina Vasilyeva, Anna Denisenko, Anastasia Kharlanova, Tatsiana Kiose, Anastasia Linnik, Liana Miroshnichenko (46 Anna Pilipenko), Yulia Slesarchik (25 Yulia Borisenko), Ekaterina Avkhimovich *(YC)*. Coach: Tatiana Volkova
Goals: Karen Carney (3, 26, 40), Ellen White (13), Natasha Dowie (60), Eniola Aluko (62)
Referee: Riem Hussein (Germany)   Attendance: 6,818.

304. 26.09.2013   FIFA World Cup 2015 Qualifiers
            Fratton Park, Portsmouth: England - Turkey 8-0 (6-0)
England: Siobhan Rebecca Chamberlain, Gemma Bonner, Lucy Bronze *(YC)*, Alex Scott, Casey Stoney (76 Steph Houghton), Karen Carney (63 Jill Scott), Jordan Nobbs, Fara Williams, Eniola Aluko (59 Natasha Dowie), Ellen White, Toni Duggan. Coach: Brent Hills
Turkey: Fatma Sahin, Sibel Duman, Didem Karagenç, Songül Ece, Sevgi Çinar, Cansu Yag (37 Emine Ecem Esen, 90 Elif Deniz), Bilgin Defterli, Esra Erol, Pinar Yalçin (70 Gamze Iskeçeli), Yagmur Uraz, Leyla Güngör. Coach: Nur Mustafa Gülen
Goals: Toni Duggan (2, 3, 37), Ellen White (30, 39), Eniola Aluko (33, 49), Natasha Dowie (75)
Referee: Olga Zadinová (Czech Republic)   Attendance: 6,293.

305. 26.10.2013   FIFA World Cup 2015 Qualifiers
            The Den Stadium, London-Millwall: England - Wales 2-0 (0-0)
England: Karen Bardsley, Lucy Bronze, Steph Houghton, Alex Scott, Casey Stoney, Karen Carney, Jordan Nobbs, Fara Williams, Eniola Aluko (62 Jill Scott), Toni Duggan (74 Natasha Dowie), Ellen White (74 Jess Clarke). Coach: Brent Hills
Wales: Nicky Davies, Kylie Davies, Sophie Ingle, Hayley Ladd, Helen Bleazard, Loren Dykes, Jessica Fishlock (58 Michelle Emma Green), Angharad James, Sarah Wiltshire (78 Hannah Keryakoplis), Alice Evans, Natasha Harding (46 Carys Hawkins). Coach: Jarmo Matikainen
Goals: Jordan Nobbs (48), Toni Duggan (57)
Referee: Stéphanie Frappart (France)   Attendance: 5,764.

306. 31.10.2013   FIFA World Cup 2015 Qualifiers
             5 Ocak Stadyumu, Adana: Turkey - England 0-4 (0-2)
Turkey: Fatma Sahin, Çigdem Belci, Didem Tas, Didem Karagenç, Esra Erol, Sibel Duman, Sevgi Çinar (78 Zübeyde Kaya), Pinar Yalçin (68 Gamze Iskeçeli), Yagmur Uraz *(YC)*, Leyla Güngör (53 Ebru Topçu), Bilgin Defterli. Coach: Nur Mustafa Gülen
England: Karen Bardsley, Gemma Bonner, Sophie Bradley-Auckland, Lucy Bronze, Alex Scott, Jordan Nobbs, Jill Scott, Fara Williams (61 Jade Moore), Eniola Aluko (79 Natasha Dowie), Toni Duggan, Ellen White (69 Jess Clarke). Coach: Brent Hills
Goals: Eniola Aluko (10), Fara Williams (17 pen), Toni Duggan (48), Jordan Nobbs (60)
Referee: Yuliya Medvedeva-Keldyusheva (Kazakhstan)   Attendance: 784.

307. 17.01.2014   La Manga (Spain): England - Norway 1-1 (1-0)
England: Karen Bardsley, Alex Scott, Demi-Lee Stokes (61 Gemma Bonner), Fara Williams, Steph Houghton, Lucy Bronze, Eniola Aluko (68 Jill Scott), Jordan Nobbs (76 Laura Bassett), Lianne Sanderson (68 Ellen White), Karen Carney, Toni Duggan (79 Gemma Davison). Coach: Mark Sampson
Norway: Cecile Fiskarstrand, Maren Mjelde (46 Catherine Hogh Dekkerhus), Trine Ronning (46 Marita Skammelsrud), Ada Stolmso Hegerberg, Caroline Graham Hansen (46 Ingrid Schjelderup), Nora Holstad Berge, Guro Reiten, Andrine Tomter, Elise Thorsnes (71 Melissa Bjaneso), Kristine Minde. Lena Mykjaland. Coach: Even Pellerud
Goals: Eniola Aluko (11) / Melissa Bjaneso (87)
Referee: Elia Maria Martinez (Spain)

308. 05.03.2014   Cyprus Cup
             Ammochostos Stadium, Larnaca (Cyprus): England - Italy 2-0 (1-0)
England: Siobhan Rebecca Chamberlain, Lucy Bronze, Steph Houghton, Alex Scott, Karen Carney, Jordan Nobbs (85 Eniola Aluko), Fara Williams, Toni Duggan *(YC)*, Lianne Sanderson *(YC)* (76 Jill Scott), Demi-Lee Stokes (80 Alex Greenwood), Ellen White (86 Laura Bassett). Coach: Mark Sampson
Italy: Laura Giuliani, Elisa Bartoli *(YC)*, Federica Di Criscio, Elena Linari, Rafaella Manieri (55 Sandy Iannella *(YC)*), Elisa Camporese, Giulia Domenichetti (87 Giulia Nasuti), Martina Rossucci, Paola Brumana (64 Marta Carissimi), Cristiana Girelli *(YC)*, Ilaria Mauro (64 Melania Gabbiadini, 75 Patrizia Panico). Coach: Antonio Cabrini
Goals: Karen Carney (45 pen), Toni Duggan (62)

309. 07.03.2014   Cyprus Cup
             GSZ Stadium, Larnaca (Cyprus): Finland - England 0-3 (0-1)
Finland: Minna Meriluoto, Susanna Lehtinen *(YC)* (63 Jenna Korhonen), Katri Mattson (Nokso-Koivisto), Katarina Naumanen, Anna Westerlund, Emmi Alanen, Nora Heroum *(YC)* (63 Sanna Saarinen), Annika Elina Kukkonen, Adelina Engman (76 Ella Vanhanen), Juliette Mikaela Kemppi, Sanna Talonen (76 Sanna Yli-Anttila), Coach: Andrée Jeglertz
England: Carly Telford (84 Lizzie Durack), Laura Bassett, Gemma Bonner, Sophie Bradley-Auckland, Anita Asante (62 Alex Scott), Alex Greenwood, Jade Moore, Jill Scott (70 Karen Carney), Eniola Aluko (76 Ellen White), Gemma Davison (70 Toni Duggan), Natasha Dowie. Coach: Mark Sampson
Goals: Anita Asante (31), Gemma Bonner (67), Eniola Aluko (72)

310. 10.03.2014   Cyprus Cup
GSP Stadium, Nicosia (Cyprus): England - Canada 2-0 (2-0)
England: Siobhan Rebecca Chamberlain, Lucy Bronze, Steph Houghton, Alex Scott, Karen Carney, Jordan Nobbs (80 Jill Scott), Fara Williams, Toni Duggan (86 Gemma Davison), Lianne Sanderson (64 Anita Asante), Demi-Lee Stokes, Ellen White (72 Natasha Dowie). Coach: Mark Sampson
Canada: Erin McLeod, Kadiesha Buchanan, Marie Eve Nault (46 Robyn Gayle), Rhian Wilkinson (79 Nkemjika Ezurike), Emily Jane Zurrer (61 Rebecca Catherine Quinn), Kaylyn Mckenzie Kyle (61 Brittany Baxter-Timko), Diana Beverly Matheson, Sophie Diana Schmidt, Josee Belanger, Adriana Kristina Leon (46 Desiree Rose Marie Scott), Christine Margaret Sinclair.   Coach: John Herdfman
Goals: Lianne Sanderson (2, 33)
Attendance: 150.

311. 12.03.2014   Cyprus Cup Final
Neo GSP Stadium, Nikosia (Cyprus): England - France 0-2 (0-2)
England: Siobhan Rebecca Chamberlain, Lucy Bronze, Steph Houghton, Alex Scott, Anita Asante (51 Jill Scott), Karen Carney (66 Kelly Jayne Smith), Demi-Lee Stokes, Fara Williams *(YC37)*, Gemma Davison (58 Eniola Aluko), Natasha Dowie (66 Lianne Sanderson), Toni Duggan.   Coach: Mark Sampson
France: Sarah Bouhaddi, Laura Georges, Jessica Houara d'Hommeaux, Griedge Mbock Bathy Nka, Wendie Renard, Camille Abily, Élise Bussaglia *(YC44)*, Louisa Necib-Cadamuro, Gaëtane Thiney (77 Marie-Laure Delie), Eugénie Le Sommer *(YC15)* (69 Kheira Hamraoui), Élodie Thomis (53 Marina Makanza).   Coach: Philippe Bergerôo
Goals: Gaëtane Thiney (6), Camille Abily (18)
Referee: Esther Staubli (Switzerland)   Attendance: 500.

312. 05.04.2014   FIFA World Cup 2015 Qualifiers
Amex Stadium, Brighton: England - Montenegro 9-0 (4-0)
England: Siobhan Rebecca Chamberlain, Lucy Bronze, Steph Houghton, Alex Scott, Karen Carney (59 Natasha Dowie), Jill Scott, Fara Williams, Eniola Aluko (64 Jade Moore), Toni Duggan, Lianne Sanderson (72 Ellen White), Demi-Lee Stokes.   Coach: Mark Sampson
Montenegro: Marija Zizic, Maja Micunovic, Zeljka Radanovic (46 Tatjana Djurkovic), Jovana Mrkic, Andreja Vidic, Darija Djukic, Jasna Djokovic (67 Nina Vujicic), Milica Vulic, Armisa Kuc, Ivana Krivokapic, Sladana Bulatovic (74 Tamara Bojat).   Coach: Zoran Mijovic
Goals: Toni Duggan (2, 13, 71), Eniola Aluko (37), Jill Scott (40), Karen Carney (49), Lianne Sanderson (55), Demi-Lee Stokes (69), Natasha Dowie (84)
Referee: Elia Maria Martínez Martínez (Spain)   Attendance: 8,908.

313. 08.05.2014   FIFA World Cup 2015 Qualifiers
Greenhous Meadow, Shrewsbury: England - Ukraine 4-0 (1-0)
England: Siobhan Rebecca Chamberlain, Lucy Bronze, Steph Houghton, Alex Scott, Jade Moore, Jill Scott (62 Laura Bassett), Fara Williams, Eniola Aluko (79 Jess Clarke), Natasha Dowie, Lianne Sanderson (62 Kelly Jayne Smith), Demi-Lee Stokes *(YC)*.
Coach: Mark Sampson
Ukraine: Iryna Zvarych, Maryna Masalska *(YC)*, Valentyna Kotyk, Iryna Vasylyuk, Daryna Apanaschenko, Tetiana Romanenko, Vira Dyatel, Olha Basanska, Lya Andrushchak (65 Olha Ovdiychuk), Valeria Aloshycheva (58 Oksana Yakovishyn), Olga Boychenko (87 Yulia Kornievets).   Coach: Anatoliy Kutsev
Goals: Natasha Dowie (41, 53), Eniola Aluko (49, 63)
Referee: Sara Persson (Sweden)   Attendance: 5,880.

314. 14.06.2014   FIFA World Cup 2015 Qualifiers
Traktor, Minsk: Belarus - England 0-3 (0-2)
Belarus: Inna Botyanovskaya, Anna Kozyupa, Daria Marinina, Yulia Borisenko (78 Elena Shevchuk), Alina Vasilyeva, Anastasia Linnik (46 Anastasia Popova), Yulia Slesarchik, Liana Miroshnichenko (57 Ekaterina Avkhimovich *(YC)*), Tatiana Markushevskaya, Anastasiya Khavanskaya, Anna Pilipenko.   Coach: Tatiana Volkova
England: Karen Bardsley, Laura Bassett, Lucy Bronze, Steph Houghton, Alex Scott, Karen Carney, Jade Moore, Fara Williams, Eniola Aluko (78 Lianne Sanderson), Natasha Dowie (66 Jess Clarke), Demi-Lee Stokes (62 Sophie Bradley-Auckland).   Coach: Mark Sampson
Goals: Eniola Aluko (31), Steph Houghton (36), Lucy Bronze (90+5)
Referee: Jana Adámková (Czech Republic)   Attendance: 350.

315. 19.06.2014   FIFA World Cup 2015 Qualifiers
Arena Lviv, Lviv: Ukraine - England 1-2 (0-2)
Ukraine: Iryna Zvarych, Valentyna Kotyk, Alla Lyshafay (89 Maryna Masalska), Iryna Vasylyuk *(YC)*, Daryna Apanaschenko, Tetiana Romanenko (58 Oksana Yakovishyn), Lyudmyla Pekur, Vira Dyatel, Olha Basanska, Olha Ovdiychuk, Olga Boychenko (85 Yulia Kornievets).   Coach: Anatoliy Kutsev
England: Karen Bardsley, Laura Bassett *(YC)*, Lucy Bronze *(YC)*, Steph Houghton, Alex Scott, Casey Stoney, Karen Carney (90 Alex Greenwood), Jade Moore, Jill Scott (69 Lianne Sanderson), Fara Williams, Eniola Aluko (79 Jess Clarke).   Coach: Mark Sampson
Goals: Olha Ovdiychuk (63) / Casey Stoney (11), Eniola Aluko (14)
Referee: Cristina Dorcioman (Romania)   Attendance: 3,757.

316. 03.08.2014   Victoria Park, Hartlepool: England - Sweden 4-0 (1-0)
England: Karen Bardsley, Alex Scott, Fara Williams (76 Jill Scott), Steph Houghton, Lucy Bronze (71 Laura Bassett), Jordan Nobbs, Karen Carney, Jodie Taylor (61 Eniola Aluko), Lianne Sanderson, Fran Kirby (61 Toni Duggan), Demi-Lee Stokes (76 Alex Greenwood).
Coach: Mark Sampson
Sweden: Hedvig Lindahl (46 Carola Söberg), Emma Berglund (69 Linda Sembrant), Nilla Fischer (34 Amanda Ilestedt), Sara Thunebro, Lotta Schelin, Kosovare Asllani (46 Lisa Dahlkvist), Sofia Jakobsson (46 Jenny Hjohlman), Hanna Folkesson, Therese Sjögran, Lina Nilsson, Caroline Seger (61 Emma Lund).   Coach: Pia Sundhage
Goals: Karen Carney (34 pen, 81), Fran Kirby (53), Lianne Sanderson (68).
Referee: Sjoukje de Jong (Netherlands)   Attendance: 4,547.

317. 21.08.2014   FIFA World Cup 2015 Qualifiers
Cardiff City Stadium, Cardiff: Wales - England 0-4 (0-4)
Wales: Nicky Davies, Nicola Cousins, Kylie Davies, Michelle Emma Green (53 Carys Hawkins), Sophie Ingle, Helen Bleazard, Loren Dykes (59 Nadia Lawrence), Jessica Fishlock, Angharad James (87 Josephine Green), Sarah Wiltshire, Natasha Harding.
Coach: Jarmo Matikainen
England: Karen Bardsley, Laura Bassett, Steph Houghton, Alex Scott, Karen Carney (68 Jill Scott), Jordan Nobbs, Fara Williams (63 Fran Kirby), Eniola Aluko (61 Jodie Taylor), Toni Duggan, Lianne Sanderson, Demi-Lee Stokes.   Coach: Mark Sampson
Goals: Karen Carney (16), Eniola Aluko (39), Laura Bassett (44), Lianne Sanderson (45)
Referee: Efthalia Mitsi (Greece)   Attendance: 3,581.

318. 17.09.2014   FIFA World Cup 2015 Qualifiers
Stadion Pod Malim Brdom, Petrovac: Montenegro - England 0-10 (0-4)
Montenegro: Iva Milacic, Marija Goranovic, Jovana Mrkic, Irena Bjelica *(YC,RC86)*, Andreja Vidic, Sanja Nedic, Jasna Djokovic (85 Jovana Zlaticanin), Marija Vukcevic, Armisa Kuc *(YC)* (90 Ivana Varagic), Ivana Krivokapic (88 Radosava Kocanovic), Sladana Bulatovic.
Coach: Zoran Mijovic
England: Carly Telford, Laura Bassett (56 Jo Potter), Gemma Bonner, Lucy Bronze, Karen Carney, Alex Greenwood, Jordan Nobbs (46 Jill Scott *(YC)*), Fara Williams *(YC)*, Eniola Aluko, Toni Duggan, Lianne Sanderson (64 Natasha Dowie).   Coach: Mark Sampson
Goals: Eniola Aluko (8, 31, 64), Karen Carney (22, 51), Lucy Bronze (37), Toni Duggan (56, 90+4), Alex Greenwood (90), Jo Potter (90+3)
Referee: Petra Chudá (Slovakia)   Attendance: 300.

Karen Carney missed a penalty kick (87)

Sent-off: Irena Bjelica (86)

319. 23.11.2014   Wembley Stadium, London: England - Germany 0-3 (0-3)
England: Karen Bardsley, Alex Scott (83 Jo Potter), Steph Houghton, Lucy Bronze (90 Laura Bassett), Fara Williams (71 Jill Scott), Jordan Nobbs, Lianne Sanderson (80 Jodie Taylor), Toni Duggan, Karen Carney, Eniola Aluko (62 Fran Kirby), Demi-Lee Stokes (83 Alex Greenwood).   Coach: Mark Sampson
Germany: Almuth Schult, Annike Krahn, Tabea Kemme (46 Luisa Wensing), Josephine Henning, Jennifer Cramer (88 Babett Peter), Melanie Leupolz (46 Anja Mittag), Simone Laudehr (78 Pauline Bremer), Lena Goeßling, Melanie Behringer (46 Dzsenifer Marozsán), Célia Sasic (88 Verena Faißt), Alexandra Popp.   Coach: Silvia Neid
Goals: Simone Laudehr (6), Célia Sasic (12, 45)
Referee: Esther Staubli (Switzerland)   Attendance: 45,619.

320. 13.02.2015   Stadium MK, Milton Keynes: England - USA 0-1 (0-1)
England: Karen Bardsley, Alex Scott, Steph Houghton, Laura Bassett (90 Jess Clarke), Demi-Lee Stokes (70 Alex Greenwood), Jordan Nobbs (81 Fara Williams), Jill Scott, Jo Potter (79 Eniola Aluko), Karen Carney, Jodie Taylor (81 Lianne Sanderson), Fran Kirby.
Coach: Mark Sampson
USA: Ashlyn Harris, Ali Krieger, Whitney Engen, Becky Sauerbrunn, Meghan Klingenberg (79 Crystal Dunn), Christen Press (90+2 Kelley O'Hara), Morgan Brian, Lauren Holiday, Carli Lloyd, Alex Morgan (90 Amy Rodriguez), Abby Wambach.   Coach: Jill Ellis
Goal: Alex Morgan (25)
Referee: Sandra Braz Bastos (Portugal)   Attendance: 14,369.

321. 04.03.2015   Cyprus Cup
GSZ Stadium, Larnaca (Cyprus): Finland - England 1-3 (0-1)
Finland: Minna Meriluoto, Tuija Annika Hyyrynen (80 Sanni Maija Franssi), Emma Koivisto, Katri Mattson (Nokso-Koivisto) (62 Annika Elina Kukkonen *(YC)*), Maija Saari, Anna Westerlund, Emmi Alanen (62 Linda Maria Sofia Ruutu), Nora Heroum, Natalia Kuikka (80 Katarina Naumanen), Adelina Engman, Juliette Mikaela Kemppi.   Coach: Andrée Jeglertz
England: Carly Telford, Laura Bassett (83 Alex Scott), Gemma Bonner, Alex Greenwood, Jade Moore, Jo Potter, Fara Williams *(YC)*, Eniola Aluko, Jess Clarke, Lianne Sanderson, Demi-Lee Stokes.   Coach: Mark Sampson
Goals: Maija Saari (89 pen) / Lianne Sanderson (21), Eniola Aluko (66), Jess Clarke (83)

Sent-off: Gemma Bonner (89)

322. 06.03.2015   Cyprus Cup
Neo GSZ, Larnaca (Cyprus): Australia - England 0-3 (0-2)
Australia: Brianna Iris Davey (74 Elizabeth Arnold Mackenzie), Laura Colleen Gloria Alleway, Stephanie Elise Catley, Katrina-Lee Gorry (61 Emily Louise van Egmond), Alanna Stephanie Kennedy (61 Nicola Marie Bolger), Yermin Servet Uzunlar (71 Hayley Raso), Larissa Crummer (71 Caitlin Jade Foord), Lisa Marie De Vanna, Michelle Pearl Heyman (84 Kyah Pam Simon), Elise Kellond-Knight, Clare Elizabeth Polkinghorne.   Coach: Alen Stajcic
England: Karen Bardsley, Laura Bassett, Steph Houghton (90 Jo Potter), Alex Scott (88 Amy Turner), Karen Carney, Katie Sarah Chapman, Alex Greenwood, Jordan Nobbs *(YC)*, Jill Scott *(YC)* (60 Fara Williams), Fran Kirby (69 Lianne Sanderson), Jodie Taylor (84 Jess Clarke).   Coach: Mark Sampson
Goals: Jodie Taylor (8, 17, 83)

323. 09.03.2015   Cyprus Cup
Neo GSP Stadium, Nikosia (Cyprus): Netherlands - England 1-1 (1-1)
Netherlands: Loes Geurts, Siri Worm *(YC58)*, Stefanie van der Gragt, Mandy van den Berg, Anouk Marieke Dekker, Vanity Tonja Caroll Lewerissa, Daniëlle van de Donk, Sherida Spitse, Desiree van Lunteren, Vivianne Miedema, Lieke Elisabeth Petronella Martens.
Coach: Roger Reijners
England: Karen Bardsley, Amy Turner *(YC45)* (63 Alex Scott), Gemma Bonner, Alex Greenwood, Katie Sarah Chapman *(YC60)*, Jade Moore (83 Fara Williams), Jordan Nobbs (63 Laura Bassett), Jo Potter, Eniola Aluko, Fran Kirby (69 Jodie Taylor), Demi-Lee Stokes.
Coach: Mark Sampson
Goals: Vivianne Miedema (19) / Eniola Aluko (43)

324. 11.03.2015   Cyprus Cup Final
GSZ Stadium, Larnaca (Cyprus): Canada - England 0-1 (0-0)
Canada: Erin McLeod, Kadeisha Buchanan, Allysha Chapman *(YC)*, Rhian Emilie Wilkinson, Ashley Lawrence (67 Jessie Fleming), Rebecca Catherine Quinn (67 Carmelina Moscato), Sophie Diana Schmidt, Desiree Rose Marie Scott, Josee Belanger (76 Janine Beckie *(YC)*), Christine Margaret Sinclair, Melissa Palma Julie Tancredi (26 Adriana Kristina Leon *(YC)*).
Coach: John Herdman
England: Siobhan Rebecca Chamberlain, Laura Bassett, Alex Scott, Karen Carney (90 Fran Kirby), Alex Greenwood, Jordan Nobbs, Claire Rafferty *(YC)* (68 Gemma Bonner), Jill Scott (68 Katie Sarah Chapman), Fara Williams, Lianne Sanderson, Jodie Taylor *(YC)* (88 Jade Moore).   Coach: Mark Sampson
Goal: Lianne Sanderson (67)
Attendance: 100.

325. 09.04.2015   Academy Stadium, Manchester: England - China 2-1 (2-1)
England: Siobhan Rebecca Chamberlain, Alex Scott, Laura Bassett, Alex Greenwood, Claire Rafferty (72 Casey Stoney), Jordan Nobbs, Fara Williams, Jill Scott (90+2 Ellen White), Jade Moore (62 Toni Duggan), Jodie Taylor (79 Lianne Sanderson), Fran Kirby (72 Eniola Aluko).
Coach: Mark Sampson
China: ZHANG Yue, TANG Jiali, (46 ZHANG Rui) LIU Shanshan, WANG Shanshan, WU Haiyan (55 RONG), LI Donga, XU Yanlu (66 PENG Han), MA Jan, WANG Shuang, TAN Ruyin, REN Guixin.   Coach: WEI Hao
Goals: Jodie Taylor (1), Fran Kirby (10) / WANG Shanshan (17)
Referee: Morag Pirie (Scotland)   Attendance: 5,665.

326. 29.05.2015   Tim Hortons Field, Hamilton: Canada - England 1-0 (1-0)
Canada: Erin McLeod, Kadeisha Buchanan, Josée Bélanger, Lauren Sesselmann (66 Carmelina Moscato), Desiree Scott, Christine Sinclair, Sophie Schmidt, Melissa Tancredi, Alyssha Champman, Adrian Leon (76 Jessie Fleming), Ashley Lawrence (76 Kaylyn Kyle).
England: Karen Bardsley, Claire Rafferty, Steph Houghton, Jill Scott, Karen Carney, Lucy Bronze, Casey Stoney, Katie Sarah Chapman, Toni Duggan, Lianne Sanderson, Ellen White.
Coach: Mark Sampson
Goal: Sophie Schmidt (24)
Attendance: 23,197.

327. 09.06.2015   FIFA World Cup 2015 Canada Group F
             Moncton Stadium, Moncton: France - England 1-0 (1-0)
France: Sarah Bouhaddi, Wendie Renard, Laure Boulleau, Laura Georges, Jessica Houara d'Hommeaux, Amandine Henry, Camille Abily, Élodie Thomis (71 Kenza Dali), Louisa Necib-Cadamuro (87 Claire Lavogez), Eugénie Le Sommer (81 Élise Bussaglia), Gaëtane Thiney.   Coach: Philippe Bergerôo
England: Karen Bardsley, Alex Scott (68 Fran Kirby), Claire Rafferty, Steph Houghton, Laura Bassett, Lucy Bronze, Fara Williams, Jill Scott, Katie Sarah Chapman (YC66) (76 Jade Moore), Eniola Aluko, Ellen White (60 Toni Duggan).   Coach: Mark Sampson
Goal: Eugénie Le Sommer (29)
Referee: Efthalia Mitsi (Greece)   Attendance: 11,686.

328. 13.06.2015   FIFA World Cup 2015 Canada Group F
             Moncton Stadium, Moncton: England - Mexico 2-1 (0-0)
England: Karen Bardsley, Claire Rafferty (53 Alex Greenwood), Steph Houghton, Laura Bassett, Lucy Bronze (85 Alex Scott), Fara Williams, Jill Scott (66 Karen Carney), Jade Moore, Eniola Aluko, Toni Duggan, Fran Kirby.   Coach: Mark Sampson
Mexico: CECILIA Aurora SANTIAGO Cisneros, Vaitiare KENTI ROBLES Salas, ALINA Lisi GARCIAMENDEZ-Rowold, BIANCA Elissa SIERRA Garcia (46 VALERIA Aurora MIRANDA Rodríguez), JENNIFER Marie Brown RUÍZ-Williams, Lydia NAYELI RANGEL Hernández, VERÓNICA Raquel PÉREZ-Murillo, Verónica CHARLYN CORRAL Ang, Sandra STEPHANY MAYOR Gutiérrez, MÓNICA OCAMPO Medina (89 Claudia FABIOLA IBARRA Muro), RENAE Nicole CUÉLLAR Cuéllar (77 MARÍA Guadalupe SÁNCHEZ Morales).   Coach: LEONARDO CUÉLLAR Rivera
Goals: Fran Kirby (71), Karen Carney (82) / Claudia FABIOLA IBARRA Muro (90)
Referee: Anna-Marie Keighley (New Zealand)   Attendance: 13,138.

329. 17.06.2015   FIFA World Cup 2015 Canada Group F
Olympic Stadium, Montreal: England - Colombia 2-1 (2-0)
England: Karen Bardsley, Alex Scott, Steph Houghton, Alex Greenwood, Casey Stoney, Fara Williams, Jordan Nobbs, Karen Carney (56 Lianne Sanderson), Jade Moore, Toni Duggan (81 Jodie Taylor), Fran Kirby (66 Jo Potter). Coach: Mark Sampson
Colombia: SANDRA Milena SEPÚLVEDA Lopera, NATALIA GAITÀN Laguado, ANGELA Corina CLAVIJO Silva, Katherine NATALY ARIAS Peña, CAROLINA ARIAS Vidal, DIANA Carolina OSPINA García (83 LEICY Maria SANTOS Herrera), DANIELA MONTOYA Quiroz, Hazleidy YORELI RINCÓN Torres (74 TATIANA ARIZA Diaz), María CATALINA USME Pineda (58 INGRID Julieth VIDAL Isaza), ORIÁNICA VELÁSQUEZ Herrera, LADY Patricia ANDRADE Rodriguez. Coach: FABIÁN Felipe TABORDA
Goals: Karen Carney (15), Fara Williams (38 pen) / INGRID VIDAL (90)
Referee: Carol-Anne Chénard (Canada)   Attendance: 13,862.

330. 22.06.2015   FIFA World Cup 2015 Canada Round of 16
TD Place Stadium, Ottawa: Norway - England 1-2 (0-0)
Norway: Ingrid Hjelmseth, Marita Lund, Maren Mjelde, Trine Bjerke Rønning (46 Maria Thorisdottir), Ingrid Moe Wold (87 Lisa-Marie Karlseng Utland), Gry Tofte Ims, Solveig Gulbrandsen, Lene Mykjåland, Kristine Minde (70 Elise Thorsnes), Isabell Herlovsen, Ada Stolsmo Hegerberg. Coach: Even Pellerud
England: Karen Bardsley, Claire Rafferty, Steph Houghton, Laura Bassett, Lucy Bronze, Fara Williams, Karen Carney, Jade Moore, Katie Sarah Chapman, Toni Duggan (63 Jodie Taylor), Fran Kirby (54 Jill Scott). Coach: Mark Sampson
Goals: Solveig Gulbrandsen (54) / Steph Houghton (61), Lucy Bronze (76)
Referee: Esther Staubli (Switzerland)   Attendance: 19,829.

331. 27.06.2015   FIFA World Cup 2015 Canada Quarter-finals
BC Place, Vancouver: England - Canada 2-1 (2-1)
England: Karen Bardsley (51 Siobhan Rebecca Chamberlain), Claire Rafferty, Steph Houghton, Laura Bassett, Lucy Bronze, Fara Williams (79 Ellen White), Jill Scott, Karen Carney (90 Casey Stoney), Jade Moore, Katie Sarah Chapman, Jodie Taylor.
Coach: Mark Sampson
Canada: Erin McLeod, Kadeisha Buchanan, Rhian Wilkinson (62 Diana Matheson), Lauren Sesselmann, Allysha Chapman, Desiree Scott (77 Kaylyn Kyle), Sophie Schmidt, Ashley Lawrence, Josée Bélanger, Christine Sinclair, Melissa Tancredi (71 Adriana Leon).
Coach: John Herdman
Goals: Jodie Taylor (11), Lucy Bronze (14) / Christine Sinclair (42)
Referee: Claudia Ines Umpierrez Rodríguez (Uruguay)   Attendance: 54,027.

332. 01.07.2015   FIFA World Cup 2015 Canada Semi-finals
Commonwealth Stadium, Edmonton: Japan - England 2-1 (1-1)
Japan: Ayumi Kaihori, Azusa Iwashimizu, Saki Kumagai, Aya Sameshima, Saori Ariyoshi, Mizuho Sakaguchi, Aya Miyama, Nahomi Kawasumi, Rumi Utsugi, Shinobu Ohno (70 Mana Iwabuchi), Yūki Nagasato. Coach: Norio Sasaki
England: Karen Bardsley, Claire Rafferty, Steph Houghton, Laura Bassett, Lucy Bronze (75 Alex Scott), Fara Williams (86 Karen Carney), Jill Scott, Jade Moore, Katie Sarah Chapman, Toni Chapman, Jodie Taylor (60 Ellen White). Coach: Mark Sampson
Goals: Aya Miyama (33 pen), Laura Bassett (90 og) / Fara Williams (40 pen)
Referee: Anna-Marie Keighley (New Zealand)   Attendance: 31,467.

333. 04.07.2015   FIFA World Cup 2015 Canada 3td place
Commonwealth Stadium, Edmonton: Germany - England 0-1 (0-0,0-0)
Germany: Nadine Angerer, Bianca Schmidt, Saskia Bartusiak, Babett Peter, Tabea Kemme, Simone Laudehr, Melanie Behringer (46 Melanie Leupolz), Lena Goeßling (101 Alexandra Popp), Sara Däbritz, Célia Sasic (73 Anja Mittag), Lena Petermann.   Coach: Silvia Neid
England: Karen Bardsley, Steph Houghton, Laura Bassett, Lucy Bronze, Alex Greenwood, Fara Williams (112 Casey Stoney), Jill Scott, Karen Carney, Katie Sarah Chapman (80 Lianne Sanderson), Jo Potter, Ellen White (61 Eniola Aluko).   Coach: Mark Sampson
Goal: Fara Williams (108 pen)
Referee: Hyang-Ok Ri (North Korea)   Attendance: 21,483.

England won after extra time.

334. 21.09.2015   EURO 2017 Qualifiers
A. Le Coq Arena, Tallinn: Estonia - England 0-8 (0-3)
Estonia: Getter Laar, Liis Lepik, Anete Paulus, Inna Zlidnis, Signy Aarna, Kristina Bannikova (75 Merily Toom), Kethy Õunpuu (55 Kairi Himanen), Kaire Palmaru (82 Liis Pello), Pille Raadik, Katrin Loo, Eneli Vals.   Coach: Keith Boanas
England: Carly Telford, Steph Houghton, Amy Turner, Jo Potter, Jill Scott (68 Eniola Aluko), Danielle Carter, Isobel Christiansen *(YC45)*, Jess Clarke (90+3 Casey Stoney), Gemma Davison (78 Ellen White), Fran Kirby, Demi-Lee Stokes.   Coach: Mark Sampson
Goals: Danielle Carter (2, 83, 90+2), Jo Potter (34), Fran Kirby (40, 81), Jill Scott (53), Isobel Christiansen (74)
Referee: Dilan Deniz Gökçek (Turkey)   Attendance: 1,342.

335. 23.10.2015   CFA International Women's Football Tournament
Chongqing (China): China - England 2-1 (2-1)
China: WANG Fei, LIU Shanshan, ZHAO Rong, LI Dongna, JIAO Xue, HAN Peng (55 WANG Lisi), LEI Jiahui (64 LOU Jiahui), TAN Ruyin (74 MEIZI Jiang), XU Yanlu (63 LI Ying), WANG Shanshan, WANG Shuang.
England: Karen Bardsley, Alex Scott, Steph Houghton, Gilly Flaherty (84 Drew Spence), Jo Potter *(YC21)*, Lucy Bronze (65 Demi-Lee Stokes), Jill Scott, Isobel Christiansen (89 Laura Coombs), Gemma Davison, Eniola Aluko, Lianne Sanderson (74 Jodie Taylor).
Coach: Mark Sampson
Goals: WANG Shuang (5, 45) / Eniola Aluko (45+3)

336. 27.10.2015   CFA International Women's Football Tournament
Chongqing (China): England - Australia 1-0 (0-0)
England: Karen Bardsley, Lucy Bronze, Steph Houghton, Gilly Flaherty, Claire Rafferty, Alex Scott, Jill Scott, Jo Potter, Demi-Lee Stokes, Isobel Christiansen (90+2 Laura Coombs), Eniola Aluko (57 Jodie Taylor).   Coach: Mark Sampson
Australia: Lydia Williams, Larissa Crummer (60 Kyah Simon), Laura Alleway, Georgia Yeoman (72 Alanna Kennedy), Stephanie Catley, Elise Kellond-Knight, Caitlin Foord, Emily van Egmond, Lisa De Vanna, Katrina Gorry (60 Tameka Butt), Samantha Kerr.
Coach: Alen Stajcic
Goal: Isobel Christiansen (60)
Referee: QIN Liang (PR China)   Attendance: 1,800.

337. 26.11.2015   Schauinsland-Reisen-Arena, Duisburg: Germany - England 0-0
Germany: Laura Benkarth, Felicitas Rauch, Babett Peter, Leonie Maier, Annike Krahn, Lina Magull (46 Tabea Kemme), Simone Laudehr (46 Melanie Leupolz), Lena Goeßling, Anna Blässe (46 Sara Däbritz), Melanie Behringer (46 Mandy Islacker), Anja Mittag (67 Dzsenifer Marozsán).   Coach: Silvia Neid
England: Karen Bardsley, Gilly Flaherty, Lucy Bronze, Steph Houghton, Alex Greenwood, Fara Williams (68 Isobel Christiansen), Demi-Lee Stokes, Jill Scott, Jordan Nobbs, Jodie Taylor (75 Jess Clarke), Fran Kirby (75 Toni Duggan).   Coach: Mark Sampson

338. 29.11.2015   EURO 2017 Qualifiers
               Ashton Gate Stadium, Bristol: England - Bosnia-Herzegovina 1-0 (0-0)
England: Karen Bardsley, Laura Bassett, Steph Houghton (84 Jemma Rose), Casey Stoney, Amy Turner *(YC71)*, Jordan Nobbs, Eniola Aluko, Isobel Christiansen (60 Toni Duggan), Jess Clarke (55 Jill Scott), Gemma Davison, Demi-Lee Stokes.   Coach: Mark Sampson
Bosnia-Herzegovina: Almina Hodzic, Aida Hadzic, Melisa Hasanbegovic, Antonela Radeljic (90+2 Tatjana Stanic), Amira Shahic, Lidija Kulis, Milena Nikolic, Marija Aleksic, Nikolina Dijakovic *(YC51)* (81 Amna Lihovic), Andjela Seslija, Alisa Spahic (90+1 Zerina Piskic). Coach: Samira Huren
Goal: Jill Scott (69)
Referee: Florence Guillemin (France)   Attendance: 13,040.

339. 03.03.2016   SheBelieves Cup 2016
               Raymond James Stadium, Tampa (USA): USA - England 1-0 (0-0)
USA: Hope Soto, Kelley O'Hara (80 Ali Krieger), Emily Sonnett, Becky Sauerbrunn, Meghan Klingenberg (90+1 Whitney Engen), Morgan Brian, Lindsey Horan (63 Christen Press), Tobin Heath, Carli Lloyd, Mallory Pugh (67 Crystal Dunn), Alex Morgan (80 Julie Johnston). Coach: Jill Ellis
ENGLAND: Karen Bardsley, Lucy Bronze, Steph Houghton, Gilly Flaherty, Alex Greenwood *(YC31)* (64 Izzy Christiansen), Fara Williams (72 Karen Carney), Jill Scott, Jordan Nobbs, Demi-Lee Stokes, Toni Duggan (88 Eniola Aluko), Jodie Taylor (78 Fran Kirby).
Coach: Mark Sampson
Goal: Crystal Dunn (72)
Referee: Tatiana Guzmán Alguera (Nicaragua)   Attendance: 13,027.

340. 06.03.2016   SheBelieves Cup 2016
               Nissan Stadium, Nashville (USA): Germany - England 2-1 (0-1)
Germany: Laura Benkarth, Saskia Bartusiak, Isabel Kerschowski (78 Lina Magull), Tabea Kemme (64 Leonie Maier *(YC72)*), Josephine Henning (53 Babett Peter), Kathrin Hendrich, Anna Blässe, Melanie Behringer (46 Lena Goeßling), Dzsenifer Marozsán (46 Sara Däbritz *(YC67)*), Alexandra Popp, Mandy Islacker (78 Anja Mittag).   Coach: Silvia Neid
England: Karen Bardsley, Alex Scott, Steph Houghton, Alex Greenwood (69 Karen Carney), Gilly Flaherty *(YC21)* (79 Casey Stoney), Fara Williams, Jill Scott, Jordan Nobbs (83 Gemma Davison), Katie Sarah Chapman, Toni Duggan (82 Fran Kirby), Demi-Lee Stokes.
Coach: Mark Sampson
Goals: Gilly Flagerty (76 og), Babett Peter (82 pen) / Toni Duggan (9)
Referee: Katja Koroleva (USA)   Attendance: 25,363.

341. 09.03.2016   SheBelieves Cup 2016
FAU Football Stadium, Boca Raton (USA): France - England 0-0
France: Meline Gérard, Laura Georges (54 Griedge Mbock Bathy Nka), Jessica Houara d'Hommeaux, Sabrina Delannoy, Camille Abily (77 Elise Bussaglia), Louisa Necib-Cadamuro (59 Eugénie Le Sommer), Kheira Hamraoui, Claire Lavogez (86 Viviane Asseyi), Amel Majri, Elodie Thomis, Marie-Laure Delie.   Coach: Philippe Bergeroo
England: Karen Bardsley, Alex Scott (69 Lucy Bronze), Casey Stoney, Steph Houghton, Claire Rafferty, Demi-Lee Stokes (71 Karen Carney), Katie Sarah Chapman, Fara Williams, Jill Scott, Jordan Nobbs, Toni Duggan (56 Eniola Aluko).   Coach: Mark Sampson
Referee: Gillian Martindale (Barbados)   Attendance: 5,000.

342. 08.04.2016   EURO 2017 Qualifiers
New York Stadium, Rotherham: England - Belgium 1-1 (0-1)
England: Karen Bardsley, Steph Houghton, Alex Scott, Casey Stoney, Katie Sarah Chapman (78 Gemma Davison), Alex Greenwood *(YC71)*, Jordan Nobbs, Jill Scott, Fara Williams, Toni Duggan (64 Eniola Aluko), Demi-Lee Stokes (56 Karen Carney).   Coach: Mark Sampson
Belgium: Justien Odeurs, Julie Biesmans, Maud Coutereels *(YC90+3)*, Laura Deloose, Heleen Jaques, Tine De Caigny (90 Sara Yuceil), Lorca van de Putte, Tessa Wullaert (90+5 Tine Schrijvers), Aline Zeler, Janice Cayman, Lenie Onzia.   Coach: Ives Serneels
Goals: Jill Scott (84) / Janice Cayman (18)
Referee: Gyöngyi Krisztina Gaál (Hungary)   Attendance: 10,550.

343. 12.04.2016   EURO 2017 Qualifiers
FA BH Football Training Centre, Zenica: Bosnia-Herzegovina - England 0-1 (0-0)
Bosnia-Herzegovina: Almina Hodzic *(YC85)*, Aida Hadzic *(YC52)*, Melisa Hasanbegovic, Antonela Radeljic, Amira Spahic, Lidija Kulis (84 Amna Lihovic), Milena Nikolic, Zerina Piskic, Marija Aleksic, Andjela Seslija (90+4 Alma Hadzic), Alisa Spahic.
Coach: Samira Huren
England: Karen Bardsley, Steph Houghton, Alex Scott (85 Toni Duggan), Casey Stoney (66 Lucy Bronze), Karen Carney, Alex Greenwood, Jordan Nobbs, Jill Scott, Fara Williams (66 Fran Kirby), Eniola Aluko, Gemma Davison.   Coach: Mark Sampson
Goal: Karen Carney (86)
Referee: Simone Ghisletta (Switzerland)   Attendance: 1,500.

344. 04.06.2016   EURO 2017 Qualifiers
Adams Park, High Wycombe: England - Serbia 7-0 (3-0)
England: Karen Bardsley, Laura Bassett, Lucy Bronze, Rachel Daly (57 Nikita Parris), Steph Houghton, Karen Carney, Alex Greenwood, Jill Scott (64 Gemma Davison), Fara Williams, Isobel Christiansen (75 Jade Moore), Ellen White.   Coach: Mark Sampson
Serbia: Susanne Nilsson, Nevena Damjanovic, Marija Ilic (55 Sanda Malesevic), Marija Jonovic (67 Dina Blagojevic), Aleksandra Kozovic, Jelena Cankovic, Tijana Krstic, Allegra Poljak, Marija Radojicic (89 Olivera Markovic), Vesna Smiljkovic, Mirela Tenkov.
Coach: Boris Arsic
Goals: Alex Greenwood (16), Karen Carney (34 pen, 60, 64), Rachel Daly (43), Ellen White (51), Isobel Christiansen (52)
Referee: Lina Lehtovaara (Finland)   Attendance: 5,903.

345. 07.06.2016   EURO 2017 Qualifiers
Sports Center of FA of Serbia, Stara Pazova: Serbia - England 0-7 (0-3)
Serbia: Susanne Nilsson, Nevena Damjanovic (75 Dina Blagojevic), Marija Ilic, Marija Jonovic, Aleksandra Kozovic, Vajda Orsoja (82 Jelena Cubrilo), Jelena Cankovic, Allegra Poljak, Marija Radojicic, Vesna Smiljkovic, Mirela Tenkov. Coach: Boris Arsic
England: Siobhan Rebecca Chamberlain, Lucy Bronze, Steph Houghton, Casey Stoney, Karen Carney, Jade Moore, Jill Scott (56 Alex Scott), Fara Williams (46 Isobel Christiansen), Gemma Davison, Demi-Lee Stokes, Ellen White (56 Nikita Parris). Coach: Mark Sampson
Goals: Jill Scott (13), Ellen White (28), Gemma Davison (41, 46), Nevena Damjanovic (53og), Nikita Parris (69, 90)
Referee: Stéphanie Frappart (France)   Attendance: 120.

346. 15.09.2016   EURO 2017 Qualifiers
Meadow Lane Stadium, Nothingham: England - Estonia 5-0 (3-0)
England: Siobhan Rebecca Chamberlain, Lucy Bronze, Steph Houghton, Karen Carney, Jordan Nobbs, Jo Potter, Jill Scott (62 Jade Moore), Danielle Carter, Gemma Davison (74 Gilly Flaherty), Nikita Parris (60 Rachel Daly), Demi-Lee Stokes. Coach: Mark Sampson
Estonia: Getter Laar, Liis Lepik, Inna Zlidnis *(90+3)*, Signy Aarna, Kristina Bannikova (70 Vlada Kubassova), Ragne Hindrimäe, Kethy Õunpuu, Kaire Palmaru (57 Aljona Sasova *(YC63)*), Pille Raadik, Eneli Vals (78 Merily Toom), Katrin Loo. Coach: Keith Boanas
Goals: Danielle Carter (9, 17, 56), Jill Scott (13), Karen Carney (90+4)
Referee: Vera Opeykina (Russia)   Attendance: 7,052.

347. 20.09.2016   EURO 2017 Qualifiers
Stadion Den Dreef, Leuven-Heverlee: Belgium - England 0-2 (0-0)
Belgium: Justien Odeurs, Julie Biesmans *(YC45)* (76 Elien Van Wynendaele), Laura Deloose, Heleen Jaques, Tine De Caigny, Lien Mermans (70 Lenie Onzia), Lorca van de Putte, Elke Van Gorp (76 Davina Philtjens), Tessa Wullaert, Aline Zeler, Janice Cayman.
Coach: Ives Serneels
England: Karen Bardsley, Lucy Bronze, Gilly Flaherty *(YC77)*, Steph Houghton, Karen Carney (90 Millie Bright), Jordan Nobbs, Jo Potter, Jill Scott *(YC35)*, Danielle Carter (46 Jade Moore), Nikita Parris (77 Rachel Daly), Demi-Lee Stokes. Coach: Mark Sampson
Goals: Nikita Parris (65), Karen Carney (85)
Referee: Inga-Lill Pernilla Larsson (Sweden)   Attendance: 6,754.

348. 21.10.2016   The Keepmoat Stadium, Doncaster: England - France 0-0
England: Karen Bardsley, Jo Potter, Steph Houghton, Demi-Lee Stokes, Lucy Bronze, Jade More, Jordan Nobbs, Jill Scott, Rachel Daly (58 Nikita Parris), Karen Carney *(YC83)* (88 Toni Duggan), Gemma Davison (71 Alex Scott). Coach: Mark Sampson
France: Sarah Bouhaddi, Wendie Renard, Laura Georges, Kheira Hamraoui, Amel Majri, Jessica Houara d'Hommeaux, Kadidiatou Diani (81 Delphine Cascarino), Elise Bussaglia *(YC5)* (69 Sandie Toletti), Claire Lavogez *(YC14)* (72 Clarisse Le Bihan), Gaëtane Thiney, Eugénie Le Sommer (90 Camille Catala). Coach: Olivier Echouafni
Referee: Graziella Pirriatore (Italy)   Attendance: 7,898.

349. 25.10.2016   Pedro Escartín, Guadalajara (Spain): Spain - England 1-2 (1-2)
Spain: Dolores Gallardo Núñez "LOLA" (46 Sandra PAÑOS García-Villamil), ANDREA PEREIRA Cejudo (73 Alexandra López Rosillo "ALE"), MARTA TORREJÓN Moya, LEILA OUAHABI El Ouhabi, IRENE Paredes Hernández, AMANDA SAMPEDRO Bustos, VIRGINIA TORRECILLA Reyes (46 BÁRBARA Latorre Viñals), María Victoria "VICKY" LOSADA Gómez, Silvia MESEGUER Bellido, ALEXIA Putellas Segura (63 MARTA CORREDERA Rueda), Jennifer "JENNI" HERMOSO Fuentes (58 María "MARI" PAZ Vilas Dono).   Coach: JORGE VILDA Rodríguez
England: Karen Bardsley, Steph Houghton, Lucy Bronze, Jill Scott (63 Isobel Christiansen), Jo Potter, Jordan Nobbs, Jade Moore, Nikita Parris (63 Toni Duggan), Gemma Davison (58 Rachel Daly), Karen Carney (73 Fara Williams), Demi-Lee Stokes.   Coach: Mark Sampson
Goals: MARTA TORREJÓN Moya (18) /
MARTA TORREJÓN Moya (13 og), Steph Houghton (15)
Referee: Elia Martínez (Spain)   Attendance: 3,000.

350. 29.11.2016   Koning Willem II Stadion, Tilburg: Netherlands - England 0-1 (0-0)
Netherlands: Loes Geurts, Desiree van Lunteren, Stefanie van der Gragt, Mandy van den Berg, Merel van Dongen, Sherida Spitse, Tessel Middag, Shanice van de Sanden, Lieke Martens (67 Jill Roord), Renée Slegers (10 Ellen Jansen), Lineth Beerebsteyn (73 Sisca Folkertsma).   Coach: Arjan van der Laan
England: Karen Bardsley, Steph Houghton, Lucy Bronze, Jordan Nobbs, Isobel Christiansen (90 Alex Scott), Jo Potter, Jade Moore, Jill Scott (58 Jodie Taylor), Toni Duggan (75 Gilly Flaherty), Karen Carney (81 Fara Williams), Demi-Lee Stokes.   Coach: Mark Sampson
Goal: Jodie Taylor (75)
Referee: Olga Zadinová (Czech Republic)   Attendance: 7,676.

351. 22.01.2017   La Manga Club, Los Belones (Spain): England - Norway 0-1 (0-1)
England: Siobhan Rebecca Chamberlain, Jo Potter, Steph Houghton, Lucy Bronze, Alex Scott, Jade Moore, Fara Williams (63 Millie Bright), Nikita Parris, Toni Duggan, Jodie Taylor (63 Ellen White), Demi-Lee Stokes.   Coach: Mark Sampson
Norway: Cecilie Fiskerstrand, Nora Holstad Berge, Ingrid Moe Wold, Elise Thorsnes, Anja Sønstevold (72 Gunhild Herregården), Maren Mjelde, Ingvild Isaksen, Andrine Stolsmo Hegerberg (63 Vilde Bøe Risa), Ada Stolsmo Hegerberg (36 Synne Jensen), Lisa-Marie Karlseng Utland, Kristine Minde.   Coach: Martin Sjögren
Goal: Ada Stolsmo Hegerberg (26)
Referee: Marta Huerta de Aza (Spain)

352. 24.01.2017   Pinatar Arena, San Pedro del Pinatar (Spain): England - Sweden 0-0
England: Siobhan Rebecca Chamberlain, Claire Rafferty (55 Gemma Davison), Gilly Flaherty *(YC62)*, Millie Bright, Gemma Bonner, Jill Scott, Jordan Nobbs, Isobel Christiansen, Rachel Williams, Rachel Daly, Karen Carney (70 Demi-Lee Stokes).   Coach: Mark Sampson
Sweden: Helvig Lindahl, Jonna Andersson (79 Hanna Glas), Linda Sembrant (65 Magdalena Eriksson), Nilla Fischer, Jessica Samuelsson, Lisa Dahlkvist (65 Hanna Folkesson), Kosovare Asllani (79 Olivia Schough), Caroline Seger, Sofia Jakobsson (46 Lotta Schelin), Stina Blackstenius (46 Pauline Hammarlund), Fridolina Rolfö.   Coach: Pia Sundhage
Referee: Marte Sørø (Norway)

Kosovare Asllani missed a penalty kick (77)

353. 01.03.2017   SheBelieves Cup 2017
              Talen Energy Stadium, Chester (USA): England - France 1-2 (1-0)
England: Karen Bardsley *(YC90+2)*, Steph Houghton, Lucy Bronze, Millie Bright *(YC44)*, Jill Scott, Jordan Nobbs (87 Isobel Christiansen), Jade Moore, Ellen White (74 Nikita Parris), Jodie Taylor (54 Rachel Williams), Rachel Daly (74 Alex Scott), Demi-Lee Stokes.
Coach: Mark Sampson
France: Sarah Bouhaddi, Ève Perisset (66 Wendie Renard), Laura Georges, Jessica Houara d'Hommeaux, Griedge Mbock Bathy Nka (83 Amel Majri), Onema Grace Geyoro, Amandine Henry, Claire Lavogez (61 Camille Abily), Gaëtane Thiney *(YC37)* (76 Élodie Thomis), Marie-Laure Delie, Kadidiatou Diani (72 Eugénie Le Sommer).   Coach: Olivier Echouafni
Goals: Jordan Nobbs (32) / Marie-Laure Delie (80), Wendie Renard (90+5)
Referee: Melissa Paola Borjas Pastrana (Honduras)   Attendance: 8,616.

354. 04.03.2017   SheBelieves Cup 2017
              Red Bull Arena, Harrison: USA - England 0-1 (0-0)
USA: Ashlyn Harris, Becky Sauerbrunn, Ali Krieger, Julie Ertz, Rose Lavelle, Samantha Mewis (77 Morgan Brian), Mallory Pugh, Crystal Dunn (64 Lynn Williams), Alex Morgan (63 Christen Press), Carli Lloyd (76 Tobin Heath), Lindsey Horan (77 Allie Long).
Coach: Jill Ellis
England: Siobhan Rebecca Chamberlain, Laura Bassett, Steph Houghton, Lucy Bronze, Fara Williams, Jordan Nobbs (90 Millie Bright), Isobel Christiansen (90 Jade Moore), Nikita Parris (77 Jodie Taylor), Toni Duggan (76 Ellen White), Karen Carney (63 Jill Scott), Demi-Lee Stokes.   Coach: Mark Sampson
Goal: Ellen White (89)
Referee: Quetzalli Alvarado Godinez (Mexico)   Attendance: 26,500.

355. 07.03.2017   SheBelieves Cup 2017
              RFK Stadium, Washington D.C. (USA): Germany - England 1-0 (1-0)
Germany: Laura Benkarth (47 Lisa Weiß), Isabel Kerschowski (61 Verena Faißt), Josephine Henning, Anna Blässe, Babett Peter, Leonie Maier (46 Kristin Demann), Sara Däbritz (90 Pauline Bremer), Dzsenifer Marozsán, Lina Magull (80 Sara Doorsoun), Alexandra Popp, Anja Mittag (83 Lena Petermann).   Coach: Steffi Jones
England: Siobhan Rebecca Chamberlain, Laura Bassett, Steph Houghton, Lucy Bronze, Fara Williams (53 Millie Bright), Jordan Nobbs, Jade Moore (73 Jill Scott), Toni Duggan, Karen Carney, Jodie Taylor (63 Ellen White), Demi-Lee Stokes.   Coach: Mark Sampson
Goal: Anja Mittag (44)
Referee: Michelle Pye (Canada)   Attendance: 10,000.

356. 07.04.2017   Vale Park, Stoke-On-Trent: England - Italy 1-1 (0-0)
England: Siobhan Rebecca Chamberlain, Steph Houghton, Lucy Bronze, Millie Bright, Demi-Lee Stokes (69 Alex Greenwood), Jordan Nobbs, Jade Moore (68 Fara Williams), Jill Scott, Toni Duggan (90 Nikita Parris), Karen Carney, Jodie Taylor.   Coach: Mark Sampson
Italy: Katja Schroffenegger, Elisa Bartoli (85 Lisa Boattin), Sara Gama, Cecilia Salvai, Elena Linari, Alia Guagni (56 Melania Gabbiadini), Cristiana Girelli (46 Valentina Cernoia), Barbara Bonansea (60 Tatiana Bonetti), Daniela Stracchi, Alice Parisi (37 Aurora Galli), Ilaria Mauro (68 Daniela Sabatino).   Coach: Antonio Cabrini
Goals: Jodie Taylor (70) / Valentina Cernoia (73)
Referee: Morag Pirie (Scotland)

357. 10.04.2017 Stadium ML, Milton Keynes: England - Austria 3-0 (1-0)
England: Siobhan Rebecca Chamberlain, Steph Houghton, Lucy Bronze, Millie Bright, Laura Bassett, Jordan Nobbs, Jade Moore, Isobel Christiansen (87 Alex Scott), Ellen White (74 Jodie Taylor), Toni Duggan (61 Karen Carney), Demi-Lee Stokes.   Coach: Mark Sampson
Austria: Manuela Zinsberger, Carina Wenninger, Viktoria Schnaderbeck, Virginia Kirchberger, Sarah Zadrazil, Sarah Puntigam, Nadine Prohaska (57 Laura Feiersinger), Verena Aschauer (80 Barbara Dunst), Lisa Makas (73 Katharina Naschenweng), Nina Burger, Nicole Billa (87 Viktoria Pinther).   Coach: Dominik Thalhammer
Goals: Ellen White (5), Lucy Bronze (67), Isobel Christiansen (85)
Referee: Gyöngyi Gaál (Hungary)   Attendance: 6,593.

358. 10.06.2017 Tissot Arena, Biel/Bienne: Switzerland - England 0-4 (0-2)
Switzerland: Gaëlle Thalmann, Rachel Rinast (51 Vanessa Bürki), Noelle Maritz, Rahel Kiwic, Jana Brunner (52 Caroline Abbé), Lia Wälti, Sandrine Mauron (60 Vanessa Bernauer *(YC65)*), Meriame Terchoun (48 Fabienne Humm), Géraldine Reuteler (60 Martina Moser), Ana-Maria Crnogorcevic, Eseosa Aigbogun.   Coach: Martina Voss-Tecklenburg
England: Karen Bardsley (75 Mary Earps), Demi-Lee Stokes, Steph Houghton (63 Jo Potter), Lucy Bronze, Millie Bright (62 Laura Bassett), Jill Scott, Jordan Nobbs, Jade Moore (63 Fara Williams), Fran Kirby (63 Karen Carney), Jodie Taylor (63 Nikita Parris *(YC71)*), Toni Duggan.   Coach: Mark Sampson
Goals: Jordan Nobbs (30), Fran Kirby (40), Jodie Taylor (50, 62)
Referee: Marte Sørø (Norway)

359. 01.07.2017 Gladsaxe Stadion, Gladsaxe: Denmark - England 1-2 (0-1)
Denmark: Stina Lykke Petersen, Mie Leth Jans, Frederikke Skjødt Thøgersen (46 Sanne Troelsgaard-Nielsen), Line Røddik Hansen, Luna Gevitz (84 Janni Arnth Jensen), Simone Boye Sørensen, Line Sigvardsen Jensen, Katrine Veje, Sofie Junge Pedersen (46 Maja Kildemoes), Stine Larsen (64 Nicoline Sørensen), Pernille Harder.   Coach: Nils Nielsen
England: Siobhan Rebecca Chamberlain (76 Carly Telford), Laura Bassett, Casey Stoney, Demi-Lee Stokes, Alex Scott, Jo Potter, Isobel Christiansen (76 Millie Bright), Fara Williams (87 Lucy Bronze), Karen Carney (83 Jordan Nobbs), Ellen White, Nikita Parris (75 Jodie Taylor).   Coach: Mark Sampson
Goals: Pernille Harder (66) / Ellen White (44, 76)
Referee: Sara Persson (Sweden)   Attendance: 437.

360. 19.07.2017 EURO 2017 Netherlands Group D
            Stadion Galgenwaard, Utrecht: England - Scotland 6-0 (3-0)
England: Karen Bardsley, Lucy Bronze, Steph Houghton, Jill Scott, Jordan Nobbs, Jade Moore, Millie Bright, Jodie Taylor (59 Toni Duggan), Ellen White (74 Karen Carney), Fran Kirby (65 Nikita Parris), Demi-Lee Stokes.   Coach: Mark Sampson
Scotland: Gemma Fay, Vaila Barsley, Ifeoma Dieke, Rachel Corsie (76 Joanne Love), Frankie Brown, Caroline Weir, Leanne Crichton, Lisa Evans, Chloe Arthur, Jane Ross (63 Erin Curthbert), Fiona Brown (46 Lana Clelland).   Coach: Anna Signeul
Goals: Jodie Taylor (11, 26, 53), Ellen White (32), Jordan Nobbs (87), Toni Duggan (90+3)
Referee: Esther Staubli (Switzerland)   Attendance: 5,578.

361. 23.07.2017   EURO 2017 Netherlands Group D
Rat Verlegh Stadion, Breda: England - Spain 2-0 (1-0)
England: Karen Bardsley, Lucy Bronze, Steph Houghton, Jill Scott, Jordan Nobbs, Jade Moore, Millie Bright, Jodie Taylor (89 Jo Potter), Ellen White (79 Toni Duggan), Fran Kirby (69 Isobel Christiansen), Demi-Lee Stokes.   Coach: Mark Sampson
Spain: Sandra PAÑOS García-Villamil, MARTA TORREJÓN Moya, IRENE Paredes Hernández, ANDREA PEREIRA Cejudo, LEILA OUAHABI El Ouhabi (89 VIRGINIA TORRECILLA Reyes), AMANDA SAMPEDRO Bustos (89 BÁRBARA Latorre Viñals), ALEXIA Putellas Segura, María Victoria "VICKY" LOSADA Gómez (73 OLGA García Pérez), Silvia MESEGUER Bellido, MARTA CORREDERA Rueda, Jennifer "JENNI" HERMOSO Fuentes.   Coach: JORGE VILDA Rodríguez
Goals: Fran Kirby (2), Jodie Taylor (85)
Referee: Carina Vitulano (Italy)   Attendance: 4,879.

362. 27.07.2017   EURO 2017 Netherlands Group D
Koning Willem II Stadion, Tilburg: Portugal - England 1-2 (1-1)
Portugal: PATRÍCIA Isabel Sousa Barros MORAIS, SÍLVIA Marisa Garcia REBELO, CAROLE da Silva COSTA, CLÁUDIA Teresa Pires NETO, TATIANA Vanessa Ferreira PINTO, DOLORES Isabel Jácome SILVA, MÉLISSA ANTUNES, ANA Catarina Marques BORGES, DIANA Micaela Abreu de Sousa e SILVA (87 LAURA José Ramos LUÍS), CAROLINA Ana Trindade Coruche MENDES (64 ANA Cristina Oliveira LEITE), SUZANE Lira PIRES (79 AMANDA Jaqueline DA COSTA).
Coach: FRANCISCO Miguel Conceição Roque NETO
England: Siobhan Rebecca Chamberlain, Jo Potter, Laura Bassett, Alex Greenwood, Alex Scott, Isobel Christiansen, Fara Williams, Millie Bright (60 Jordan Nobbs), Karen Carney, Nikita Parris, Toni Duggan (81 Demi-Lee Stokes).   Coach: Mark Sampson
Goals: Carolina Mendes (17) / Toni Duggan (7), Nikita Parris (48)
Referee: Kateryna Monzul (Ukraine)   Attendance: 3,335.

363. 30.07.2017   EURO 2017 Netherlands Quarter-finals
Stadion De Adelaarshorst, Deventer: England - France 1-0 (0-0)
England: Karen Bardsley (75 Siobhan Rebecca Chamberlain), Lucy Bronze, Steph Houghton, Demi-Lee Stokes, Jill Scott *(YC62)*, Jordan Nobbs, Jade Moore, Millie Bright, Jodie Taylor, Ellen White, Fran Kirby.   Coach: Mark Sampson
France: Sarah Bouhaddi, Laura Georges, Jessica Houara d'Hommeaux, Griedge Mbock Bathy Nka *(YC82)*, Sakina Karchaoui, Amandine Henry, Camille Abily (78 Claire Lavogez), Onema Grace Geyoro, Eugénie Le Sommer, Marie-Laure Delie (90 Clarisse Le Bihan), Kadidiatou Diani (65 Élodie Thomis).   Coach: Olivier Echouafni
Goal: Jodie Taylor (60)
Referee: Esther Staubli (Switzerland)   Attendance: 6,283.

364. 03.08.2017   EURO 2017 Netherlands Semi-finals
De Grolsch Veste, Enschede: Netherlands - England 3-0 (1-0)
Netherlands: Sari van Veenendaal, Desiree van Lunteren, Stefanie van der Gragt (70 Kelly Zeeman), Kika van Es, Anouk Dekker, Sherida Spitse, Daniëlle van de Donk (90+1 Jill Roord), Jackie Groenen, Shanice van de Sanden (89 Renate Jansen), Vivianne Miedema, Lieke Martens.   Coach: Sarina Wiegman
England: Siobhan Rebecca Chamberlain, Lucy Bronze, Steph Houghton, Jordan Nobbs, Fara Williams (67 Toni Duggan), Jade Moore (76 Karen Carney), Millie Bright, Jodie Taylor, Ellen White, Fran Kirby, Demi-Lee Stokes.   Coach: Mark Sampson
Goals: Vivianne Miedema (22), Daniëlle van de Donk (62), Millie Bright (90+3 og)
Referee: Stéphanie Frappart (France)   Attendance: 27,093.

365. 19.09.2017   FIFA World Cup 2019 Qualifiers
             Prenton Park, Birkenhead: England - Russia 6-0 (4-0)
England: Siobhan Rebecca Chamberlain, Steph Houghton, Lucy Bronze, Jordan Nobbs, Jade Moore, Millie Bright, Jodie Taylor (65 Ellen White), Nikita Parris (60 Karen Carney), Fran Kirby (70 Isobel Christiansen), Toni Duggan, Demi-Lee Stokes.   Coach: Mark Sampson
Russia: Tatyana Shcherbak, Ksenia Tsybutovich, Anna Kozhnikova, Kseniya Kovalenko, Elvira Ziyastinova, Ekaterina Sochneva (79 Ekaterina Pantyukhina), Nadezhda Smirnova, Elena Morozova, Anna Cholovyaga (33 Anna Belomyttseva), Marina Fedorova, Elena Danilova.   Coach: Elena Fomina
Goals: Nikita Parris (11), Jodie Taylor (14), Jordan Nobbs (36), Lucy Bronze (44), Toni Duggan (57, 84)
Referee: Stéphanie Frappart (France)   Attendance: 7,047.

Fran Kirby missed a penalty kick (31)

Sent-off: Ksenia Tsybutovich (30)

366. 20.10.2017   Stade du Hainaut, Valenciennes: France - England 1-0 (0-0)
France: Sarah Bouhaddi, Wendie Renard, Hawa Cissoko, Amel Majri, Marion Torrent, Inès Jaurena (69 Léa Le Garrec), Aminata Diallo, Onema Grace Geyoro, Valérie Gauvin (69 Ouleymata Sarr), Eugénie Le Sommer, Kadidiatou Diani (81 Viviane Asseyi).
Coach: Corinne Diacre
England: Siobhan Rebecca Chamberlain, Millie Bright, Steph Houghton, Lucy Bronze, Demi-Lee Stokes, Jill Scott, Fara Williams *(YC39)* (61 Jade Moore), Jordan Nobbs, Jodie Taylor (84 Nikita Parris), Toni Duggan (84 Isobel Christiansen), Karen Carney (62 Melissa Lawley).
Coach: Mo Marley
Goal: Viviane Asseyi (89)
Referee: Jana Adamkova (Czech Republic)   Attendance: 20,059.

367. 24.11.2017   FIFA World Cup 2019 Qualifiers
             Banks's Stadium, Walsall: England - Bosnia-Herzegovina 4-0 (1-0)
England: Siobhan Rebecca Chamberlain, Lucy Bronze, Steph Houghton, Alex Greenwood, Millie Bright, Jordan Nobbs, Isobel Christiansen (73 Jo Potter), Danielle Carter, Nikita Parris (81 Melissa Lawley), Fran Kirby, Toni Duggan.   Coach: Mark Sampson
Bosnia-Herzegovina: Almina Hodzic, Melisa Hasanbegovic, Andjela Seslija (46 Valentina Sakotic), Amira Spahic (90 Nikolina Milovic), Antonela Radeljic, Alisa Spahic (77 Aida Hadzic), Lidija Kulis *(YC85)*, Amela Krso, Marija Aleksic, Dajana Spasojevic, Milena Nikolic *(YC60)*.   Coach: Samira Huren
Goals: Steph Houghton (19, 54), Nikita Parris (46), Fran Kirby (83 pen)
Referee: Ewa Augustyn (Poland)   Attendance: 10,026.

368. 28.11.2017   FIFA World Cup 2019 Qualifiers
                Weston Homes Community Stadium, Colchester: England - Kazakhstan 5-0 (1-0)
England: Karen Bardsley, Gemma Bonner, Steph Houghton, Alex Greenwood, Lucy Bronze (77 Danielle Carter), Jill Scott, Fara Williams (63 Isobel Christiansen), Keira Walsh, Jodie Taylor (63 Fran Kirby), Nikita Parris, Melissa Lawley.   Coach: Mark Sampson
Kazakhstan: Oksana Zheleznyak (46 Irina Sandalova), Bibigul Nurusheva, Yekaterina Krasyukova, Shokhista Khojasheva, Aida Gaistenova *(YC45)* (70 Anastassiya Vlassova), Yekaterina Babshuk *(YC64)*, Karina Zhumbaikyzy, Begaim Kirgizbaeva, Adilya Vyldanova, Saule Karibayeva (81 Asselkhan Turlybekova), Svetlana Bortnikova.
Coach: Aitpay Jamantayev
Goals: Melissa Lawley (15), Fran Kirby (64 pen), Nikita Parris (68, 75), Isobel Christiansen (76)
Referee: Lois Otte (Belgium)   Attendance: 9,643.

369. 01.03.2018   SheBelieves Cup
                MAPFRE Stadium, Columbus (USA): England - France 4-1 (3-0)
England: Karen Bardsley (83 Carly Telford), Anita Asante (14 Abbie McManis), Demi-Lee Stokes (87 Alex Greenwood), Millie Bright *(YC52)*, Lucy Bronze, Jill Scott, Fran Kirby (71 Isobel Christiansen), Nikita Parris (61 Melissa Lawley), Toni Duggan (71 Ellen White), Keira Walsh, Jodie Taylor.   Coach: Phil Neville
France: Karima Benameur, Ève Périsset, Sakina Karchaoui, Laura Georges, Griedge Mbock Bathy Nka, Faustine Robert (61 Gaëtane Thiney), Amandine Henry, Aminata Diallo, Eugénie Le Sommer, Kadidiatou Diani (61 Viviane Asseyi), Ouleymata Sarr (74 Valérie Gauvin).
Coach: Corinne Diacre
Goals: Toni Duggan (7), Jill Scott (28), Jodie Taylor (39), Fran Kirby (46) / Gaëtane Thiney (77)
Referee: Christina Unkel (United States)   Attendance: 7,566.

370. 04.03.2018   SheBelieves Cup
                Red Bull Arena, New Jersey (USA): Germany - England 2-2 (1-1)
Germany: Almuth Schult, Kathrin Hendrich, Verena Faißt, Lena Goeßling (87 Johanna Elsig), Tabea Kemme (90 Sara Doorsoun), Svenja Huth (75 Lea Schüller), Sara Däbritz (72 Mandy Islacker), Linda Dallmann (46 Lina Magull), Dzsenifer Marozsán, Hasret Kayikci (46 Anna Blässe), Alexandra Popp.   Coach: Steffi Jones
England: Siobhan Rebecca Chamberlain, Millie Bright, Lucy Bronze, Abbie McManus, Demi-Lee Stokes, Fara Williams (59 Keira Walsh), Fran Kirby (90 Jodie Taylor), Jill Scott (67 Isobel Christiansen), Melissa Lawley *(YC84)* (84 Rachel Daly), Ellen White, Toni Duggan (67 Nikita Parris).   Coach: Phil Neville
Goals: Hasret Kayikci (17), Millie Bright (51 og) / Ellen White (18, 73)
Referee: Karen Abt (United States)   Attendance: 7,882.

371. 07.03.2018   SheBelieves Cup
                Orlando City Stadium, Orlando (USA): USA - England 1-0 (0-0)
USA: Alyssa Naeher, Abby Dahlkemper, Emily Sonnett, Crystal Dunn, Tierna Davidson, Allie Long (74 Sofia Huerta), Lindsey Horan (74 Morgan Brian), Carli Lloyd, Alex Morgan, Megan Rapinoe (80 Savannah McCaskill), Mallory Pugh (90+2 Lynn Williams).   Coach: Jillian Ellis
England: Karen Bardsley, Millie Bright, Abbie McManus, Demi-Lee Stokes (87 Hannah Blundell), Lucy Bronze, Ellen White, Melissa Lawley (52 Toni Duggan), Isobel Christiansen, Fran Kirby (75 Rachel Daly), Keira Walsh (86 Jill Scott), Jodie Taylor (52 Nikita Parris).
Coach: Phil Neville
Goal: Karen Bardsley (58 og)
Referee: Carol Anne Chenard (Canada)   Attendance: 12,351.

372. 06.04.2018   FIFA World Cup 2019 Qualifiers
St. Mary's Stadium, Southampton: England - Wales 0-0
England: Carly Telford, Lucy Bronze, Steph Houghton *(YC25)*, Abbie McManus *(YC29)*, Demi-Lee Stokes, Jordan Nobbs, Keira Walsh, Fran Kirby, Nikita Parris (55 Melissa Lawley), Jodie Taylor (55 Ellen White), Toni Duggan (80 Beth Mead).   Coach: Phil Neville
Wales: Laura O'Sullivan, Loren Dykes, Sophie Ingle *(YC85)*, Rhiannon Roberts, Natasha Harding *(YC45)*, Angharad James, Kayleigh Green, Jessica Fishlock, Rachel Rowe, Hayley Ladd, Charlotte Estcourt.   Coach: Jayne Ludlow
Referee: Inga-Lill Pernilla Larsson (Sweden)   Attendance: 25,603.

373. 10.04.2018   FIFA World Cup 2019 Qualifiers
Nogometni kamp Reprezentacije BiH, Zenica: Bosnia-Herzegovina - England 0-2 (0-0)
Bosnia-Herzegovina: Envera Hasanbegovic, Amira Spahic *(YC39,YC59)*, Melisa Hasanbegovic, Antonela Radeljic, Alisa Spahic (90+2 Merjema Medic), Amela Krso (66 Selma Kapetanovic), Aida Hadzic *(YC12)*, Lidija Kulis, Milena Nikolic, Marija Aleksic, Valentina Sakotic (74 Marina Lukic).   Coach: Samira Hurem
England: Carly Telford, Steph Houghton, Lucy Bronze, Alex Greenwood *(YC43,YC47)*, Abbie McManus, Jade Moore, Isobel Christiansen (80 Rachel Daly), Jordan Nobbs, Ellen White, Toni Duggan (87 Jodie Taylor), Melissa Lawley (57 Beth Mead).   Coach: Phil Neville
Goals: Toni Duggan (56), Jodie Taylor (90+3 pen)
Referee: Andromachi Tsiofliki (Greece)   Attendance: 340.

374. 08.06.2018   FIFA World Cup 2019 Qualifiers
Sapsan Arena, Moskva: Russia - England 1-3 (1-3)
Russia: Yulia Grichenko, Anastasia Akimova, Irina Podshibyakina, Anna Kozhnikova *(YC49)*, Anna Belomyttseva *(YC82)*, Lina Yakupova (46 Margarita Chernomyrdina), Elvira Ziyastinova, Nadezhda Smirnova *(YC64)*, Elena Morozova, Ekaterina Pantyukhina *(YC44)* (72 Nelli Korovkina), Elena Danilova (81 Ekaterina Sochneva).   Coach: Elena Fomina
England: Carly Telford, Abbie McManus, Lucy Bronze, Millie Bright, Keira Walsh (84 Leah Williamson), Jill Scott, Ellen White (67 Jodie Taylor), Nikita Parris, Fran Kirby, Toni Duggan (62 Beth Mead), Rachel Daly.   Coach: Phil Neville
Goals: Elena Danilova (31) / Nikita Parris (22), Jill Scott (27, 36)
Referee: Riem Hussein (Germany)   Attendance: 1,859.

375. 31.08.2018   FIFA World Cup 2019 Qualifiers
Rodney Parade, Newport: Wales - England 0-3 (0-0)
Wales: Laura O'Sullivan, Loren Dykes, Hayley Ladd, Rhiannon Roberts, Natasha Harding (90 Ffion Morgan), Jessica Fishlock, Sophie Ingle, Angharad James, Kayleigh Green, Kylie Nolan (61 Elise Hughes), Helen Ward (73 Peyton Vincze).   Coach: Jayne Ludlow
England: Karen Bardsley, Steph Houghton, Lucy Bronze, Alex Greenwood, Millie Bright, Jill Scott (83 Keira Walsh), Jordan Nobbs, Toni Duggan, Nikita Parris, Jodie Taylor (77 Isobel Christiansen), Fran Kirby (88 Rachel Daly).   Coach: Phil Neville
Goals: Toni Duggan (57), Jill Scott (60), Nikita Parris (69)
Referee: Katalin Kulcsár (Hungary)   Attendance: 5,053.

376. 04.09.2018   FIFA World Cup 2019 Qualifiers
Ortaliq Stadion, Pavlodar: Kazakhstan - England 0-6 (0-2)
Kazakhstan: Oksana Zheleznyak, Yulia Myasnikova, Bibigul Nurusheva, Kundyz Kozhakhmet, Anastassiya Vlassova (52' Adilya Vyldanova), Alexandra Burova, Begaim Kirgizbaeva, Kamila Kulmagambetova *(YC33)* (74 Svetlana Bortnikova), Karina Zhumbaikyzy *(YC88)*, Asselkhan Turlybekova, Saule Karibayeva (43 Aida Gaistenova *(YC90+4)*).
Coach: Razia Nurkenova
England: Mary Earps (67 Carly Telford), Hannah Blundell, Gabrielle George, Abbie McManus, Isobel Christiansen, Lauren Bruton, Lucy Staniforth, Leah Williamson, Keira Walsh (62 Lucy Bronze), Beth Mead, Rachel Daly (71 Toni Duggan).   Coach: Phil Neville
Goals: Beth Mead (9 pen, 82), Rachel Daly (35), Isobel Christiansen (54), Lucy Staniforth (66), Lucy Bronze (86)
Referee: Hristiana Guteva (Bulgaria)   Attendance: 6,842.

Beth Mead missed a penalty kick (70)

377. 06.10.2018   Meadow Lane Stadium, Nottingham: England – Brazil 1-0 (1-0)
England: Carly Telford, Steph Houghton, Lucy Bronze *(YC45)*, Alex Greenwood, Millie Bright, Isobel Christiansen, Jordan Nobbs (70 Fara Williams *(YC90)*), Toni Duggan (60 Beth Mead), Nikita Parris (74 Lucy Staniforth), Rachel Daly, Fran Kirby (75 Melissa Lawley). Coach: Phil Neville
Brazil: BÁRBARA Micheline do Monte Barbosa, MÔNICA Hickmann Alves (75' Kathellen SOUSA FEITOZA), Bruna Benites "BETIS" (41 DAIANE Limeira Santos Silva), CAMILA Martins Pereira (66 TAMIRES Cassia Dias Gomes), LETICIA SANTOS de Oliveira, Mirailldes Maciel Mota "FORMIGA" (77 Andressa Cavalari Machry "ANDRESSINHA"), Débora Cristiane de Oliveira "DEBINHA" (57 KEROLIN Nicoli Israel Ferraz), Thaysa de Moraes Rosa Moreno "ISA", MARTA Vieira da Silva (22 RAQUEL Fernandes dos Santos), ANDRESSA ALVES da Silva, LUDMILA da Silva.
Coach: Oswaldo Fumeiro Alvarez "VADÃO"
Goal: Fran Kirby (2)
Referee: Sandra Braz Bastos (Portugal)   Attendance: 7,864.

378. 09.10.2018   Craven Cottage, London: England – Australia 1-1 (1-0)
England: Mary Earps, Steph Houghton, Lucy Bronze, Alex Greenwood, Abbie McManus (86 Leah Williamson), Jordan Nobbs, Lucy Staniforth (63 Rachel Daly), Keira Walsh, Toni Duggan, Beth Mead (62 Nikita Parris), Fran Kirby (76 Fara Williams).   Coach: Phil Neville
Australia: Mackenzie Arnold, Clare Polkinghorne, Stephanie Catley, Ellie Carpenter, Elise Kellond-Knight, Tameka Butt, Chloe Logarzo (81 Alexandra Chidiac), Amy Sayer (55 Emily Gielnik), Lisa De Vanna (66 Mary Fowler), Caitlin Foord *(YC89)*, Princess Ibini (66 Larissa Crummer).   Coach: Alen Stajcic
Goals: Fran Kirby (21) / Clare Polkinghorne (84)
Referee: Florence Guillemin (France)   Attendance: 6,068.

379. 08.11.2018   BSFZ-Arena, Maria Enzersdorf: Austria – England 0-3 (0-1)
Austria: Manuela Zinsberger, Carina Wenninger, Virginia Kirchberger, Verena Aschauer, Sophie Maierhofer (55 Yvonne Weilharter), Nadine Prohaska (55 Barbara Dunst), Sarah Puntigam, Laura Feiersinger, Sarah Zadrazil, Nina Burger (76 Viktoria Pinther), Nicole Billa (87 Jennifer Klein). Coach: Dominik Thalhammer
England: Mary Earps (79 Ellie Roebuck), Hannah Blundell, Gabrielle George, Abbie McManus, Karen Carney, Lucy Staniforth, Leah Williamson, Toni Duggan (78 Chloe Kelly), Melissa Lawley (65 Nikita Parris), Chioma Ubogagu (59 Rachel Daly), Georgia Stanway.
Coach: Phil Neville
Goals: Chioma Ubogagu (26), Georgia Stanway (71), Rachel Daly (81)
Referee: Lucie Sulcová (Czech Republic)   Attendance: 1,000.

380. 11.11.2018   AESSEAL New York Stadium, Rotherham: England – Sweden 0-2 (0-2)
England: Carly Telford, Steph Houghton, Lucy Bronze *(YC27)*, Alex Greenwood, Millie Bright, Jill Scott (83 Lucy Staniforth), Isobel Christiansen (73 Georgia Stanway), Jordan Nobbs, Nikita Parris, Beth Mead (46 Toni Duggan), Rachel Daly (73 Melissa Lawley).
Coach: Phil Neville
Sweden: Hedvig Lindahl, Linda Sembrant, Jonna Andersson, Amanda Ilestedt, Jessica Samuelsson (61 Nathalie Björn), Magdalena Ericsson, Caroline Seger (79 Hanna Folkesson), Elin Rubensson (90+3 Julia Roddar), Anna Anvegård (61 Fridolina Rolfö), Kosovare Asllani (90+3 Olivia Schough), Sofia Jakobsson (79 Lina Hurtig).   Coach: Peter Gerhardsson
Goals: Sofia Jakobsson (20), Anna Anvegård (33)
Referee: Petra Pavlikova (Slovakia)   Attendance: 9,161.

381. 27.02.2019   SheBelieves Cup
    Talen Energy Stadium, Chester (USA): England - Brazil 2-1 (0-1)
England: Carly Telford, Abbie McManus, Steph Houghton, Alex Greenwood, Lucy Bronze (YC27), Isobel Christiansen (66 Rachel Daly), Keira Walsh, Karen Carney (66 Beth Mead), Ellen White (76 Toni Duggan), Nikita Parris, Fran Kirby (87 Lucy Staniforth).
Coach: Phil Neville
Brazil: ALINE Villares Reis, JUCINARA Thaís Soares Paz (83 THAISA de Moraes Rosa Moreno), MÔNICA Hickmann Alves (90+2 KATHELLEN Sousa Feitoza), LETÍCIA SANTOS de Oliveira, ÉRIKA Cristiano dos Santos, Miraildes Maciel Mota "FORMIGA", ANDRESSA ALVES da Silva, ADRIANA Leal da Silva, MARTA Vieira da Silva (70 GEYSE da Silva Ferreira), LUDMILA Da Silva (35 Débora Cristiane de Oliveira "DÉBINHA"), BEATRIZ Zaneratto João (69 RAQUEL Fernandes dos Santos).
Coach: Oswaldo Fumeiro Alvarez "VADÃO"
Goals: Ellen White (49), Beth Mead (75) / Andressa Alves (16 pen).
Referee: Katja Koroleva (USA)   Attendance: 5,954.

382. 02.03.2019   SheBelieves Cup
    Nissan Stadium Nashville: USA – England 2-2 (1-1)
USA: Adrianna Franch, Julie Ertz, Tierna Davidson, Kelley O'Hara (60 Becky Sauerbrunn), Crystal Dunn (87 Carli Lloyd), Abby Dahlkemper, Tobin Heath, Megan Rapinoe, Rose Lavelle (64 Samantha Mewis), Mallory Pugh (55 Christen Press), Alex Morgan.   Coach: Jill Ellis
England: Karen Bardsley, Demi Stokes, Abbie McManus, Steph Houghton, Rachel Daly, Lucy Bronze, Keira Walsh, Ellen White (80 Georgia Stanway), Nikita Parris (88 Jodie Taylor), Fran Kirby (73 Beth Mead), Toni Duggan.   Coach: Phil Neville
Goals: Megan Rapinoe (33), Tobin Heath (67) / Steph Houghton (36), Nikita Parris (52).
Referee: Marianela Araya Cruz (Costa Rica)

383. 05.03.2019   SheBelieves Cup
Raymond James Stadium, Tampa (USA): Japan – England 0-3 (0-3)
Japan: Erina Yamane, Risako Oga (46 Yuka Momiki), Risa Shimizu (80 Asato Miyagawa), Aya Sameshima, Moeka Minami, Moeno Sakaguchi (46 Rikako Kobayashi), Arisa Matsubara, Hina Sugita, Yui Hasegawa, Jun Endo (46 Kumi Yokoyama), Mayo Ikejiri (46 Narumi Miura). Coach: Asako Takakura
England: Carly Telford, Steph Houghton *(YC85)*, Alex Greenwood, Lucy Bronze, Isobel Christiansen (39 Georgia Stanway), Leah Williamson, Keira Walsh (59 Gemma Bonner), Lucy Staniforth (81 Fran Kirby), Karen Carney (65 Toni Duggan), Jodie Taylor (51 Ellen White), Beth Mead (65 Chioma Ubogagu).   Coach: Phil Neville
Goals: Lucy Staniforth (12), Karen Carney (23), Beth Mead (30).
Referee: Christina Unkel (USA)

384. 05.04.2019   Academy Stadium, Manchester: England – Canada 0-1 (0-0)
England: Karen Bardsley, Demi Stokes, Abbie McManus, Steph Houghton, Rachel Daly (73 Jill Scott), Lucy Bronze, Keira Walsh, Karen Carney (64 Beth Mead), Jodie Taylor (73 Ellen White), Nikita Parris, Toni Duggan (84 Georgia Stanway).   Coach: Phil Neville
Canada: Stephanie Labbé, Shelina Zadorsky, Allysha Chapman *(YC34)* (56 Jayde Riviere), Kadeisha Buchanan, Desiree Scott, Sophie Schmidt (75 Julia Grosso), Ashley Lawrence, Jessie Fleming, Christine Sinclair, Nichelle Prince (81 Deanne Rose), Janine Beckie (90+3 Shannon Woeller).   Coach: Kenneth Heiner-Møller
Goal: Christine Sinclair (81).
Referee:

385. 09.04.2019   The County Ground, Swindon: England – Spain 2-1 (1-0)
England: Ellie Roebuck (46 Mary Earps), Alex Greenwood, Rachel Daly (67 Gemma Bonner), Jill Scott *(YC19)*, Jade Moore (54 Lucy Staniforth), Millie Bright, Leah Williamson, Ellen White, Georgia Stanway (67 Keira Walsh), Beth Mead (83 Nikita Parris), Toni Duggan (54 Chioma Ubogagu).   Coach: Phil Neville
Spain: SANDRA PAÑOS García-Villamil, ANDREA PEREIRA Cejudo, MARÍA Pilar LEÓN Cebrián *(YC20)* (52 LEILA OUAHABI El Ouhabi), IRENE PAREDES Hernández (52' IVANA Andrés Sanz), María Victoria "VICKY" LOSADA Gómez (79 ÁNGELA SOSA Martín), SILVIA MESEGUER Bellido (39 VIRGINIA TORRECILLA Reyes), AMANDA SAMPEDRO Bustos (63 AITANA BONMATÍ Conca), María Francesca "MARIONA" CALDENTEY Oliver, Jennifer "JENNI" HERMOSO Fuentes, MARTA CORREDERA Rueda, ALEXIA PUTELLAS Segura.   Coach: JORGE VILDA
Goals: Beth Mead (36), Ellen White (46) / AITANA BONMATÍ Conca (67).
Referee:

386. 25.05.2019   Banks's Stadium, Walsall: England – Denmark 2-0 (1-0)
England: Karen Bardsley, Demi Stokes, Rachel Daly, Jill Scott, Jade Moore, Millie Bright, Leah Williamson, Ellen White, Georgia Stanway (61 Fran Kirby), Nikita Parris (61 Karen Carney), Beth Mead (80 Lucy Staniforth).   Coach: Phil Neville
Denmark: Katrine Abel, Sofie Svava, Rikke Sevecke, Stine Ballisager Pedersen, Janni Arnth, Sofie Junge Pedersen, Sanne Troelsgaard (75 Julie Tavlo-Petersson), Nicoline Sørensen (75 Frederikke Thøgersen), Pernille Harder, Signe Bruun (64 Rikke Madsen), Emma Snerle (41 Mille Gejl Jensen).   Coach: Lars Søndergaard
Goals: Nikita Parris (45+1), Jill Scott (59).
Referee: Désirée Grundbacher (Switzerland)

387. 01.06.2019   Amex Stadium, Brighton: England – New Zealand 0-1 (0-0)
England: Carly Telford, Abbie McManus, Steph Houghton, Alex Greenwood, Lucy Bronze, Keira Walsh (89 Georgia Stanway), Lucy Staniforth (68 Jill Scott), Jodie Taylor (75 Ellen White), Nikita Parris (68 Beth Mead), Fran Kirby, Toni Duggan (54 Karen Carney).
Coach: Phil Neville
New Zealand: Erin Nayler, Catherine Bott (84 Paige Satchell), Rebekah Stott, Alexandra Riley *(YC56)*, Meikayla Moore, Abby Erceg, Ria Percival, Betsy Hassett (73 Annalie Longo), Katie Bowen, Rosie White (73 Olivia Chance), Sarah Gregorius (64 Hannah Wilkinson).
Coach: Tom Sermanni
Goal: Sarah Gregorius (50).
Referee:

388. 09.06.2019   FIFA World Cup 2019 Group D
            Allianz Riviera, Nice: England – Scotland 2-1 (2-0)
England: Karen Bardsley, Lucy Bronze, Alex Greenwood, Steph Houghton, Keira Walsh, Millie Bright (55 Abbie McManus), Jill Scott, Nikita Parris, Fran Kirby (82 Georgia Stanway), Ellen White, Beth Mead (71 Karen Carney).   Coach: Phil Neville
Scotland: Lee Alexander, Nicola Docherty *(YC47)* (55 Kirsty Smith), Rachel Corsie, Sophie Howard (75 Chloe Arthur), Jennifer Beattie *(YC43)*, Kim Little, Caroline Weir, Erin Cuthbert, Lisa Evans, Christie Murray (87 Lizzie Arnot), Claire Emslie.   Coach: Shelley Kerr
Goals: Nikita Parris (14 pen), Ellen White (40) / Claire Emslie (79).
Referee: Jana Adámková (Czech Republic)   Attendance: 13,188.

389. 14.06.2019   FIFA World Cup 2019 Group D
            Stade Océane, Le Havre: England – Argentina 1-0 (0-0)
England: Carly Telford, Lucy Bronze, Alex Greenwood, Steph Houghton, Abbie McManus, Jill Scott, Jade Moore *(YC45+2)*, Nikita Parris (87 Rachel Daly), Jodie Taylor, Fran Kirby (89 Karen Carney), Beth Mead (81 Georgia Stanway).   Coach: Phil Neville
Argentina: Vanina Correa, Agustina Barroso *(YC69)*, Eliana Stábile, Adriana Sachs, Aldana Cometti *(YC39)*, Linda Bravo, Florencia Bonsegundo, Estefanía Banini (68 Mariana Larroquette), Miriam Mayorga, Lorena Benítez (77 Vanesa Santana), Sole Jaimes (90' Yael Oviedo).   Coach: Carlos Borrello
Goal: Jodie Taylor (61).
Referee: Liang Qin (China)   Attendance: 20,294.

Nikita Passis missed a penalty kick (28).

390. 19.06.2019   FIFA World Cup 2019 Group D
            Allianz Riviera, Nice: Japan – England 0-2 (0-1)
Japan: Ayaka Yamashita, Aya Sameshima, Saki Kumagai, Nana Ichise, Risa Shimizu, Hina Sugita, Emi Nakajima, Jun Endo (85 Saori Takarada), Mana Iwabuchi, Rikako Kobayashi (62 Narumi Miura), Kumi Yokoyama (61 Yuika Sugasawa).   Coach: Asako Takakura
England: Karen Bardsley, Lucy Bronze, Steph Houghton, Demi Stokes, Rachel Daly, Keira Walsh (72 Jade Moore), Millie Bright, Jill Scott, Toni Duggan (83 Nikita Parris), Ellen White, Georgia Stanway (74 Karen Carney).   Coach: Phil Neville
Goals: Ellen White (14, 84).
Referee: Claudia Umpiérrez (Uruguay)   Attendance: 14,319.

391. 23.06.2019   FIFA World Cup 2019 Eight-finals
Stade du Hainaut, Valenciennes: England – Cameroon 3-0 (2-0)
England: Karen Bardsley, Lucy Bronze, Alex Greenwood, Steph Houghton, Keira Walsh, Millie Bright, Jill Scott (78 Lucy Staniforth), Nikita Parris (84 Leah Williamson), Fran Kirby, Toni Duggan, Ellen White (64 Jodie Taylor).   Coach: Phil Neville
Cameroon: Annette Ngo Ndom, Augustine Ejangue (64 Ysis Sonkeng), Estelle Johnson, Marie-Aurelle Awona, Yvonne Leuko *(YC4)*, Raissa Feudijo, Jeannette Yango, Gaëlle Enganamouit (53 Alexandra Takounda *(YC90+10)*), Ajara Nchout, Gabrielle Aboudi Onguéné, Michaela Abam (68 Ninon Abena).   Coach: Alain Djeumfa Defrasne
Goals: Steph Houghton (14), Ellen White (45+4), Alex Greenwood (58).
Referee: Liang Qin (China)   Attendance: 20,148.

392. 23.06.2019   FIFA World Cup 2019 Quarter-finals
Stade Océane, Le Havre: Norway – England 0-3 (0-2)
Norway: Ingrid Hjelmseth, Ingrid Wold (85 Synne Skinnes Hansen), Maria Thorisdóttir *(YC88)*, Maren Mjelde, Vilde Bøe Risa, Caroline Graham Hansen, Ingrid Engen, Guro Reiten (74 Amalie Eikeland), Kristine Minde, Karina Sævik (64 Lisa-Marie Karlseng Utland), Isabell Herlovsen.   Coach: Martin Sjögren
England: Karen Bardsley, Lucy Bronze, Steph Houghton, Demi Stokes, Keira Walsh, Millie Bright, Jill Scott, Nikita Parris (88 Rachel Daly), Fran Kirby (74 Georgia Stanway), Toni Duggan (54 Beth Mead), Ellen White.   Coach: Phil Neville
Goals: Jill Scott (3), Ellen White (40), Lucy Bronze (57).
Referee: Lucila Venegas (Mexico)   Attendance: 21,111.

Nikita Parris missed a penalty kick (83).

393. 02.07.2019   FIFA World Cup 2019 Semi-finals
Groupama Stadium, Décines-Charpieu: England – USA 1-2 (1-2)
England: Carly Telford, Lucy Bronze, Steph Houghton, Demi Stokes, Rachel Daly (89 Georgia Stanway), Keira Walsh (71 Jade Moore), Millie Bright *(YC40,YC86)*, Jill Scott, Nikita Parris *(YC90+5)*, Ellen White, Beth Mead (58 Fran Kirby).   Coach: Phil Neville
USA: Alyssa Naeher, Becky Sauerbrunn *(YC83)*, Kelley O'Hara (87 Ali Krieger), Crystal Dunn, Abby Dahlkemper, Julie Ertz, Rose Lavelle (65 Samantha Mewis), Tobin Heath (80 Carli Lloyd), Lindsey Horan *(YC47)*, Alex Morgan, Christen Press.   Coach: Jill Ellis
Goals: Ellen White (19) / Christen Press (10), Alex Morgan (31)
Referee: Edina Alves Batista (Brazil)   Attendance: 53,512.

Steph Houghton missed a penalty kick (84).

394. 06.07.2019   FIFA World Cup 2019 Third Place Match
Allianz Riviera, Nice: England – Sweden 1-2 (1-2)
England: Carly Telford, Lucy Bronze, Alex Greenwood, Steph Houghton, Abbie McManus (83 Rachel Daly), Jill Scott, Jade Moore *(YC90+4)*, Nikita Parris (74' Karen Carney), Fran Kirby, Ellen White, Beth Mead (50 Jodie Taylor).   Coach: Phil Neville
Sweden: Hedvig Lindahl *(YC85)*, Linda Sembrant, Nilla Fischer, Magdalena Eriksson, Nathalie Björn (72 Amanda Ilestedt), Hanna Glas, Caroline Seger, Kosovare Asllani (46 Julia Zigiotti Olme), Sofia Jakobsson, Stina Blackstenius, Fridolina Rolfö (27 Lina Hurtig).   Coach: Peter Gerhardsson
Goals: Fran Kirby (31) / Kosovare Asllani (11), Sofia Jakobsson (22).
Referee: Anastasia Pustovoytova (Russia)   Attendance: 20,316.

395. 29.08.2019 King Power at Den Dreef Stadion, Heverlee:
Belgium – England 3-3 (2-2)
Belgium: Nicky Evrard, Julie Biesmans *(YC29)*, Davina Philtjens *(YC16)* (66 Shari Van Belle), Heleen Jaques (79 Chloe Van De Velde), Laura Deloose (76 Kassandra Missipo), Laura Deneve (66 Justine Vanhaevermaet), Janice Cayman, Tine De Caigny, Tessa Wullaert (87 Elke Van Gorp), Ella Van Kerkhoven, Elena Dhont (46 Davinia Vanmechelen).
Coach: Ives Serneels
England: Carly Telford (63' Mary Earps), Lucy Bronze, Alex Greenwood, Steph Houghton, Abbie McManus *(YC90+3)*, Keira Walsh (87 Leah Williamson), Nikita Parris (75' Lucy Staniforth), Jodie Taylor (75' Beth England), Beth Mead, Rachel Daly, Georgia Stanway (56' Fara Williams). Coach: Phil Neville
Goals: Carly Telford (38 og), Ella Van Kerkhoven (45+2, 55) /
Jodie Taylor (22), Beth Mead (26), Nikita Parris (75 pen).
Referee:

396. 03.09.2019 Brann Stadion, Bergen: Norway – England 2-1 (0-1)
Norway: Ingrid Hjelmseth (86 Cecilie Fiskerstrand), Ingrid Wold, Maria Thorisdóttir, Maren Mjelde, Karina Sævik, Guro Reiten, Kristine Minde, Frida Maanum (56 Ingrid Engen), Caroline Graham Hansen, Vilde Bøe Risa, Amalie Eikeland (69 Lisa-Marie Karlseng Utland).
Coach: Martin Sjögren
England: Carly Telford (78 Ellie Roebuck), Demi Stokes, Steph Houghton, Rachel Daly (77 Leah Williamson), Lucy Bronze, Millie Bright, Keira Walsh, Jodie Taylor (77 Beth England), Georgia Stanway (89 Fara Williams), Nikita Parris (83 Beth Mead), Toni Duggan.
Coach: Phil Neville
Goals: Frida Maanum (53), Caroline Graham Hansen (89) / Georgia Stanway (10)
Referee:

397. 05.10.2019 Riverside Stadium, Middlesbrough: England – Brazil 1-2 (0-0)
England: Mary Earps, Steph Houghton, Alex Greenwood, Lucy Bronze, Jill Scott, Jordan Nobbs (58 Rachel Daly *(YC65)*), Leah Williamson, Keira Walsh, Jodie Taylor (74 Beth England), Nikita Parris (74 Lucy Staniforth), Beth Mead. Coach: Phil Neville
Brazil: BÁRBARA Micheline do Monte Barbosa, GIOVANNA Campiolo Rocha (46 MÔNICA Hickmann Alves), TAMIRES Cassia Dias Gomes, KATHELLEN Sousa Feitoza, ÉRIKA Cristiano dos Santos, LUANA BERTOLUCCI Paixão (87 VICTORIA Kristine Albuquerque de Miranda), Miraildes Maciel Mota "FORMIGA" (71 THAISA de Moraes Rosa Moreno), Francisleide dos "CHÚ" SANTOS Barbosa (46 LUDMILA Da Silva *(YC57)*), MARTA Vieira da Silva *(YC35)* (46 MARIA APARECIDA Souza Alves), Débora Cristiane de Oliveira "DÉBINHA", BEATRIZ Zaneratto João (71 ALINE MILENE De Lima *(YC80)*).
Coach: Oswaldo Fumeiro Alvarez "VADÃO"
Goals: Beth England (80) / Débora Cristiane de Oliveira "DÉBINHA" (49, 67).
Referee: Riem Hussein (Germany)   Attendance: 29,238.

398. 08.10.2019   Estádio do Bonfim, Setúbal: Portugal – England 0-1 (0-0)
Portugal: PATRÍCIA Isabel Sousa Barros MORAIS, CAROLE da Silva COSTA, SÍLVIA Marisa Garcia REBELO, MÓNICA Soraia Amaral MENDES, MATILDE Mota Veiga Santiago FIDALGO, DOLORES Isabel Jácome SILVA *(YC53)*, JÉSSICA Lisandra Manjenje Nogueira SILVA (83 TATIANA Vanessa Ferreira PINTO), FÁTIMA Alexandra Figueira PINTO *(YC15)*, VANESSA MARQUES Malho (83 MÉLISSA Ferreira GOMES), CAROLINA Ana Trindade Coruche MENDES (63 ANDREIA Alexandra NORTON), ANA Catarina Marques BORGES (73 CLÁUDIA Teresa Pires NETO).
Coach: FRANCISCO NETO.
England: Ellie Roebuck, Lucy Bronze, Steph Houghton, Alex Greenwood, Rachel Daly (65 Jodie Taylor), Beth England (65 Jordan Nobbs), Leah Williamson, Keira Walsh, Lucy Staniforth (80 Melissa Lawley), Nikita Parris, Beth Mead (86 Lauren Hemp).
Coach: Phil Neville
Goal: Beth Mead (72)
Referee: Lucia Abruzzese (Italy)

399. 09.11.2019   Wembley Stadium, London: England – Germany 1-2 (1-1)
England: Mary Earps, Lucy Bronze, Steph Houghton, Alex Greenwood, Jill Scott, Jordan Nobbs (77 Georgia Stanway), Leah Williamson, Keira Walsh, Ellen White (73 Jodie Taylor), Nikita Parris (73 Lauren Hemp), Beth Mead (73 Rachel Daly).   Coach: Phil Neville
Germany: Merle Frohms *(YC36)*, Sophia Kleinherne *(YC53)*, Kathrin-Julia Hendrich, Sara Doorsoun *(YC30)*, Dzsenifer Marozsán, Lina Magull (84 Lena Lattwein), Lena Oberdorf (46 Marina Hegering), Sara Däbritz (70 Melanie Leupolz), Sandra Starke (65 Turid Knaak), Alexandra Popp (65 Pauline Bremer), Klara Bühl.   Coach: Martina Voss-Tecklenburg
Goals: Ellen White (44) / Alexandra Popp (9), Klara Bühl (90).
Referee: Stéphanie Frappart (France)   Attendance: 77,768.

Nikita Parris missed a penalty kick 36).

400. 12.11.2019   Fotbalový stadion Strelecký ostrov, Ceské Budejovice:
                    Czech Republic – England 2-3 (2-2)
Czech Republic: Barbora Votíková, Petra Bertholdová, Eliska Sonntágová, Jana Petríková, Tereza Szewieczková (71 Michaela Khýrová), Klára Cahynová, Lucie Vonková, Karerina Svitková, Andrea Stasková (85 Kamila Dubcová), Lucie Martínková, Andrea Jarchovská.
Coach: Karel Rada
England: Carly Telford, Demi Stokes, Lucy Bronze, Jill Scott, Beth England (77 Rachel Daly), Millie Bright, Leah Williamson, Keira Walsh, Lucy Staniforth (76 Jordan Nobbs *(YC84)*), Nikita Parris (64 Lauren Hemp), Beth Mead.   Coach: Phil Neville
Goals: Tereza Szewieczková (15, 27) /
Beth England (17), Beth Mead (20), Leah Williamson (86).
Referee: Ewa Augusstyn (Poland)

401. 05.03.2020   SheBelieves Cup 2020
                    Exploria Stadium, Orlando: USA – England 2-0 (0-0)
USA: Alyssa Naeher, Julie Ertz, Crystal Dunn, Becky Sauerbrunn, Kelley O'Hara, Abby Dahlkemper, Carli Lloyd (90 Jessica McDonald), Tobin Heath (70 Lynn Williams), Rose Lavelle (70 Samantha Mewis), Christen Press (62 Megan Rapinoe), Lindsey Horan.
Coach: Vlatko Andonovski
England: Carly Telford, Steph Houghton, Alex Greenwood, Leah Williamson, Millie Bright, Georgia Stanway (71 Toni Duggan), Jill Scott (65 Jordan Nobbs), Keira Walsh, Ellen White (78 Beth England), Nikita Parris (89 Chloe Kelly), Lauren Hemp.   Coach: Phil Neville
Goals: Christen Press (53), Carli Lloyd (55).
Referee: Odette Hamilton (Jamaica)

402. 08.03.2020   SheBelieves Cup 2020
Red Bull Arena, Harrison (USA): Japan – England 0-1 (0-0)
Japan: Sakiko Ikeda, Mayo Doko, Risa Shimizu (46 Jun Endo), Shiori Miyake, Narumi Miura, Hina Sugita *(YC61)*, Emi Nakajima, Yuka Momiki, Asato Miyagawa, Mina Tanaka (76 Mami Ueno), Mana Iwabuchi (66 Riko Ueki).   Coach: Asako Takakura
England: Ellie Roebuck, Demi Stokes, Steph Houghton, Millie Bright, Jordan Nobbs (90+2 Jill Scott), Beth England (69 Ellen White), Keira Walsh (60 Leah Williamson), Georgia Stanway (69 Lucy Staniforth), Chloe Kelly *(YC54)* (60 Nikita Parris), Lauren Hemp (60 Toni Duggan), Rachel Daly.   Coach: Phil Neville
Goal: Ellen White (83).
Referee: Katja Koroleva (USA)

403. 10.03.2020   SheBelieves Cup 2020
Toyota Stadium, Frisco (USA): England – Spain 0-1 (0-0)
England: Carly Telford, Abbie McManus, Alex Greenwood, Leah Williamson *(YC78)*, Millie Bright (46 Steph Houghton), Jill Scott *(YC72)* (87 Keira Walsh), Jordan Nobbs (62 Georgia Stanway), Ellen White (70 Chloe Kelly), Nikita Parris, Toni Duggan (70 Alessia Russo), Rachel Daly.   Coach: Phil Neville
Spain: SANDRA PAÑOS García-Villamil, AINHOA Vicente MORAZA, MARÍA Pilar LEÓN Cebrián, LEILA OUAHABI El Ouhabi *(YC12)* (46 MARTA CORREDERA Rueda), ANDREA PEREIRA Cejudo, ÁNGELA SOSA Martín (46 MARTA CARDONA de Miguel), AMANDA SAMPEDRO Bustos (68 Jennifer "JENNI" HERMOSO Fuentes), "PATRI" Patricia Guijarro Gutiérrez (57 VIRGINIA TORRECILLA Reyes), AITANA BONMATÍ Conca, LUCÍA GARCÍA Córdoba (90+4 ALBA María REDONDO Ferrer), María Francesca "MARIONA" CALDENTEY Oliver (46 ALEXIA PUTELLAS Segura).
Coach: JORGE VILDA
Goal: ALEXIA PUTELLAS Segura (83).
Referee: Danielle Chesky (USA)

xxx. 27-10-2020   Wiesbaden: Germany – England **not played**

xxx. 01.12.2020   Bramall Lane, Sheffield: England – Norway **not played**

404. 23.02.2021   St George's Park National Football Centre, Burton upon Trent:
England – Northern Ireland 6-0 (3-0)
England: Ellie Roebuck (61 Sandy MacIver), Lucy Bronze, Leah Williamson (75 Carlotte Wubben-Moy), Steph Houghton, Alex Greenwood, Rachel Daly (84 Ebony Salmon), Jill Scott, Jordan Nobbs (46 Ella Toone), Georgia Stanway, Ellen White (76 Beth England), Lauren Hemp (61 Chloe Kelly).   Coach: Hege Riise
Northern Ireland: Rebecca Flaherty, Julie Nelson, Abbie Magee, Rebecca Holloway (83 Toni Finnegan), Nadene Caldwell (84 Kelsie Burrows), Sarah Robson (84 Samantha Kelly), Chloe McCarron (57 Rebecca McKenna *(YC90+4)*), Rachel Furness, Marissa Callaghan (58' Ciara Watling), Lauren Wade (73 Louise McDaniel), Simone Magill.   Coach: Kenny Shiels
Goals: Ellen White (18, 23, 49), Lucy Bronze (29), Rachel Daly (67), Ella Toone (75 pen).
Referee: Lorraine Watson (Scotland)   Attendance: 0

405. 09.04.2021   Stade Michel d'Ornano, Caen: France – England 3-1 (1-0)
France: Pauline Peyraud-Magnin, Aïssatou Tounkara, Marion Torrent *(YC77)* (85 Ève Périsset), Perle Morroni, Élisa De Almeida, Ella Palis *(YC58)* (60 Inès Jauréna), Grace Geyoro, Sandy Baltimore, Marie-Antoinette Katoto, Valérie Gauvin (59 Viviane Asseyi), Kadidiatou Diani (85 Kenza Dali).   Coach: Corinne Diacre
England: Ellie Roebuck, Leah Williamson (64 Carlotte Wubben-Moy), Alex Greenwood (46 Niamh Charles), Rachel Daly *(YC90)*, Keira Walsh, Jill Scott (73 Jordan Nobbs), Millie Bright, Ellen White (74 Beth England), Nikita Parris (46 Chloe Kelly), Beth Mead *(YC17)* (64 Lauren Hemp), Fran Kirby.   Coach: Hege Riise
Goals: Sandy Baltimore (32), Viviane Asseyi (63 pen), Marie-Antoinette Katoto (82) / Fran Kirby (79 pen).
Referee: Sara Persson (Sweden)

406. 13.04.2021   bet365 Stadium, Stoke-on-Trent: England – Canada 0-2 (0-1)
England: Carly Telford (46 Karen Bardsley), Leah Williamson, Demi Stokes (32 Alex Greenwood), Rachel Daly (64 Lucy Bronze), Beth England (64 Chloe Kelly), Jordan Nobbs, Millie Bright, Georgia Stanway, Fran Kirby (46 Ella Toone), Lauren Hemp, Nikita Parris (80 Ellen White).   Coach: Hege Riise
Canada: Stephanie Labbé, Ashley Lawrence, Vanessa Gilles, Allysha Chapman, Shelina Zadorsky *(YC28)*, Desiree Scott (66 Jayde Riviere), Rebecca Quinn (82 Sophie Schmidt), Jessie Fleming, Évelyne Viens (59 Jordyn Huitema), Deanne Rose (59 Nichelle Prince), Janine Beckie.   Coach: Bev Priestman
Goals: Évelyne Viens (3), Nichelle Prince (86).
Referee: Cheryl Foster (Wales)

407. 17.09.2021   World Cup Qualifiers 2021/2022, Europe Group D
   Saint Mary's Stadium, Southampton: England – North Macedonia 8-0 (3-0)
England: Mary Earps, Leah Williamson, Demi Stokes, Alex Greenwood, Rachel Daly (82 Niamh Charles), Millie Bright (63 Carlotte Wubben-Moy), Georgia Stanway (71 Beth England), Ellen White (72 Jill Scott), Ella Toone, Beth Mead, Lauren Hemp (63 Nikita Parris). Coach: Sarina Wiegman-Goltzbach
North Macedonia: Suarta Dervishi, Pavlinka Nikolovska, Natasa Andonova, Polozani Sindis, Julija Zivic *(YC66)*, Sara Kolarovska, Afrodita Saliihi (78 Kristina Petrushevska), Gentjana Roçi, Hava Mustafa (86 Katerina Mileska), Aleksandra Markovska (46 Rabija Dervishi), Ulza Maksuti *(YC68)* (90+1 Teodora Dimoska).   Coach: Kiril Izov
Goals: Ella Toone (12), Ellen White (42, 67 pen), Julija Zivic (45 og), Beth England (77, 90), Sara Kolarovska (79 og), Beth Mead (90+1).
Referee: María Dolores Martínez (Spain)

408. 21.09.2021   World Cup Qualifiers 2021/2022, Europe Group D
   Stade de Luxembourg, Luxembourg: Luxembourg – England 0-10 (0-4)
Luxembourg: Lucie Schlimé, Isabel Albert, Emma Kremer, Laura Miller *(YC78)*, Gabriela De Lemos Crespo (78 Martine Schon), Jessica Berscheid, Marisa Soares Marques (89 Aldina Dervisevic), Marta Estévez García (62 Jill De Bruyn *(YC83)*), Edina Kocan (46 Noemie Raths), Julie Marques Abreu (89 Kelly Mendes Garcia), Kimberley Dos Santos.
Coach: Daniel Santos
England: Mary Earps, Leah Williamson, Demi Stokes, Alex Greenwood (59 Carlotte Wubben-Moy), Rachel Daly, Millie Bright, Ellen White (58 Beth England), Ella Toone (81 Jill Scott), Nikita Parris, Fran Kirby (71 Georgia Stanway), Lauren Hemp (59 Beth Mead *(YC66)*).
Coach: Sarina Wiegman-Glotzbach
Goals: Ellen White (12, 17), Nikita Parris (27), Alex Greenwood (37, 47), Jessica Berscheid (61 og), Millie Bright (78, 90+1), Rachel Daly (90+3), Beth England (90+4).
Referee: Aleksandra Cesen (Slovania)

409. 23.10.2021   World Cup Qualifiers 2021/2022, Europe Group D
Wembley Stadium, London: England – Northern Ireland 4-0 (0-0)
England: Mary Earps, Leah Williamson, Demi Stokes (46 Keira Walsh), Alex Greenwood (80 Lucy Staniforth), Rachel Daly (64 Beth Mead), Millie Bright, Ellen White, Ella Toone, Nikita Parris (63 Beth England), Fran Kirby (80 Carlotte Wubben-Moy), Lauren Hemp.
Coach: Sarina Wiegman-Glotzbach
Northern Ireland: Jacqueline Burns, Demi Vance, Julie Nelson, Kelsie Burrows *(YC60)* (73 Ciara Watling), Sarah McFadden, Chloe McCarron, Rachel Furness (74 Louise McDaniel), Marissa Callaghan (81 Emily Wilson), Lauren Wade (81 Kerry Beattie), Rebecca McKenna, Caragh Hamilton (64 Kirsty McGuinness).   Coach: Kenny Shiels
Goals: Beth Mead (64, 74, 78), Beth England (72)
Referee: Ivana Martincic (Croatia)

410. 26.10.2021   World Cup Qualifiers 2021/2022, Europe Group D
Daugavas Stadionā, Riga: Latvia – England 0-10 (0-4)
Latvia: Enija Anna Vaivode, Ligita Tumāne (77 Dzeina Eglīte), Anastasija Rocāne (86 Kristīne Girzda), Karlīna Miksone, Arta Lubina, Sofija Gergeleziu, Tatjana Baliceva (77 Alīna Silova), Olga Sevcova, Viktorija Zaicikova, Sandra Voitāne, Renāte Fedotova (69 Alise Gaike).   Coach: Romans Kvacovs
England: Mary Earps, Leah Williamson, Alex Greenwood (46 Demi Stokes), Millie Bright, Keira Walsh, Beth England, Ellen White (46 Rachel Daly), Ella Toone (69 Carlotte Wubben-Moy), Beth Mead, Fran Kirby (46 Georgia Stanway), Lauren Hemp (46 Nikita Parris).
Coach: Sarina Wiegman-Glotzbach
Goals: Ella Toone (8, 12, 68), Ellen White (25), Millie Bright (32), Beth Mead (55), Rachel Daly (70, 82), Leah Williamson (79), Georgia Stanway (81)
Referee: Katarzyna Lisiecka-Sek (Poland)

Ellen White missed a penalty kick (38).

411. 27.11.2021   World Cup Qualifiers 2021/2022, Europe Group D
Stadium of Light, Sunderland: England – Austria 1-0 (1-0)
England: Mary Earps, Demi Stokes (90+2 Jess Carter), Alex Greenwood, Rachel Daly, Millie Bright, Keira Walsh, Ellen White, Ella Toone (63 Georgia Stanway), Beth Mead (70 Nikita Parris), Fran Kirby, Lauren Hemp.   Coach: Sarina Wiegman-Glotzbach
Austria: Manuela Zinsberger, Laura Wienroither, Carina Wenninger, Katharina Naschenweng (60 Katja Wienerroither *(YC62)*), Virginia Kirchberger, Sarah Zadrazil, Sarah Puntigam, Maria Plattner (89 Marie Höbinger), Verena Hanshaw, Barbara Dunst, Nicole Billa (87 Stefanie Enzinger).   Coach: Irene Fuhrmann
Goal: Ellen White (39).
Referee: Kateryna Monzul (Ukraine)   Attendance: 9,160.

412. 30.11.2021   World Cup Qualifiers 2021/2022, Europe Group D
Keepmoat Stadium, Doncaster: England – Latvia 20-0 (8-0)
England: Mary Earps, Carlotte Wubbe-Moy, Alex Greenwood, Millie Bright (46 Jess Carter), Keira Walsh (71 Katie Zelem), Beth England, Georgia Stanway (60 Jill Scott), Ellen White (60 Alessia Russo), Ella Toone (46 Jordan Nobbs), Beth Mead, Lauren Hemp.
Coach: Sarina Wiegman-Glotzbach
Latvia: Laura Sinutkina (46 Alīna Sklemenova), Ligita Tumāne *(YC52)*, Arta Lubina, Sofija Gergeleziu, Alise Gaike (46 Selga Vitmore), Tatjana Baliceva (85 Ērika Gricienko), Anna Gornela, Signija Senberga (68 Viktorija Vengrevica), Evelīna Freidenfelde (56 Diāna Skribina), Viktorija Zaicikova, Sandra Voitāne.   Coach: Romans Kvacovs
Goals: Beth Mead (3, 12, 23), Ellen White (6, 9, 49), Lauren Hemp (18, 44, 76, 88), Ella Toone (42), Georgia Stanway (52 pen), Jess Carter (56), Beth England (61, 84), Jill Scott (67), Alessia Russo (71, 81, 82), Jordan Nobbs (80)
Referee: Veronika Kovarova (Czech Republic)

413. 17.02.2022   Four Nations Tournament
Riverside Stadium, Middlesbrough: England – Canada 1-1 (1-0)
England: Mary Earps, Leah Williamson (65 Nikita Parris), Demi Stokes, Alex Greenwood (65 Jess Carter), Millie Bright, Keira Walsh, Alessia Russo (75 Ellen White), Ella Toone (46 Georgia Stanway), Fran Kirby, Lauren Hemp (66 Beth Mead), Rachel Daly (65 Lucy Bronze).
Coach: Sarina Wiegman-Glotzbach
Canada: Kailen Sheridan, Jayde Riviere (66 Chloé Lacasse), Ashley Lawrence *(YC48)*, Vanessa Gilles, Kadeisha Buchanan *(YC85)*, Desiree Scott, Julia Grosso (59 Nichelle Prince), Jessie Fleming, Deanne Rose (80 Victoria Pickett), Jordyn Huitema (59 Rebecca Quinn), Janine Beckie.   Coach: Bev Priestman
Goals: Millie Bright (22) / Janine Beckie (55).
Referee: Lina Lehtovaara (Finland)   Attendance: 8,769.

414. 20.02.2022   Four Nations Tournament
Carrow Road, Norwich: England – Spain 0-0
England: Hannah Hampton, Alex Greenwood, Lucy Bronze, Jill Scott (62 Leah Williamson), Jordan Nobbs (62 Keira Walsh), Jess Carter, Georgia Stanway *(YC66)* (80 Ella Toone), Ellen White, Nikita Parris (46 Lauren Hemp), Beth Mead *(YC48)* (72 Fran Kirby), Rachel Daly.
Coach: Sarina Wiegman-Glotzbach
Spain: "MISA" María Isabel Rodríguez Rivero, ONA BATLLE Pascual (62 OLGA CARMONA García), MARÍA Pilar LEÓN Cebrián, IVANA Andrés Sanz *(YC32)*, AITANA BONMATÍ Conca, "PATRI" Patricia Guijarro Gutiérrez, SHEILA García García, MARTA CARDONA de Miguel (46 ATHENEA del Castillo Belvide), LUCÍA GARCÍA Córdoba (74 AMAIUR SARRIEGI Isasa), Jennifer "JENNI" HERMOSO Fuentes (87 ESTHER González Rodríguez), ALEXIA PUTELLAS Segura.   Coach: JORGE VILDA
Referee: Iuliana Elena Demetrescu (ROM)   Attendance: 14,284.

415. 23.02.2022   Four Nations Tournament
Molineux Stadium, Wolverhampton: England – Germany 3-1 (1-1)
England: Ellie Roebuck, Leah Williamson, Alex Greenwood *(YC40)*, Lucy Bronze (82 Ella Toone), Millie Bright, Keira Walsh, Jess Carter (34 Rachel Daly), Georgia Stanway (61 Nikita Parris), Ellen White (82 Alessia Russo), Fran Kirby, Lauren Hemp.
Coach: Sarina Wiegman-Glotzbach
Germany: Merle Frohms, Maximiliane Rall, Sophia Kleinherne, Lina Magull (72 Linda Dallmann), Fabienne Dongus (72 Chantal Hagel), Sara Däbritz, Giulia Gwinn, Jana Feldkamp, Nicole Anyomi (46 Jule Brand *(YC79)*), Lea Schüller, Klara Bühl (88 Selina Cerci).
Coach: Martina Voss-Tecklenburg
Goals: Ellen White (15), Millie Bright (84), Fran Kirby (90+4) / Lina Magull (41)
Referee: Emikar Calderas (Venezuela)   Attendance: 14,463.

416. 08.04.2022   World Cup Qualifiers 2021/2022, Europe Group D
Rose Proeski National Arena,Skopje: North Macedonia – England 0-10 (0-5)
North Macedonia: Viktorija Pancurova, Pavlinka Nikolovska (80 Kristina Petrushevska), Ane Boseska, Natasa Andonova (75 Aleksandra Markovska *(YC90)*), Sara Velkova *(YC84)*, Hristina Joshevska, Gentjana Roçi *(YC44)* (54 Afrodita Saliihi *(YC75)*), Elena Petrovska (55 Angela Stojkovska), Hava Mustafa (46 Elma Shemsovikj), Ulza Maksuti *(YC79)*, Eli Jakovska.
Coach: Kiril Izov
England: Hannah Hampton, Demi Stokes, Lucy Bronze (71 Rachel Daly), Millie Bright, Keira Walsh (71 Katie Zelem), Jess Carter, Georgia Stanway (61 Jill Scott), Ellen White (71 Alessia Russo), Ella Toone, Beth Mead, Lauren Hemp (60 Nikita Parris).
Coach: Sarina Wiegman-Glotzbach
Goals: Beth Mead (5, 12, 47, 53), Ella Toone (24, 74, 78), Ellen White (41), Georgia Stanway (45, 56)
Referee: Vivian Peeters (Netherlands)

417. 12.04.2022   World Cup Qualifiers 2021/2022, Europe Group D
Windsor Park, Belfast: Northern Ireland – England 0-5 (0-1)
Northern Ireland: Jacqueline Burns, Demi Vance *(YC72)*, Julie Nelson, Abbie Magee (82 Caragh Hamilton), Kelsie Burrows (76 Rebecca McKenna), Sarah McFadden, Rachel Furness (61 Chloe McCarron), Joely Andrews (75 Nadene Caldwell), Marissa Callaghan, Lauren Wade (62 Kirsty McGuinness), Simone Magill.   Coach: Kenny Shiels
England: Mary Earps, Leah Williamson, Lucy Bronze, Millie Bright, Keira Walsh, Jess Carter (66 Rachel Daly), Georgia Stanway (87 Jordan Nobbs), Ellen White (65 Beth England), Ella Toone, Beth Mead (71 Nikita Parris), Lauren Hemp.   Coach: Sarina Wiegman-Glotzbach
Goals: Lauren Hemp (26, 60), Ella Toone (52), Georgia Stanway (70, 79)
Referee: Riem Hussein (Germany)

418. 16.06.2022   Molineux Stadium, Wolverhampton: England – Belgium 3-0 (0-0)
England: Mary Earps, Carlotte Wubben-Moy (46 Alex Greenwood), Leah Williamson, Demi Stokes (46 Rachel Daly), Lucy Bronze *(YC49)*, Millie Bright, Keira Walsh, Georgia Stanway (61 Fran Kirby), Ellen White (61 Beth England), Beth Mead (46 Chloe Kelly), Lauren Hemp (81 Nikita Parris). Coach: Sarina Wiegman-Glotzbach
Belgium: Nicky Evrard, Julie Biesmans (73 Davinia Vanmechelen), Davina Philtjens (61 Kassandra Missipo), Sari Kees (46 Charlotte Tison), Laura Deloose, Laura Deneve (46 Amber Tysiak), Marie Minnaert, Féli Delacauw (61 Elena Dhont), Tessa Wullaert, Sarah Wijnants (73 Jody Vangheluwe), Tine De Caigny.   Coach: Ives Serneels
Goals: Chloe Kelly (62), Rachel Daly (66), Nicky Evrard (83 og).
Referee: Sara Persson (Sweden)   Attendance: 9,598.

419. 24.06.2022   Elland Road, Leeds: England – Netherlands 5-1 (1-1)
England: Mary Earps, Leah Williamson, Alex Greenwood *(YC51)* (63 Georgia Stanway), Lucy Bronze, Millie Bright, Beth England (63 Alessia Russo), Keira Walsh, Chloe Kelly (46 Beth Mead), Fran Kirby (64 Ella Toone), Lauren Hemp (81 Nikita Parris), Rachel Daly (75 Jess Carter).   Coach: Sarina Wiegman-Glotzbach
Netherlands: Sari van Veenendaal, Lynn Wilms (81 Kerstin Casparij), Dominique Janssen, Stefanie van der Gragt (46 Caitlin Dijkstra), Aniek Nouwen *(YC29)*, Sherida Spitse (73 Damaris Egurrola), Victoria Pelova (63 Esmee Brugts), Jackie Groenen, Jill Roord, Lineth Beerensteyn *(YC45+2)* (63 Vivianne Miedema), Lieke Martens (46 Daniëlle van de Donk). Coach: Mark Parsons
Goals: Lucy Bronze (32), Beth Mead (53, 90), Ella Toone (72), Lauren Hemp (74) / Lieke Martens (22)
Referee: Sandra Braz Bastos (Portugal)   Attendance: 19,365.

Sherida Spitse missed a penalty kick (52).

420. 30.06.2022   Stadion Letzigrund, Zürich: Switzerland – England 0-4 (0-0)
Switzerland: Seraina Friedli, Viola Calligaris *(YC44)*, Noelle Maritz, Ana-Maria Crnogorcevic (46 Lara Marti), Luana Bühler, Coumba Sow, Sandy Maendly (79 Riola Xhemaili), Lia Wälti (46 Sandrine Mauron), Ramona Bachmann (65 Fabienne Humm), Eseosa Aigbogun (79 Rachel Rinast), Géraldine Reuteler (87 Meriame Terchoun).   Coach: Nils Nielsen
England: Mary Earps, Leah Williamson, Alex Greenwood (62 Jess Carter), Millie Bright, Keira Walsh, Alessia Russo *(YC45+1)* (61 Beth England), Georgia Stanway *(YC69)* (79 Jill Scott), Beth Mead (62 Chloe Kelly), Fran Kirby (61 Ella Toone), Lauren Hemp (75 Nikita Parris), Rachel Daly.   Coach: Sarina Wiegman-Glotzbach
Goals: Alessia Russo (56), Georgia Stanway (74 pen), Beth England (76), Jill Scott (90+4).
Referee: Ainara Acevedo (Spain)

421. 06.07.2022   EURO 2022 England, Group A
       Old Trafford, Manchester: England – Austria 1-0 (1-0)
England: Mary Earps, Lucy Bronze, Leah Williamson, Keira Walsh, Millie Bright, Georgia Stanway, Rachel Daly, Beth Mead (64 Chloe Kelly), Ellen White (64 Alessia Russo), Lauren Hemp, Fran Kirby (63 Ella Toone).   Coach: Sarina Wiegman-Glotzbach
Austria: Manuela Zinsberger, Katharina Naschenweng (59 Julia Hickelsberger), Carina Wenninger, Viktoria Schnaderbeck (77 Marina Georgieva), Laura Wienroither, Verena Hanshaw, Barbara Dunst, Sarah Zadrazil, Laura Feiersinger (87 Marie Höbinger), Sarah Puntigam, Nicole Billa.   Coach: Irene Fuhrmann
Goal: Beth Mead (16).
Referee: Marta Huerta de Aza (Spain)   Attendance: 68,671.

422. 11.07.2022   EURO 2022 England, Group A
       Amex Stadium, Brighton and Hove: England – Norway 8-0 (6-0)
England: Mary Earps, Lucy Bronze, Leah Williamson, Keira Walsh, Millie Bright, Georgia Stanway (80 Jill Scott), Rachel Daly (57 Alex Greenwood), Beth Mead, Ellen White (57 Alessia Russo), Lauren Hemp (70 Chloe Kelly), Fran Kirby (58 Ella Toone).
Coach: Sarina Wiegman-Glotzbach
Norway: Guro Pettersen, Maria Thorisdóttir, Tuva Hansen, Maren Mjelde, Ingrid Engen, Vilde Bøe Risa (59 Frida Maanum *(YC87)*), Caroline Graham Hansen (75 Amalie Eikeland), Guro Reiten (84 Elisabeth Terland), Julie Blakstad *(YC56)*, Karina Sævik (46 Guro Bergsvand), Ada Stolsmo Hegerberg (75 Celin Ildhusøy *(YC77)*).   Coach: Martin Sjögren
Goals: Georgia Stanway (12 pen), Lauren Hemp (15), Ellen White (29, 41), Beth Mead (34, 38, 81), Alessia Russo (66)
Referee: Riem Hussein (Germany)   Attendance: 28,847.

423. 15.07.2022   EURO 2022 England, Group A
Saint Mary's Stadium, Southampton: England – Northern Ireland – England 0-5 (0-2)
Northern Ireland: Jacqueline Burns, Demi Vance, Julie Nelson (87 Ashley Hutton), Rebecca Holloway (66 Abbie Magee), Laura Rafferty (66 Kelsie Burrows), Sarah McFadden, Marissa Callaghan (87 Emily Wilson), Rachel Furness (80 Nadene Caldwell), Rebecca McKenna, Kirsty McGuinness, Lauren Wade. Coach: Kenny Shiels
England: Mary Earps, Lucy Bronze (74 Jess Carter), Leah Williamson, Keira Walsh, Millie Bright (46 Alex Greenwood), Georgia Stanway (46 Ella Toone), Rachel Daly, Beth Mead, Ellen White (46 Alessia Russo), Lauren Hemp (60 Chloe Kelly), Fran Kirby.
Coach: Sarina Wiegman-Glotzbach
Goals: Fran Kirby (40), Beth Mead (44), Alessia Russo (48, 53), Kelsie Burrows (76 og).
Referee: Esther Staubli (Switzerland)   Attendance: 30,785.

424. 20.07.2022   EURO 2022 England, Quarter-finals
Amex Stadium, Brighton and Hove: England – Spain 2-1 (0-0,1-1)
England: Mary Earps, Lucy Bronze, Leah Williamson, Keira Walsh (116 Jill Scott), Millie Bright, Georgia Stanway, Rachel Daly (82 Alex Greenwood *(YC119)*), Beth Mead (58 Chloe Kelly), Ellen White (58 Alessia Russo), Lauren Hemp (117 Nikita Parris), Fran Kirby (64 Ella Toone).   Coach: Sarina Wiegman-Glotzbach
Spain: SANDRA PAÑOS García-Villamil, ONA BATLLE Pascual, IRENE PAREDES Hernández, MARÍA Pilar LEÓN Cebrián *(YC45)*, OLGA CARMONA García, AITANA BONMATÍ Conca, María Francesca "MARIONA" CALDENTEY Oliver (100 AMAIUR SARRIEGI Isasa), "PATRI" Patricia Guijarro Gutiérrez, TERESA Abelleira Dueñas (71 LAIA ALEIXANDRI López), ESTHER González Rodríguez (77 SHEILA García García), MARTA CARDONA de Miguel (46 ATHENEA del Castillo Belvide).   Coach: JORGE VILDA
(Not used sub: "MISA" María Isabel Rodríguez Rivero *(YC88)*).
Goals: Ella Toone (84), Georgia Stanway (96) / ESTHER González Rodríguez (54)
Referee: Stéphanie Frappart (France)   Attendance: 28,994.

England won following extra-time.

425. 26.07.2022   EURO 2022 England, Semi-finals
Bramall Lane, Sheffield: England – Sweden 4-0 (1-0)
England: Mary Earps, Lucy Bronze, Leah Williamson, Keira Walsh, Millie Bright, Georgia Stanway *(YC85)* (87 Jill Scott), Rachel Daly (87 Alex Greenwood), Beth Mead (86 Chloe Kelly), Ellen White (57 Alessia Russo), Lauren Hemp, Fran Kirby (79 Ella Toone).
Coach: Sarina Wiegman-Glotzbach
Sweden: Hedvig Lindahl, Linda Sembrant (76 Hanna Bennison), Hanna Glas, Magdalena Eriksson, Amanda Ilestedt (55 Jonna Andersson), Nathalie Björn *(YC73)*, Filippa Angeldahl (51 Caroline Seger), Kosovare Asllani, Sofia Jakobsson (52 Johanna Rytting Kaneryd), Stina Blackstenius (76 Lina Hurtig), Fridolina Rolfö.   Coach: Peter Gerhardsson
Goals: Beth Mead (34), Lucy Bronze (48), Alessia Russo (68), Fran Kirby (76).
Referee: Esther Staubli (Switzerland)   Attendance: 28,624.

426. 31.07.2022 EURO 2022 England, Final
Wembley Stadium, London: England – Germany 2-1 (0-0, 1-1)
England: Mary Earps, Lucy Bronze, Leah Williamson, Keira Walsh, Millie Bright, Georgia Stanway *(YC23)* (88 Jill Scott), Rachel Daly (88 Alex Greenwood), Beth Mead (64 Chloe Kelly *(YC111)*), Ellen White *(YC23)* (56 Alessia Russo *(YC100)*), Lauren Hemp (120 Nikita Parris), Fran Kirby (55 Ella Toone). Coach: Sarina Wiegman-Glotzbach
Germany: Merle Frohms, Kathrin-Julia Hendrich, Marina Hegering (103 Sara Doorsoun), Felicitas Rauch *(YC40)* (113 Lena Lattwein), Lena Oberdorf *(YC57)*, Sara Däbritz (73 Sydney Lohmann), Giulia Gwinn, Lina Magull (90 Linda Dallmann), Jule Brand (46 Tabea Waßmuth), Lea Schüller *(YC57)* (67 Nicole Anyomi), Svenja Huth. Coach: Martina Voss-Tecklenburg
Goals: Ella Toone (62), Chloe Kelly (110) / Lina Magull (79)
Referee: Kateryna Monzul (UKR)   Attendance: 87,192.

England won following extra-time and became European Champions for the first time.

427. 03.09.2022   World Cup Qualifiers Europa 2021/2022, Group D
Wiener Neustadt Arena, Vienna: Austria – England 0-2 (0-1)
Austria: Manuela Zinsberger, Laura Wienroither, Carina Wenninger, Marina Georgieva, Sarah Zadrazil, Sarah Puntigam, Julia Hickelsberger (69 Katharina Naschenweng), Verena Hanshaw, Laura Feiersinger (88 Marie Höbinger), Barbara Dunst (88 Lisa Kolb), Nicole Billa (79 Katja Wienerroither). Coach: Irene Fuhrmann
England: Mary Earps, Leah Williamson (79 Jess Carter), Alex Greenwood, Lucy Bronze (84 Rachel Daly), Millie Bright, Keira Walsh, Alessia Russo (62 Beth England), Georgia Stanway, Ella Toone (79 Lauren James), Beth Mead (62 Nikita Parris), Lauren Hemp.
Coach: Sarina Wiegman-Glotzbach
Goals: Alessia Russo (7), Nikita Parris (69).
Referee: Iuliana Demetrescu (ROM)   Attendance: 2,600.

428. 06.09.2022   World Cup Qualifiers Europa 2021/2022, Group D
bet365 Stadium, Stoke-on-Trent: England – Luxembourg 10-0 (5-0)
England: Ellie Roebuck, Leah Williamson (46 Millie Bright), Alex Greenwood, Lucy Bronze, Rachel Daly (61 Demi Stokes), Keira Walsh, Alessia Russo (46 Beth England), Georgia Stanway (46 Katie Zelem), Ella Toone, Nikita Parris, Beth Mead (60 Lauren Hemp).
Coach: Sarina Wiegman-Glotzbach
Luxembourg: Lucie Schlimé, Jessica Becker (79 Noemi Tiberi), Mariana Lourenço (46 Isabel Albert), Emma Kremer, Catherine Have, Laura Miller, Marisa Soares Marques (46 Kelly Mendes Garcia), Charlotte Schmidt, Joana Lourenco (79 Edina Kocan), Caroline Jorge Magalhaes (66 Julie Marques Abreu), Kimberley Dos Santos. Coach: Daniel Santos
Goals: Georgia Stanway (12 pen, 26), Alessai Russo (18), Rachel Daly (38), Beth Mead (40), Beth England (48, 90+2), Nikita Parris (59), Ella Toone (73 pen), Lauren Hemp (90).
Referee: Simona Ghisletta (SUI)   Attendance: 24,174.

429. 07.10.2022   Wembley Stadium, London: England – USA 2-1 (2-1)
England: Mary Earps, Rachel Daly, Alex Greenwood, Millie Bright *(YC45)*, Lucy Bronze, Keira Walsh, Georgia Stanway, Chloe Kelly (90+1 Lauren James), Fran Kirby (68 Ella Toone), Beth Mead, Lauren Hemp. Coach: Sarina Wiegman-Glotzbach
USA: Alyssa Naeher, Emily Fox (22 Hailie Mace *(YC32)*), Naomi Girma (83 Becky Sauerbrunn), Alana Cook, Sofia Huerta (63 Sam Coffey), Andi Sullivan (63 Crystal Dunn), Lindsey Horan, Trinity Rodman *(YC48)* (83 Ashley Sanchez), Megan Rapinoe (83 Alyssa Thompson), Sophia Smith, Rose Lavelle. Coach: Vlatko Andonovski
Goals: Lauren Hemp (10), Georgia Stanway (33 pen) / Sophia Smith (28).
Referee: Riem Hussein (GER)   Attendance: 76,893.

430. 11.10.2022   Amex Stadium, Brighton and Hove: England – Czech Republic 0-0
England: Mary Earps, Demi Stokes (82 Rachel Daly), Lucy Bronze, Alex Greenwood, Millie Bright (62 Esme Morgan), Keira Walsh, Ella Toone, Chloe Kelly (46 Beth Mead), Fran Kirby, Lauren Hemp, Lauren James (63 Ebony Salmon).   Coach: Sarina Wiegman-Glotzbach
Czech Republic: Olivie Lukásová, Petra Bertholdová, Simona Necidová, Klára Cahynová, Tereza Krejciríková (75 Lucie Martínková), Katerina Svitková, Tereza Szewieczková (57 Michaela Khýrová), Kamila Dubcová, Eliska Sonntágová, Gabriela Slajsová (75 Anna Dlasková), Andrea Stasková (75 Miroslava Mrázová).   Coach: Karel Rada
Referee: Alexandra Collin (FRA)   Attendance: 21,222.

431. 11.11.2022   Pinatar Arena, San Pedro del Pinatar (ESP): England – Japan 4-0 (1-0)
England: Mary Earps, Millie Bright, Niamh Charles, Esme Morgan, Keira Walsh (89 Katie Zelem), Georgia Stanway (89 Jess Park), Ella Toone (83 Nikita Parris), Beth Mead, Rachel Daly, Chloe Kelly (64 Lauren James), Alessia Russo (64 Ebony Salmon).
Coach: Sarina Wiegman-Glotzbach
Japan: Ayaka Yamashita, Shiori Miyake (70 Saori Takarada), Risa Shimizu, Moeka Minami, Saki Kumagai, Man Iwabuchi (58 Mina Tanaka), Hina Sugitu, Yui Hasegawa, Fuka Nagano, Hinata Miyazawa (71 Aoba Fujino), Jun Endo.   Coach: Futoshi Ikeda
Goals: Rachel Daly (38), Chloe Kelly (53), Ella Toone (78), Jess Park (90).
Referee: Zuzana Valentová (SVK)

432. 15.11.2022   Pinatar Arena, San Pedro del Pinatar (ESP): England – Norway 1-1 (1-0)
England: Ellie Roebuck, Alex Greenwood (63 Alessia Russo), Millie Bright (46 Esme Morgan), Niamh Charles, Maya Le Tissier, Keira Walsh (46 Katie Zelem), Ella Toone, Nikita Parris (83 Katie Robinson), Rachel Daly, Chloe Kelly, Lauren James (46 Georgia Stanway).
Coach: Sarina Wiegman-Glotzbach
Norway: Aurora Mikalsen, Anja Sønstevold *(YC66,YC72)*, Guro Bergsvand, Mathilde Harviken, Guro Reiten, Amelie Eikeland (73 Vilde Bøe Risa), Lisa Naalsund (61 Frida Maanum), Ingrid Syrstad Engen, Thea Bjelde (73 Maria Thorisdóttir), Emilie Haavi (46 Julie Blakstad), Sophie Roman Haug.   Coach: Hege Riise
Goals: Rachel Daly (33), Frida Maanum (80).
Referee: Zuzana Valentová (SVK)